· ON A SPACESHIP WITH BEELZEBUB ·

# On a Spaceship
# With Beelzebub
## By a Grandson of Gurdjieff

## BY DAVID KHERDIAN

*Frontispiece by the author after a passage from G.I. Gurdjieff's*
ALL AND EVERYTHING: BEELZEBUB'S TALES TO HIS GRANDSON

GLOBE PRESS BOOKS / NEW YORK

This book is available at a special discount
when ordered in bulk quantites.

*First Edition*

Publisher's Cataloging in Publication
*(Prepared by Quality Books, Inc.)*

Kherdian, David.
   On a spaceship with Beelzebub : by a grandson of Gurdjieff / by
David Kherdian. —
   p. cm.
   ISBN 0-936385-20-0 (hardcover)
   ISBN 0-936385-10-3 (pbk.)
   1. Kherdian, David—Biography. 2. Authors, American—20th
century—Biography. 3. Spiritual formation. 4. Gurdjieff, Georges
Ivanovitch, 1872-1949. I. Title.

PS3561.H4                              811'.54
                                              90-85646

10  9  8  7  6  5  4  3  2
Manufactured in the United States

*Dedicated to all those I studied with, and fought with, and with whom I prayed: for whether in agreement, disagreement, hostility or accord, they were the course of study to be passed through on the way to liberation and personal freedom.*

*And to G.I. Gurdjieff, who provided the means.*

## BOOKS BY DAVID KHERDIAN

*Poetry*

On the Death of My Father and Other Poems
Homage to Adana
Looking Over Hills
The Nonny Poems
I Remember Root River
The Farm
Taking the Soundings on Third Avenue
The Farm: *Book Two*
Place of Birth
Threads of Light
The Dividing River / The Meeting Shore

*Novels*

The Road From Home
It Started with Old Man Bean
Beyond Two Rivers
Finding Home
The Song in the Walnut Grove
The Mystery of the Diamond in the Wood
Bridger: The Story of a Mountain Man
A Song for Uncle Harry (novella)

*Nonfiction*

Six San Francisco Poets
Root River Run (memoir)
On a Spaceship with Beelzebub:
*By a Grandson of Gurdjieff*

*It was the very essence of Gurdjieff's teaching that the pupil must stand on his own feet and he took every measure, sometimes apparently harsh and brutal, to break down any tendency towards dependence upon himself. He would go to the length of depriving himself of much-needed helpers in his work rather than allow a relationship of dependence, or subordination. At the same time, he took for granted that a teacher is necessary and made it clear why this is so. No man can work alone until he knows himself, and no one can know himself until he can be separate from his own egoism. The teacher is always needed to apply the knife, to sever the true from the false, but he can never work for his pupil, nor understand for him, nor be for him. We must work, and understand, and be, for ourselves.*

J.G. Bennett from TALKS ON BEELZEBUB'S TALES, page 14

## · PROLOGUE ·

This is the story of my discovery of the Gurdjieff work—the most powerful, effective and meaningful system of esoteric teaching ever to come to the West. It is also the story of my search for someone who could pass on to me Gurdjieff's powerful method of self-development, who could teach it in the way that he had intended it to be taught.

Freedom. To be free. Inside myself. Freedom—and all that it means to me—is what ultimately brought me to the door of the Gurdjieff work. When I began my search, it was an idea that seemed to imply a possibility that nothing in life could answer. And although I was trapped in life, there was a part of me that yearned for something that would set me free. Now, having searched for, and found, an answer of my own to the question of inner freedom, my meaning of freedom is simply this: to know why I am here, and what I was intended for.

I have pondered for a long time the mission of Gurdjieff's "Fourth Way" teaching because I need to understand the obligation I have assumed by practicing his ideas. I had begun to do this work from my own egoistic needs, but Gurdjieff had said, "You must first be out and out egoist before you can become altruist." Although I can see the egoistic side, my experiences in the work have not answered the question of what the altruistic side means, especially since the Gurdjieff work, as it is today, has no intention of taking its place in the world.

But before I can properly tell my story, I ought to address one obvious question: Who exactly was Gurdjieff? He was, and remains today, a mysterious figure. Perhaps this is so because he was on a higher level than we are, and we are unable to judge—or even see—anyone who is on a higher level than ourselves. And Gurdjieff was many steps removed from the platform on which the rest of his disciples stood.

He was born in the Caucasus, and raised in the city of Kars, a melting pot of Christian and non-Christian races. Gurdjieff's question, the 'idee fixe' of his inner world, that arose in his mind in early youth, was this: *What is the sense and significance of life on the earth in general and of human life in particular?* While still a young man his travels took him to Persia, Turkestan, Tibet, India, the Gobi desert and Egypt, in an unremitting search for a "real and universal knowledge." His travels in search of hidden knowledge carried him deeper and deeper into Asia, and eventually led him to a source of wisdom in which others before him had also been initiated.

Gurdjieff was unusual not only because he was able to weld a diversity of esoteric disciplines into a single method, but because the method that he conceived was tailored for the West. To participate in an Eastern teaching, with which the West has been fairly inundated, the student must change their garment of culture and memorize a lexicon of foreign words and prayers. But in Gurdjieff's method, the essential work of translation had already been done—by Gurdjieff. He was able to make his ideas palatable to the psychologically and scientifically oriented Westerner who was suspicious of anything that hinted of religion or dogma. The religious and spiritual sources of his method were therefore well hidden, and the true meaning and purpose of his "Work"—as he called it—had to be discovered privately and individually by the seeker. If the student could not find his way for himself, he soon became another "rat for my experiments," as Gurdjieff liked to boast, for he had his own mission, of which he never spoke.

Gurdjieff did not become a visible presence until around 1912, when he appeared in St. Petersburg, surrounded by students. It was soon after that P.D. Ouspensky met Gurdjieff, having searched on his own for esoteric knowledge. Ouspensky was a Russian journalist who meticulously recorded the teaching as Gurdjieff gave it during the early years in Russia, and on the long flight from Russia to the West.

The First World War obliterated Gurdjieff's plans to found an institute in Russia. His flight from Russia to the West is recorded in Thomas de Hartmann's *Our Life with Mr. Gurdjieff*, the most heartfelt of all the books about Gurdjieff.

Together with his band of pilgrims, Gurdjieff founded his Institute for the Harmonious Development of Man at the Chateau du Prieure, near Fontainebleau, in 1922. He would devote the rest of his life to bringing to the West what he had discovered in the East. To do this he created an exact language and, with de Hartmann as his amanuensis, produced the haunting melodies needed for his movements, the sacred dances he had observed in the temples of the East, and that he had reformulated for the purposes of his teaching.

These movements, more than any other method, conveyed by direct experience what Gurdjieff meant by "balancing the centers." He contended that we were not *normal* because our emotional, mental and physical centers were not in accord, for the reason that they had not been properly educated and trained. The movements, although they could not be called sacred dances as practiced by his pupils, *did* impart a feeling of spirituality that words by themselves could not convey. These were not only an embodiment of the Work in action, but proof of its result.

His Russian pupils were joined by members of the English nobility, as well as English and American writers, artists, and intellectuals. These were his earliest students. Gurdjieff was concerned to make his ideas and his presence known to the West. He had come on a mission, as a "Herald of the Coming Good," the title of the one book he issued in his lifetime. Among his early pupils, in addition to Ouspensky, who was already a famous writer in Russia, and Thomas de Hartmann, the composer, also famous in Russia, were Alexandre de Salzmann, an artist and stage designer; his wife Jeanne, a dancer; and A.R. Orage, the editor of *The New Age*, whom George Bernard Shaw had called the world's best living editor. Orage not only assisted in the translation of Gurdjieff's monumental work, *All and Everything: Beelzebub's Tales to His Grandson*, but it is questionable whether that work would have achieved its final, completed form without his assistance. There were also Jane Heap and Margaret Anderson, artist and writer, who together edited *The Little Review*, the most influential literary magazine of its time. Other writers of significance who would spread the ideas were Kathryn Hulme, Fritz Peters, and Jean Toomer.

In books, articles and letters, Katherine Mansfield, Olgivanna Lloyd Wright, Fritz Peters, Jean Toomer and others have given us first-hand reports of life at the Prieure, where the relationships of the people were imbued with brotherly love. No one has satisfactorily explained how and why this quality became lost among subsequent groups, and particularly among those to whom he entrusted his work before he died, and who later established the Gurdjieff Foundation in his name.

Ouspensky's *In Search of the Miraculous*, published in 1949, is a monumental treatise on the teaching that was instrumental in attracting countless young people into the work during the consciousness-raising sixties. Although the work had gone through a fallow period prior to this, those that Gurdjieff had trained, as well as many who had not been trained, were now in a position to pass on the teaching to a new and eager generation of seekers.

The Gurdjieff teaching soon became known as the Fourth Way, in contradistinction to the ways of the fakir, the yogi and the monk, which were each concentrated on only one of the three centers of man; the fakir being the way of bodily discipline and control, the yogi being the training of the mind, and the monk that of the heart. The Fourth Way incorporated all of these, and on its Way one had but to swallow a pill. That pill, that proved to be too bitter for most, was Conscious Labor and Intentional Suffering. "I teach these two things only," Gurdjieff had said, but if we could understand that— and it could only be understood through our own effort and earned experience—we would also understand, in his words, "That when it rains, the streets get wet."

But what exactly did Gurdjieff mean by Conscious Labor and Intentional Suffering? No two people have ever given an identical answer or formulation for the reason that, like all of Gurdjieff's ideas, our understanding is dependent on our effort and experience, as well as the level of our own being. Conscious labor quite obviously called for an effort we were not accustomed to make in our ordinary (un-normal) lives, for the reason that we were still asleep, according to Gurdjieff. Intentional Suffering, equally, could not occur when our Conscience had not been awakened. The two aspects of the formulation were correlated because Consciousness and Conscience could not be separated.

There are now countless "fourth way" methods in life, all of them partial and incomplete, and all of them borrowing, if not stealing directly from Gurdjieff, who has also exercised a great, abiding influence on many of the Eastern gurus who have followed in his footsteps. But I doubt that Gurdjieff would have been disappointed by any of this. On the contrary, I believe he would have considered it proof that his mission was being accomplished. He once stated that *All and Everything* would be read from the pulpit one day, and that modern myths would be concocted based on a partial understanding of his book. Today we see more than one Christian order of monks and nuns writing books and practicing the ideas embodied in Gurdjieff's Enneagram. His work has entered the marketplace, as well as the church, with more than one major industry putting ideas of his into training programs for their employees. EST, Arica, The Diamond Path, to name a few of those who, in many instances, would have had no basis for existence had it not been for Gurdjieff. His yeast is alive, and the bread is rising in unexpected places, and with unexpected results; and we may never know the ultimate result, except to believe that it will be beneficent.

Unfortunately, those who have clung to the old form of the Work, deifying Gurdjieff or the current leaders of the Foundation, seem to have forgotten their original aim.

If Gurdjieff did not share his mission with his students and disciples he did share his method, which he handed out piecemeal, for he needed their participation for his own advancement, and he resisted any attempt to systematize his ideas, for good reason. In countless ways, he urged and prodded his followers to experience themselves in new ways, for only then could they begin to see themselves *as they were*, as opposed to their imagined pictures of themselves. It soon became evident that his teaching was based on a spiritual psychology, and although self-knowledge was not its end, it was certainly the means: the first stage in self-development and the beginning of man's awakening from sleep.

While his students studied themselves, he was studying them, for if the West was to change—become spiritualized, as it would have to do in order for the world to survive—it would have to have a "change of mind", and for this to be possible it would have to know itself. Gurdjieff was a student of the human psyche as no one before him had been, but this knowledge was only a means to an end, and the end was for a purpose that individually we would have to find for ourselves. And that of course was the point: to find in the work what we needed for *our* lives, just as he had found what he needed for his life, and in that discovery and achievement had provided us with an unheard of possibility.

Whatever may occur to the form he left us—that was ever in transition while he lived—his ideas and his example remain pure and will always be available for those who seek it, both in his books, where it is permanently preserved, and in whatever real groups that may survive.

I

# THE GURDJIEFF FOUNDATION

## · CHAPTER ONE ·

The year was 1960, and now, with college behind me, the Army behind me, and a brief flirtation with Europe—where I thought I would settle and live—also behind me, I moved to San Francisco to resume my apprenticeship as a writer.

One of the friends I made there, also a budding writer, was Jacob (Jerry) Needleman. I had just compiled a bibliography of William Saroyan that was about to be published. Oyez, a new, small press in the Bay Area had approached me to do a series of portraits and checklists of some of the new San Francisco poets. Apparently, a poetry renaissance had begun, but the only poetry I had read was in college, and though I had been moved by the poetry of Yeats, and some of the poems of Eliot and Wilfred Owen, as well as A.E. Housman, I could make no sense of Hart Crane and Wallace Stevens, and most of the other American poets we were given to read.

During the 60s everyone was riding on a wave of cosmic energy, and ironically, as it turned out, I rode out on the Wave of Poetry, and very mysteriously became a poet myself, when poetry was the last kind of writing I had wanted to do.

Jerry, in the meantime, was writing short stories, and one day decided to produce a literary magazine. I would be his coeditor. He swore me to secrecy on the title, *Poor Old Tired Horse*. He was so convinced of its merit that he was certain the title would be stolen if word got out. "We need a manifesto," he declared. I put a sheet of clean paper in the typewriter, and presto, with no more than a word or two about the direction we were to go in, I produced "a perfect piece of work," according to Jerry, who from that day on was convinced I was a natural writer, born to the trade. I returned the compliment by stealing a line from one of his short stories for my description of the Beat poet, David Meltzer, for the first monograph I would publish with Oyez. When Jerry's wife, Carla Needleman, read the booklet I presented them with (having received ten complimentary copies, and a $50.00 advance, my first earnings as a writer), she said, "You've been hiding your light under a bushel."

Carla had been married before, and the large photograph of Gurdjieff that highlighted their library had come from her former husband. I didn't have to be told that Gurdjieff was Armenian (mother Armenian, father Greek). But although he looked like one of several types I was familiar with, there was nevertheless something about the suffering in his face that was not like the suffering in the faces of all the other old Armenians I knew.

Carla said he was a mystic philosopher. It was never clear to me if Carla's former husband knew Gurdjieff, or had simply studied his ideas, but it was clear that Gurdjieff was someone who had played an important part in their lives. It never occurred to me that he might be a part of their lives still.

I was struck by Gurdjieff's bald head, that had been shaved clean, and the sad eyes, completely lacking in self-pity. The bald head and large mustache suggested a Magus, but that may have only been an affected appearance or pose to hide something else. The Oriental mind, as I well knew, never moved directly at its target. He had been photographed in his undershirt, with the top button showing. This didn't surprise me, as my own father often walked around, both inside the house, and outside, when wandering through or working in his garden, barefooted and in his B.V.D.s. It made me wonder if Gurdjieff had not also come from peasant stock.

At Fields Bookstore in San Francisco, where I often went to search for books for my William Saroyan collection, I was handed a mimeo newsletter that Mr. Fields asked me to deliver to Saroyan the next time I went to Fresno. The request didn't surprise me because Mr. Fields had published a limited edition of one of Saroyan's books back in the thirties. I assumed they were friends. But I didn't know until I delivered the envelope that the newsletter had to do with Gurdjieff, and it would be years before I would learn that Fields Bookstore was a point of connection for people in the work.

Saroyan and I decided Gurdjieff was a charlatan, though how we came to this conclusion I can't imagine now. Having recently reread Saroyan's letters to me I find that I had been reading Gurdjieff at that time, or perhaps shortly after, and that his work had struck something in me. I had forgotten this, perhaps because it hadn't taken me anywhere at the time, and being absorbed by my own work I found his writings disturbing or distracting, because I was certain of only one thing at that time: I wanted to be a writer.

It wasn't long after this that my sister, who was much closer to the Needlemans than I was, joined a Gurdjieff group in the Bay Area, and it was only then that I learned that Jerry and Carla were also in the work. I was about to leave San Francisco, and it would be many years before I would see the Needlemans again, and under very different circumstances than those that first brought us together.

The book I wrote next would be titled *Homage to Adana*, after my father's birthplace. I had already begun my own small press, that I had named after the region of Cilicia, once a notable Armenian kingdom, when Adana was its capitol city. But the "homage" was not strictly speaking to Adana *or* the old country, but rather to the men and women who had transplanted old values in this new land, and had placed my heritage in front of me as a boy, that I had inherited at my birth, but that I was only now beginning to come to terms with.

All my life the existence of my people, as well as my place in their midst, had puzzled me, even at times tormented me, because their suffering had occurred elsewhere, in another world and time, that they could not forget but that I did not want to learn about. My mother had been the sole survivor of her family of the attempted genocide of the Armenian nation by the Turks during the First World War.

Like all those of my generation, I came into myself very late, which meant that I would come to my work late, my marriage late, and the meaning of my life very, very late.

I had blamed my unhappiness on my birthplace—Racine, Wisconsin—but as I began to move out and inhabit a larger world, a world I was sure I needed, I found myself, from the very beginning—for I had left at the age of twenty—needing to return to continue my search for something I could neither name nor understand. Something had been deposited there, some secret mystery, to which I must return again and again if I was to fathom the meaning of my existence on Earth. This I knew, and this was all I knew, but I knew it with such instinctive certainty that nothing could prevent me from my search, even though I knew I was working in the dark.

Finally, with the writing of the poems that became *Homage to Adana* I began to sense a movement, and I realized I was *directing* that movement, and that at last my search had acquired an intelligence and a purpose.

I had to recover my life before I could inherit it. This was the burden of my writing. This was the life I was finding in these poems, and to my surprise I began to see patterns that I had never known were there.

From an early age I knew that I required guides, examples, some intelligent outer force that could show me, even move me in a direction that was meaningful. My spirit cried out for something more than I had seen and been given, or could ever expect to receive. But what that was I couldn't know. Had I known it was simply my birthright that I was seeking I could have dropped the rancor and resentment.

*Homage to Adana* gave my life a direction it had lacked before. I had not only found my voice as a writer, but I had—though I didn't know it at the time—prepared the ground in my search for a teaching, for what I had discovered that I hadn't yet put a name to—work on myself—was manifest in a teaching, and specifically for me, the Gurdjieff teaching.

No doubt because I was ready, Carlos Castaneda's *The Teachings of Don Juan* fell into my hands. If Theodore Dreiser's *The Stoic* had put me on my path, *Don Juan* made it possible for me stay on the path I was on, although in the long view—that is much more apparent to me now—it was just another step on the endless Path that I had entered with this birth. But as yet I hadn't known that I was either on or searching for a spiritual path or direction, or for that matter that the deliverance to another dimension of reality was even possible. But here was a book that opened onto a world I had never suspected was there. I did not, in one quick leap, go from tunnel vision to clear sight, but I was aware, almost instantly, that the world I had been living in was not enough, that there were worlds within worlds within worlds, and it was clear that I had encountered very few of these worlds in my short life. Don Juan moved comfortably between worlds because he was at home in both. This seemed miraculous to me, and years later I would know why, for Gurdjieff had said that the manifestation of the laws of one cosmos in another cosmos constitute what *we* call a *miracle*. Don Juan was such a miracle for me.

Most of my life—certainly all of adult life—I had been consumed with the need for fame. Fame was to be my ticket to the larger world I was seeking, my entry card, the proof-positive of my arrival. It would also validate me, the son of immigrant parents, and certify me American, artist, citizen of the world. But I had another side to me that I didn't see nearly as clearly, that would not accept anything from the outside, a side that was determined to make life as difficult as possible, to seek discomfort the moment comfort appeared, a side that would never be relaxed or at home anywhere, a side that knew that this Earth was not home and would never be home. Gurdjieff had also said that every stick has two ends, and that life's two-sided stick appears in all things, including the inner life of man. I could understand that the law of opposites was absolute, but what I did not see, for myself, was which end of the stick I was holding at any given time—or even which end I wished to grasp.

What I did understand of all this was that I had just had my first flirtation with fame. Through my press I had edited and published an anthology of twenty Fresno poets. Up until this time it had always been assumed that New York was the proper arbiter and judge of things literary. At best, magazines or journals were produced in the hinterland, but with their sights clearly aimed at mecca. But Fresno was rife with poets, and when one of them suggested that my press produce a journal, I suggested an anthology instead. There were poets everywhere, all waiting to break into the big time, and here was a new opportunity, because what my anthology—*Down at the Santa Fe Depot: 20 Fresno Poets*—really heralded was a celebration of place and time and people, all of whom were as valid as anyone, anywhere.

The book was so successful among the literati, both nationally and locally, that I was on the verge of becoming a local celebrity. Within two months of the book's publication, and after I had produced a second printing, I left Fresno, never to return. This effectively ended my long relationship with Saroyan, who never forgave me my departure. I had wanted to tell him, but couldn't, that my brush with fame had had a shrinking effect on me—instead of an enlarging one. I had felt pigeon-holed, marked down and defined, and anything—even total obscurity—would have been better than that.

If this was not what I wanted, what was it then that I was seeking? Did I know, did I even know to ask? A failed marriage behind me, Fresno behind me, the Armenians presumably behind me, wherefore and to what was I headed? I didn't know. I was taking the next step, and the next step was the Berkshires in Massachusetts, where I soon began writing the poems that would become the book, *Looking Over Hills*.

Although I didn't know it at the time, I had to leave everything behind before it would be possible for something completely new to appear. And this newness was ostensibly only a change in my poetry—from people to nature, from outer to inner. I didn't see it as a progression because what I was confronted with was so much bigger, that I could see nothing but it. There was a declaration behind the vision that produced the poems, which were poems about the invisible, interconnected fabric of the universe and life, and what I not only sensed but knew, was this: I have become a channel, a radio that can transmit messages between stations, but this "glory" is not mine, it is temporary, and nothing of its quality will accrue to me if I leave it at that; that is, if I accept this and do not take a step beyond this, into a dimension where I can make something that *is* mine, and that *will* not, *can* not be taken away.

I knew that this glory or attunement that I was feeling, although temporary and belonging to the poet, not to me, could be permanently achieved if I could put aside my attachment to being the poet and work to make this state of raised consciousness a permanent reality. Surely this is what Don Juan had been speaking about, and this is what the apprentice, Castaneda, had been seeking.

## · CHAPTER TWO ·

It has taken me a very long time to understand that we can never know more than the next step, with the ledge we are standing on being the step already taken. But about this one step we are able to be relatively certain. And we can only know it by feeling. We must trust our hearts.

Somewhere in Castaneda, he speaks of the leap into the abyss. In a sense, every step we make is that, but some more dramatic—more important and urgent—than others. On the step we are on we incorporate what we have understood, which must then be actualized. The previous step is a preparation for the one that will follow. We are stopped—if we are—by thinking in terms of conclusions or results, instead of seeing that our life is a series of steps, the outcome of which is unknown to us because we neither know where we came from nor where we are going.

I was about to make two successive steps, both of which I had prepared for, but in totally different ways.

Something in me knew that my work with the Armenians was not over, that a great deal of psychological material had to be put in order. *Homage to Adana* had revealed this, and in doing so had pointed me in a direction. *Ararat*, an Armenian-American literary magazine, where I had published many of my early poems, was about to lose its editor, and applications were being taken. Shortly after finishing *Looking Over Hills* I drove down to New York to apply for the job, which meant meeting with the assistant editors and the publisher, and presenting a verbal proposal. I was very eager to have the job, and I was both passionate and persuasive during the interview. I made a number of promises: I would introduce photographic covers, institute a series of oral tape recordings of the survivors of the Massacres, travel to Armenia for a special issue, and do special issues, as well, on Arshille Gorky and General Antranik. And I would double the circulation and bring the magazine back on schedule.

I was given the job.

The next step was far more decisive and important. I was about to meet the woman who would become my wife and partner, as well as my best friend. Years later, my teacher would say that the reason our marriage was so successful was that we had married with our heads. It put me in mind then, as it does now, of my first marriage, which was as different from my second marriage as day is to night. Although I knew by the time the first marriage ended that it never could have survived, no matter what effort either of us would have made, I also knew that because I was much older than she, that the fault for its dissolution, as well as our uniting, had to fall to me. In my heart and mind I took full responsibility for its failure, and I suffered not only that but all the unhappiness I had caused her. For two weeks I hardly moved from my chair, while I absorbed with full cognizance and responsibility the pain and harm I had inflicted on her, putting aside as completely as I could, my own anguish and sorrow.

The first call I made from the office of my new job with *Ararat* was to Nonny Hogrogian. I had known and admired her illustrative work for some years, and I wanted not only to have her work for the magazine, to which she had contributed in the past, but I also wanted her to do the cover for *Homage to Adana*.

Like me she had trouble working for and with the Armenians. She refused, by apologizing for her busy schedule and claiming a current deadline. She recommended another Armenian artist and hung up. But before I could dial the other number, she called back. She apologized again, this time for her brusqueness, and asked if I would send her my manuscript. She explained later that she had felt she had been rude in not asking to at least see my work. She failed to tell me that she had admired my poetry and had clipped one of my poems from a magazine and pinned it to her wall.

We met within a fortnight at a reception that was given by the board of *Ararat* to introduce me as their new editor. She said she was very taken with my book of poems and wanted to illustrate the cover. She would call me when it was done. I told her how much I admired her book of Armenian folk tales, but I did not tell her that I had been intrigued by the book into wishing to meet the artist. I didn't know that she felt the same way about me.

She had also been taken by my boisterous self-confidence. I had told her that *Homage to Adana* was a great book, believing that that made up for the fact that I couldn't pay her. She understood all this without either of us saying a word about it. We both had hidden motives.

When she called to tell me that the art work was ready, she invited me to stay for lunch. She had made a special soup, that she nearly ruined in her nervousness by watering it down for fear it would not be enough—she rightly assumed that a hearty appetite went with my inflated self-importance. I brought two bottles of California riesling, which complemented—in my vanity—my corduroy coat and stetson.

As she liked to tell the story, my first question in the door was, "How old are you, and how come you never married?"

"Thirty-seven," she had answered, "and I plan to—soon!" I waited until I was seated before I asked her her sun sign. When she told me, I said, "It will never work, my first wife was a Taurus."

She wrote the next day—I had moved my office to Westport— that she had cancer rising. "Will that help?"

I consulted my sister Virginia, the expert, and wrote back that it made a big difference.

Thirty days later we were married, on the very day following the completion of her deadline. She had told the truth.

I had never been with an Armenian woman before. The Armenian community I had been raised in was so tightly-knit that I had thought of the Armenian girls as sisters, and I had regarded mating with them a form of incest. But there was more to it than that. Nonny was my equal, and in the past I had only been attracted to women who were passive and shy to the point of being mousy.

I didn't understand at the time that our relationship had been made possible by the suffering I had been through over the failure of my first marriage. It would be years before I would understand how and why this was so. What I had known instinctively—that had never actually touched my consciousness—was that by standing in front of my life and seeing myself *as I was* had the effect of—in this case—maturing me.

This seeing, if rightly conducted, could be transformative. I had been lucky so far, but if my luck was to continue I would need to be joined to a real teaching.

We moved to New Hampshire and began our life together. In the month that we were alone in New York, while Nonny finished the etchings for her book of tales from Grimm, I wrote what would become the first section of *The Nonny Poems*. My art was growing and changing with each book because it followed the changing experiences in my life. There was a movement from past to present that interested me, and now, with these new poems, I was deliberately attempting to make poems out of the lived moment in its occurrence, which I attempted to transmute for the page into a living work of art. It was one thing to rearrange the past in tranquility, with time, experience and acquired understanding being the arbiter, and quite another to see the beauty in the hour and to hold it fast on the page in an indestructible work of art.

The writing of these poems also evoked in me a tension and pull between the past and the present—between the needs of the moment and the unfulfilled requirements of the past.

At the same time, I was moving ahead with my first issue of *Ararat*, and Nonny had become my art director.

Our days were active and full and happy. We had scraped together enough money to make a down payment on a house in what felt like the wilderness. We were up a dirt road, protected by an area reserved for forestation, with no other home in sight. Except for occasional hikers on the Appalachian Trail, that circled our back yard and went by our home, we had complete privacy. After years of city living we both craved a period of isolation from the noise and clamor of city life.

My aim to find a teacher or teaching kept nagging at me. Despite the fullness of my life—or perhaps because of it—I felt that something was missing, that my spiritual nature, so long denied, had surfaced and was begging to be attended to. But I had no idea how or where to begin. My problem was compounded by Nonny's suspicions, as well as her doubts, for whenever the subject came up she would challenge it by saying that our life was good and satisfying as it was. Like me, she had been anti-religious all of her life. She had felt threatened by my need for something "spiritual" in my life. With her marriage she had felt fulfilled as a woman, at last. She had already experienced a measure of fame as a children's book illustrator, and this had meant nothing to her beyond an opportunity to exercise her artistic gifts, for she had known from around the age of five that she wanted to be—was in fact—an artist. She derived as much pleasure from cooking as from art work, and even preferred it to doing books because there was no pressure, no reward or punishment, no career hanging over her head. She took to gardening with the same intensity and passion, and in a very short time she became a good gardener as well.

All this seemed to satisfy her. She had already been a liberated woman, which she also took for granted. What mattered was being married. She also hoped to be a mother.

Much later she would look back on this time and say that her life was standing in the way of her life. But at the moment everything seemed perfect.

Her indifference to fame was unable to provide an example for me. I needed fame to replace the self-confidence that the circumstances of my life had cheated me of, for I had always felt that the Armenians in the community in which I was raised were backward, and that the factory town that engulfed that community was equally, in its own way, behind the times. I wasn't aware then that fame would also have the effect of providing the approval I had never received from my father.

It was becoming obvious that my pull toward something more than ordinary life could provide was being held up by my wish for its very opposite: instead of reality, I was unconsciously seeking an illusion or appearance of something from the outside in order to replace what was missing on the inside.

What happened next helped bring both of us closer to the truth of our existence. Our experiences, although strangely opposite, were moving us toward the same conclusion, as well as toward a new resolve.

Macmillan, for whom I had edited two contemporary American poetry anthologies, had accepted *The Nonny Poems* for publication. I felt that I had made it at last. A big part of me had never wanted anything more than this, a fixed and permanent place in the literary world. But now that it seemed to be coming true, I saw that it was meaningless in terms of a deeper need, that seemed to grow as the superficial need became realized. How could I know what I needed if I couldn't even achieve what I thought I wanted? If only the deeper part of me had a voice and could speak, and somehow provide a direction out of the labyrinth my assumed life had been weaving for me.

Once, on one of the long walks I had taken with Saroyan, he stopped in the street to make a point. It was a moment that had remained forever etched in my memory. We had been talking about writing, and he had said that the previous winter he had set himself the program of working on several projects simultaneously, just as he had done when he was "new to the game. Thirty years ago, exactly," he said, "and so it was time to test myself again, to see where I stood."

We continued walking while he explained that he had pulled it off, writing a story a day for a fixed period, as well as a preface for each of the earlier stories that had made his name. At the same time, he also wrote a play. Therefore, he concluded, "I still knew I had it." As we went on with our walk I tried to consider what it was he thought he still had. And then, from somewhere deep inside of me, a place as incorruptible as conscience, a voice said, in answer to Saroyan's assessment, "Is that all you understand?"

But what did the voice mean? I knew the truth of it at once, but with all of me—I had thought—I wanted to be everything that Saroyan was, a writer who could produce, who had become world famous, who could travel, and with two or three homes around the world. And money. I had nothing to show for my life at that time but a small unknown book of poems. But to my great surprise, something inside of me had mysteriously rejected all that I aspired to on the outside. The memory of that day had never left me.

Nonny had developed a lump on one of her breasts that she had been assured was benign, but one day, about one and half years after we were married, while examining herself, she noted a slight change in its composition. Our doctor wanted to perform the biopsy while she was under anaesthesia. If it proved to be malignant, he would perform a mastectomy.

The suspense was hideous, even though we agreed that for her own piece of mind it was just as well she didn't know ahead of time. She would come out of the operating room unscathed, or with a deformed body and a possible death sentence hanging over her head.

I wandered the grounds of Mary Hitchcock hospital in Hanover, unable to do anything but walk, in a need to use some part of myself other than my mind. It felt to me as if the world had become a very unfamiliar place. I was suddenly alone inside my skin, and frightened, with nothing recognizable to turn to, to look at, or to find a relation with. I was sinking into a void, with nothing to think about or to hold on to. I couldn't remember what my life meant anymore. I saw that I was defenseless, at the complete mercy of circumstances and conditions I could neither understand nor change.

All I wanted was her safety and her health. With each hour that went by I knew I was moving closer and closer to what I didn't want to face. At last I was called in to see the doctor. He told me what I knew I was going to hear, that her breast had been removed, along with her lymph nodes. "There is no sign that the cancer has spread. The prognosis is good."

I stared at him. I didn't know that I was in shock. I was aware of my body heaving before I realized that I was sobbing uncontrollably. The doctor got up from his chair. I still hadn't spoken. He mumbled something about my needing to be alone, and hurriedly left.

I didn't get up from my chair until I had control over my body. I went out into the lobby and waited to be told what room they would be taking Nonny to.

On the day I brought her home from the hospital Nonny took off her bandages and made me look at her scar. "It doesn't matter," I said, but I couldn't stop her crying. I knew what she was feeling: we had been married such a short time, and now this. But it made no difference to me; if anything I treasured her even more for feeling I might have lost her, and from knowing, too, that I might lose her still.

A long time went by before we were able to talk about our fears and concerns for each other and the future. She had taken a different interest now in my need for spiritual answers to our questions about life. One day she told me that when she had come out of the anaesthesia, and had instinctively reached her hand up to her chest—and in the instant realized what had happened—a voice inside her said, "This isn't it, this isn't what my life is about."

I told her then about my experience with Saroyan. "Something knows when nothing else does," she said. "We have to learn to listen more carefully from now on."

## · CHAPTER THREE ·

The following year we moved from New Hampshire to upstate New York. Shortly after our move I found a copy of *The Fiery Fountains* by Margaret Anderson. I didn't know when I began reading it that she had been a student of Gurdjieff's. I had known of her, as I had known of Jane Heap, as co-editors of the famous literary magazine, "The Little Review." I had never been able to get my hands on her own record of that period, that she had recorded in *My Thirty Years War*, but I was hoping this book would put me in touch with that period and its history.

Instead of that, I found the Gurdjieff work. Her book was more about Gurdjieff and his teaching then about her literary life. Or rather, what she had to say about herself and her activities seemed terribly unimportant—even to her—once she met the teaching.

Why, I asked myself now, had I not gone back and reread Gurdjieff? Had I been put off by the people in the work that I had met through my sister in Berkeley, Warwick and Santa Fe, the various places she had been in groups? What I had not seen in all these people, what I could not have seen, of course, was Gurdjieff himself, the man. But Margaret Anderson had brought him alive for me—his teaching, his relation to his pupils and, finally, his presence and his being.

I was also deeply moved by Jane Heap's letters that were quoted throughout the book. Serious, compassionate and wise, their sincerity was beyond anything I had encountered in my readings in literature. They seemed to open a door into another world, and standing in that doorway was Gurdjieff.

For some reason, I didn't tell Nonny about the book. Soon after I finished reading it we had the Hausmans over for dinner. Gerry Hausman and I had started our careers as poets together, publishing our poems in a joint pamphlet that we followed with readings in Las Vegas and Santa Fe, New Mexico. It was the Hausmans who had given me the copy of *Don Juan*, and I knew that Gerry had had a passing interest in Gurdjieff. He had once read Thomas de Hartmann's, *Our Life with Mr. Gurdjieff*. In describing the book he seemed to remember best that Gurdjieff had made them pound rocks, and then had taken them over a mountain pass without provisions or proper clothing. He shook his head in disbelief. His interest in Gurdjieff, I knew, had ended there.

Nonny had heard us talking about the Margaret Anderson book, and the next day she picked it up and read it without saying anything to me. When she had finished it she confessed that she had been intrigued and also jealous when she overheard me telling Gerry about the book. "You were so passionate about it, and I couldn't understand why you had never mentioned it to me."

"Well, I hadn't planned not to," I said, and laughed, "but anyhow, it worked. So what did you think?"

"I loved it! I didn't know that all this spiritual stuff was going to be like *this*."

From that day forward we read all the books we could find on Gurdjieff and his teaching. Nonny told me now that in the past, when my sister and I talked about Gurdjieff her ears would perk up, but that none of the other teachings we talked about interested her. "All those different costumes...but I just read where Gurdjieff said his work had to take place in life. I like that. It makes sense. We don't have to change our religion...."

"No, in fact, in one of his lectures he says something about our conscience being connected to our religion. Or does he say faith? Anyhow, what he's saying is that if you take a man's religion away you take his faith away, and if you do that you deprive him of his spiritual possibilities, because faith and conscience are inextricably connected. He also says that to outrage anybody's religious feeling is contrary to all morality."

A year of reading went by. We had felt for a long time that our life was changing because Gurdjieff had opened to us the possibilities inherent in our being, but so deeply submerged as to be unattainable without guidance. And yet, for all our reading, our believing, we had to admit that on the outside nothing had really changed. We confessed to different feelings, beliefs and attitudes, but ideas alone were not enough. I felt no more free than before, and my relations with people really hadn't changed. If I was practicing the ideas at all, I was doing so in conjunction with discoveries I was making on my own, which meant that I was lacking direction from the outside, from a trained observer, someone who could see and clear my own path enough for me to begin to venture on it in earnest. The Path was an intriguing idea, but I had to admit that after a year of reading I was no closer to being on my path then I had been before I met these ideas.

Gurdjieff seemed to put a special emphasis on two things in his writings: the awakening of conscience, and remorse. I knew from my own experience that when conscience is awakened the truth of one's actions was clear and irrefutable, and one had no choice but to accept oneself as one was—or at least had been in that situation. Conscience had a way of removing all of our buffers at once, and as Gurdjieff had said, we could then see our contradictions. It was our psychological buffers that kept us from seeing these contradictions.

He seemed also to be saying that we could experience remorse through and by our own efforts. Jane Heap had said that half of our waking life should be spent in pondering.

Although she had not explained how this was to be done, I remembered that in the Bible, Mary had pondered with her heart. This told me that one had to have a feeling for one's life, and a belief that it was possible to know, instinctively, what was needed if one could trust one's deepest feelings, and that by pondering one could *reach* those feelings.

I began to practice this, and whenever I came to something that either puzzled me or that I had a feeling for, I would ponder it. As a result of this, and with Nonny's help and with the insights into my character that had resulted from my work as a writer, I began to detect a pattern in my life that had resulted because of my difficulties with my father. Never having received his approval, or so it had always seemed to me, I found myself being both competitive and often combative with other men. What I seemed to be fighting for was something I felt I should have received earlier, and that I needed now as compensation. I wasn't able to get a handle on the convoluted nature of all this until I perceived one day that with all men I had one of two relations: either they were my father, and I was seeking to extract something from them that he hadn't given me, or I became the father (often to male friends much younger than myself) and became ultimately disappointed in them, as I felt I was to my father. In either case, I saw that my method of dealing with men was neurotic, and was one of the things that spoiled my life.

By constantly facing this in myself, and observing its occurrence, it began to change by itself. As a result I began to realize that in a school, where we would be regarded as broken and damaged machines in need of repair, this kind of work, in controlled circumstances, with a guide or guides who knew their way through the territory, one could make quicker strides than we were able to make alone.

We began to feel at one and the same time that we needed to find a group to work with.

Our desperation was matched by our reluctance to seek help. As artists we had always worked alone and for ourselves. Our work was our joy and salvation, and the only purpose we had found in life. That and our marriage and families. Until Gurdjieff, I had always believed that man's highest activity was art. One of the hardest things to swallow about Gurdjieff was his contempt for art in all its forms. "I was once sick man for art," he had stated, underscoring his point. To make matters worse, he declared that there *was* an objective art, which he claimed was mathematical, and could produce on all people alike its intended effect. He pointed to certain cathedrals, ceremonies and architectural monuments. It became clear to me in time that his music and movements, as well as his writings, in particular, *All and Everything: Beelzebub's Tales to His Grandson*, were all objective works of art.

And then there was subjective art, the stuff that *we* were making. As difficult as it was to accept his verdict, I could see that at the very least one could not justify one's life through one's art alone. I had to admit that all the artists I knew personally had been failures as human beings. This did not mean that the two were synonymous, but I had begun to smell a rat long before Gurdjieff pushed it under my nose.

Jane Heap had said that the trouble with artists is that they work to perfect their art instead of themselves. I had no trouble agreeing with this, and yet it was through my art that I was *trying* to perfect myself. The problem, as my year of reading had begun to show me, was that my art was slowly turning into something else. My intentions in the beginning were fairly pure, but I was already consumed with the idea of fame, a career, a place in the literary firmament. I had already begun to lose my original intention.

According to the universal laws which Gurdjieff discussed at great length, and particularly the Law of Seven, shown in his diagram, the Enneagram, everything becomes its opposite in time. This was lawful because life was obliged to repeat itself endlessly—for life had no place to go, except round and round—and wasn't this the Buddha's message? Life was the experience that made evolution possible. Taken by itself, it didn't lead anywhere, but if rightly understood and correctly engaged in, it could lead to a permanent change, and that change had to do with Being. The planet had a destiny, as did the individual, although it was quite doubtful that the ultimate destiny of either or each would ever be revealed to me in this lifetime. But this did not alter the truth of it, and it was clear to me that things did turn into their opposites. Gurdjieff said that this could be avoided by conscious shocks occurring at appropriate intervals. In our own case, his work was the shock we needed, but this too could run down if we didn't take the next step.

"What are we going to do?" Nonny announced one morning. "We've got to do something beside read books and talk to each other."

"I've been thinking about it."

"And."

"I thought I'd call Jerry Needleman—tonight." We looked at each other across the table, while a smile of relief appeared on both our faces. The decision had finally been made. I told Nonny now of my experience of the day before, when I had been sitting at this same chair and table. I had just finished my daily reading from Gurdjieff's *Beelzebub's Tales*, and had walked into the kitchen, where Nonny was preparing lunch. When I sat down I found myself looking out the window, gazing into the sky, my eyes unfocused, and turned more inward than out. Deep in the sky, but without form or seeming substance, Gurdjieff appeared, invisible and yet unmistakably himself, and said—not outside of me but somewhere deep inside—"It is all right, everything is going to be all right." It was an eternal moment, that because of its force lasted for several Earthly minutes. I knew that it *was* Gurdjieff, and I understood by those few words all that I needed to know: I could continue my search. *I would be protected.*

I called the Needlemans that evening. Carla answered the phone. She was happy to hear from me, and both surprised and pleased to learn why I was calling, although I detected a slight change in her voice when the subject of Gurdjieff came up. She went to get Jerry but came back to say that he couldn't come to the phone. "Perhaps," she said, "you could call later."

I called the next day but he was out, Carla said. I asked what the best time would be to call on the following day. I called again, and again he was unavailable.

"Why didn't you ask Carla for a name or phone number?" Nonny asked, after I had hung up.

"I don't know. I guess I couldn't believe that Jerry wouldn't come to the phone."

"I wish your sister Virginia wasn't out of the country."

"You know, when Virginia was in Warwick, I visited her and got to know someone in a bookstore. I'm just remembering a conversation we had back then. He was telling me how, each morning, he swept out his shop and dusted the books and furniture. He was obviously trying to bring order into life, and the quiet, unobtrusive way he had found to go about it impressed me. He was clearly practicing something he had learned in the work. I think I'll call him."

A week after our final call to the Needlemans we were sitting in a cafe in Warwick, New York, across from James Farr. We were seated at a round table, partially covered by our three cups of tea, whose steam rose silently between us, that I was secretly hoping would obscure my nervousness. After all this waiting I didn't know what to say, nor what to ask. "We've been reading the books," I said again, repeating the statement I had made over the phone. James had been waiting for one of us to speak. He was playing a role, that I was only vaguely aware he was uncomfortable in. Possibly it was a role he had never been in before. He reached over for the sugar bowl and slowly filled his spoon: once, twice, three times, and then gradually stirred the contents without looking in the cup. "Here we always walk around with a pebble in our shoe," he said, and placed the spoon on his napkin and looked at me. When I didn't answer, he said, "We have to change alarm clocks often." This time I understood him. I remembered reading about this in Ouspensky, who said that man was asleep, but that even exercises (alarm clocks) had to be changed often, otherwise, because of our nature, we would dream that we were awake without realizing that the very thing that awoke us had imperceptibly turned into a new form of sleep.

"Do you take turns waking each other up?" I asked. He looked at me, I thought a little dismayed.

"I can't find anything in Ouspensky," I said, "or anywhere else that indicates how to work. I agree with practically everything that's said, but when it comes to actually trying something, I forget before I remember."

"I don't even know what it is we are suppose to practice—or try,"

Nonny interjected.

"Don't be anxious. What we are trying is not easy. Here we have a teacher, other people, reminding factors."

"I find if I take just one idea and ponder what it means, and how it fits into my own life, my understanding does increase," I said. "But then I don't always know what all the thoughts that come to me mean, or how to apply them to my situation."

"That's right," James agreed. "That's why we need a common language. Also, we must become grounded in the ideas, so that when we have an experience we have something to refer it to. Gurdjieff has presented us with a complete cosmology."

"Does that mean that the work will speak to anything and everything in my life?" Nonny asked.

"Yes, it can, certainly. But here we must work on rightly conducted self-observation. Until we can do that nothing else is possible."

I had to admit again that I didn't know what he was talking about. "That's all right," James said, "the important thing at first is to just read the books, take in all you can, you have to know the work first with your mind, everything follows after that. Do you know what *metanoia* means?"

"No."

"It means change of mind. Think about that."

Driving home we felt both elated and disappointed. It was good to talk to someone who knew more than we did, but much of what he said we didn't understand, and nothing he had said had inspired us. We had hoped that the meeting would have settled something in us, and would help us to see what we needed, but it hadn't.

James had invited us for the weekend, which would include a lecture by his teacher, Mr. Nyland, a former pupil of Gurdjieff's, on Saturday night, and a work day on Sunday.

We both liked James Farr and had trusted him because of his obvious sincerity. When we drove back to Warwick on that Saturday we had felt encouraged, but the result of that weekend made us know that we would have to continue to look elsewhere for our search for a group. Instead of lecturing, Mr Nyland improvised on the piano for nearly an hour. Gurdjieff had said, verify everything for yourself, trust no one. Nonny and I pooled our verifications and decided his playing was not only abysmal, but his improvisations were meaningless.

That night we were put in a small, barren and dirty room, after we had been outfitted with sleeping bags. The next morning we had icy showers. Gurdjieff had prided himself on his hospitality, which of course was, quite apart from his teaching, a part of his culture—the same culture we had come out of. He had also said that "the work should at least be on the level of life." This meant to me that life was the beginning point, as well as the point of departure—but only if one had achieved a certain standard of life. Gurdjieff defined that "certain standard" with the term "good householder," which these people clearly were not. They may have made conditions purposefully difficult for us but it seemed more a kind of poverty—physical and emotional—that we didn't understand, especially since we had seen Mr. Nyland's home and it seemed palatial compared to the homes of the others in the Warwick group.

The next day we went to work: I was assigned to a demolition crew, with inadequate tools, although we were issued safety helmets, while Nonny was given the task of making muffins without a recipe or any knowledge of the kitchen or its contents.

We asked to meet with Mr. Nyland but were told we could not. Without discussing it, both Nonny and I knew that this was not the place for us.

We had made the first important step by deciding to find a group, but the actual finding of a group was not so easy as we had thought. We had been so concentrated on our resistance to joining that it had never occurred to us that something might be resisting us.

· CHAPTER FOUR ·

Without wasting any time I wrote to my sister in England. She had just completed a course of study with John Bennett at Sherbourne. Bennett and Madame de Salzmann were considered two of the most developed of Gurdjieff's pupils, and we heard that shortly after Madame took charge of the work, following the death of Gurdjieff, she removed Bennett from the Gurdjieff Foundation, the official body of the work. His experimentation with other systems and teachings was apparently considered heretical and, combined with his reputation of being mercurial and unpredictable, resulted in his being considered a threat to the established work. His behavior—and with it his reputation—didn't seem so different from Gurdjieff's, who had developed his system out of many esoteric teachings. Bennett had written a number of important books on Gurdjieff and his ideas, and I had read most of them. It seemed to me that, if anything, he had separated himself from the official work by the force and individuality of his own work, and by doing so he had stepped out of the form and into himself.

Virginia wrote that we shouldn't lose heart. She would speak to Bennett at the first opportunity, but in the meantime she gave us his address and encouraged us to write him a letter—"from your heart," she said.

Bennett's response was warm and inviting. He said we could come to Sherbourne and look into the possibility of taking one of his courses. A letter from Virginia followed, in which she told us that Bennett had said, in reference to Nonny's experience, that cancer is sometimes a door into the work.

We were both very moved by his letter. Nonny felt that he had not only understood her experience but was encouraging her to find her next step from within that experience. Having put it that way, she was able to see it as something positive, a growing point for her life instead of something that had ended.

We accepted his invitation and began making preparations to fly to London when Nonny, quite unexpectedly, had to go back to the hospital for another biopsy. She was dismissed with a clean bill of health, but before we could purchase our tickets, Bennett's wife, Elizabeth, wrote to say that her husband had died.

The following day we received a letter from Virginia saying she had returned to Sherbourne to help out, but that she would soon be back in the States. "Sit tight," she wrote, "we'll think of something when I get back."

In her next letter Virginia said that Bennett had been planning to transplant his work in America and had looked into a site in West Virginia just months before his death. It had since been purchased and was being worked on. She wanted to check it out when she returned and suggested we join her.

Charles Town, West Virginia was named after the man who owned the mansion that Bennett had purchased—Charles Washington, the brother of our first President. It was located on 450 acres, most of it scrub forest, but with a large milk barn and other out buildings.

Upon Virginia's return we wasted no time in driving to Claymont—as the property had been christened. Virginia was more impressed with Claymont than either Nonny or I. She had told us about Bennett's vision of a community that would be based in large part on The Sermon on the Mount. Bennett was convinced that we were headed for a global disaster that only a community from the New Age could survive. One that was built on the principle of a higher order, or demiurgic source, that everyone in the community could relate to. He was certain that all other communities would fall into disagreement and dissolution. He had implanted this idea in his people and had charged them with the obligation to carry it out. Only time would tell if his vision were true.

Although Bennett's mission did not touch our wish, which was by comparison, wholeheartedly selfish, we did not feel threatened by it, or even put off by it, providing the teaching at Claymont could provide whatever it was we felt would be right for us.

We had arrived at the cottage where Virgil Ort, the man in charge, was staying. "It's a temporary appointment," Virginia had explained earlier. She added that Pierre Elliott, the person who would be heading the work here, wouldn't arrive until everything had been put in place. When I asked who that was, Virginia said he was the man who had found a watermelon for Gurdjieff in the dead of winter in Paris. Nonny remembered the story. "Didn't Gurdjieff say that having done that he could stay?" "Yes," Virginia said, "that's Pierre. That was thirty-five or forty years ago, and he is one of the elders now."

Virgil Ort answered the door and ushered us in without smiling. "Please to sit down," he said in a German accent, indicating the chairs he had arranged for us. The wall was lined with photographs of himself in various poses, as well as several with children that, for some reason, I didn't think were his. He was a little younger than Nonny and I but older than Virginia, who was the age of the majority of the people I had seen working on the grounds. After my experience at Warwick, I wondered if this wasn't the common age of people in the work now: late twenties and early thirties.

Nonny and I were ignored while Virginia and Virgil Ort spoke about Bennett's sudden death. Despite the common sorrow that everyone at Claymont was experiencing, there was a feeling in the air of something being renewed, an energy that came out of a hope and a plan for the future. I had felt it as we walked around the grounds and observed the people at work. Everyone seemed both serious and lighthearted, and I wondered if their buoyancy didn't come from their having work to do that they believed in and that gave their life a purpose.

Virgil was saying now, perhaps for our benefit, that Bennett had not died like a dog. He called him "Mister" which had the effect of making his incomprehensible statement doubly offensive.

After we left and I had registered a string of meaningless complaints to Virginia, I said that what really bothered me about Virgil Ort was the same thing that disturbed me about James Farr. "They seem not to know how to talk to someone new."

"They're intimidated themselves," Virginia said. "Everyone below a certain level of spiritual development feels inadequate, and almost everyone is below that magic level."

"I can accept that, but why wouldn't Nyland speak to us? We asked for an interview and were refused."

"I don't think that came from him. He was being protected."

"From what? Can a teacher exist without pupils? Don't tell me he's gone into retirement with *those* people..."

"You have different requirements," Virginia said, "and there are very few people coming into the work who are your age."

"It isn't that, it's just that I don't feel the teaching either here or there. Something is missing."

"Things will be different when Pierre gets here."

"The watermelon man?"

Virginia laughed. "Yes, the watermelon man. He has made something. I think you would agree that he has. But that doesn't mean he would be right for you."

We spent the night in a motel, and the next morning drove back for one last look before returning to our home in New Concord. Virginia was living with us for now. It was evident to both Nonny and me that she had learned something from her time with Bennett. We were aware that she was doing some kind of morning exercise every day without fail, and her working habits had improved. And there was something in her seriousness that was different. It had deepened because it had been strengthened by her own being efforts.

Instead of being disheartened by our experiences at Claymont and Nyland's place, I felt somehow reassured. My serious doubts about working with others was being confirmed. But Virginia saw through my attitude. She called it negative, and reminded me again of my need. "There is always the Gurdjieff Foundation," she said now. "I don't think they take well to renegades and rebels, but I heard that Peter Brook and Pamela Travers, who are in the work in England, sometimes go to Armonk when they are in the States. So there must be a place for artists."

"Armonk?"

"A small town just north of Manhattan where they have their Sunday work. The man in charge of the Foundation, that Gurdjieff himself appointed, is Lord Pentland."

"It sounds very organizational." Nonny said.

"Perhaps it is, but how will you know if it's not for you if you don't check it out for yourselves?"

## · CHAPTER FIVE ·

We were sitting in the office of British Electric Company, looking up at a photograph of Queen Elizabeth. The two chairs provided for us seemed to have been arranged for our visit, which meant that British Electric neither had nor needed an anteroom. Our choice of things to look at was confined to the photo of the Queen and the man and woman sitting at adjoining desks, both of which faced in our direction. It was a bland, nondescript room, out of keeping with the posh neighborhood of the Upper East Side of Manhattan.

Was this Lord Pentland's business, I wondered, or merely a front for the work? It didn't occur to me that the head of the Gurdjieff Foundation would have a job and need to make a living. I had always assumed in my naivete that nobility and wealth went hand in hand.

The woman hadn't once lifted her face from her work, while the man seemed to be looking at everything *but* the contents on his desk. But despite their differences, they seemed to have something in common. Was it a detached indifference, or concealed curiousity? Or was this the face of the work?

The one enclosed chamber inside this large, drab office space obviously belonged to Lord Pentland, the person we had made an appointment to see.

I looked up at the photo again, and then over at Nonny to see if she was as amused by the hanging presence of Queen Elizabeth as I was. Nonny smiled back, knowingly.

We were still smiling when the door of Lord Pentland's chamber opened. His door faced the desk furthest from us. We could not see him from where we were sitting, but we were aware that he had signaled to the man at the desk, who quietly rose from his chair and walked over to us. "Lord Pentland will see you now," he said.

Lord Pentland was standing beside his chair when we entered, and greeted us by motioning to two chairs at the side of his desk. He closed the door and sat down.

"So, you've been reading the books," he said, questioningly. I meant to respond to the question in his voice, but said instead, "I feel desperate!" I was startled by my statement, but realized instantly that he was someone we could speak to. His presence and inner authority were unmistakable.

"About what?" he asked. There was a smile of amused interest on his face, as well as a look of concern.

"I want to be free."

"You want, or you wish?"

"What's the difference?" Nonny asked.

"One belongs to personality, the other to essence. Wish is the most powerful force a man can make in himself: to wish, truly, with one's whole being. But to want—one thing today, another tomorrow, hmn?"

I didn't know what to say. He was looking at me now, waiting, in complete patience, and without expectation. I suddenly felt that he knew what I was feeling, that if he wished he could reveal to me my own thoughts, and even more than that, my desires.

No one had ever given me their complete attention before. I felt disarmed. He broke the silence by saying, "You must first have an aim. Your aim is to be free. Good! But what is an aim? Do you wish the Gurdjieff work, do you need this work, or do you only want the work?" He paused. "You ring me up. But what if I am not here? You call once, twice, three times, hmn? Then what do you do?"

"We called on several people before you," Nonny said. His eyes lit up. "Ah, and what happened?"

"David wrote to John Bennett first. His sister had studied with him at Sherbourne in England, and she gave us his address." While Nonny spoke I watched Lord Pentland. I had been struck first by his height, which I saw now was exaggerated by his emaciated thinness. His forehead was furrowed, and his dark eyes were deeply set in their sockets. But it was only his flesh that looked aged; he was otherwise as sprightly as a man in his thirties—which was certainly half his actual age. He just missed being rumpled, but I didn't know if this was undeveloped taste, indifference, or a form of English casualness I didn't understand. He looked a bit like a benevolent giraffe.

"After Bennett died," I heard Nonny saying, "we went out and had a look at Claymont."

"Yes, Claymont, hmn, tell me about it," Lord Pentland said. "There were a lot of people running around," Nonny said, "planting, digging, cooking what looked like vegetarian food. I don't know what the spiritual life is suppose to look like, but it didn't feel right for me. We're over forty, our life is established, we didn't think we should have to move backward in order to have the work."

"The man in charge referred to Bennett as Mister," I said, "and in the half day we were there, he must have said at least ten times that Mister didn't die like a dog."

"He said it again in the morning, before we left," Nonny said, and laughed.

"You didn't fancy Claymont, then."

"I'd remembered reading about 'not dying like a dog,' by Gurdjieff, but I just couldn't understand why he kept saying it."

"To die like a man is to die consciously, aware of one's death and the meaning of one's life, that one has intentionally lived," Lord Pentland said.

"Well, that should be obvious to everyone!" Nonny exclaimed. "We have two words for death in the Armenian language, *merneel*, meaning human death, and *satkeel*, for animal death. The greatest personal insult is to say to someone, *satkeese!*, or 'may you die like a dog.'"

"So, it is in the language then," Lord Pentland mused. A look of amazed delight on his face.

"Yes," Nonny and I said in unison.

"But that explains so much. Gurdjieff made a very big thing of it, but it was there in the language and culture all the time—for him, I mean. This is obvious to you. You're both Armenian, Gurdjieff was Armenian..." his voice trailed off, "but for us, for whom it had to be provided...."

I didn't want to admit that it was important to me that Gurdjieff was Armenian. Now that I had come this far, it really didn't matter anymore, but I don't know if I would have gotten this far if Gurdjieff hadn't been Armenian. The quality in his work, including the music, had an Armenianness to it that both Nonny and I understood because of our shared heredity.

"Then you came here," Lord Pentland said, referring to our discussion about Claymont.

"No," I answered, "we also went to Nyland's place in New York state. They call it Chardovogne Barn. It wasn't so different from Claymont, at least on the outside."

Lord Pentland gave a short laugh, which caused me to stop short. "Look at this," he said, and handed me a letter that had been sitting on top of his desk. I recognized at once the landmark used for the logo.

"This just came from Wilhem Nyland," he said, with unmistakable relish. "He wants our help with the movements." To my surprise, he was indicating with his hand that he wanted me to read the letter. "I was the one to tell Nyland he had to leave the Foundation."

I was taken aback. Why was he telling us all this? I could see that he wasn't bragging, but rather trying to prove something.

"Aren't the movements the Sacred Dances that Gurdjieff brought back from the East?" Nonny asked.

"Reformulated for the West would be more accurate," Lord Pentland said.

To my surprise, I broke into what he was saying. "Lord Pentland, we need a group to work with. We can't go any further on our own." I was aware that Nonny was looking at me, and I could feel her support.

I had gone over everything in my mind—our past failures to find a group, along with the growing feeling that we might not find one, coupled with my growing reluctance to sign up with anyone, anywhere—and yet I knew that our need wasn't being fulfilled, now that we had gotten all we could from the books that were available. Lord Pentland was quite obviously an unusual man, with capacities that were beyond my judgment. I was beginning to feel an emotional connection.... Perhaps I could give him my trust, perhaps I could learn what I needed from him and achieve the freedom I craved. Gurdjieff had said that his work was for the sly man, and Lord Pentland's operation was certainly that. In every way, what I had seen and heard so far conformed to my notion of what the Gurdjieff work should look like, at least on the outside.

"We have something for beginners," Lord Pentland was saying. He paused to consider, and then said, "For now, go on with your reading of *All and Everything.*

"In the morning," he continued, speaking very slowly, "after you have washed, but before breakfast, sit in a chair, alone in a room facing a window, with your eyes nearly closed, and dropping all thoughts, lower your attention to your center. Here," he said, indicating with his hand, "just below the navel. Ten minutes, in the morning—for now."

I reviewed the exercise in my mind before speaking. "How about Armonk?" I asked.

"Oh, that's for older people," he said, flapping his right hand in the air, as if our request were out of the question.

"We will have to be put in a group," I said. He looked at me from under his bushy eyebrows. For the first time I noticed that he was bald. He took out a pad and wrote down an address. "Next Friday," he said, "at 7 P.M."

But we didn't get up to leave. He fingered the pad before returning it to its place. Then he said something very surprising. Looking into my eyes, he said, "You need to go on writing." And then, turning to Nonny, "And you need to cook."

I don't know what shocked me more, that he knew my work, or that he had somehow read my fear, for I had been feeling for some time that if I entered the work I would have to give up my art. I realized now that it was one of the things that had been holding me back.

I was feeling dazed when we stood up to say good-bye. I had forgotten to ask if it was a real group that we would be entering, or only something for beginners. "Come here anytime you wish," he said now, "I want you to think of this as your home."

We left the office and walked to the elevator. My eyes were beginning to fill up, and Nonny was already crying. "No one ever said that to me..." Nonny started to say, but she was too choked up to continue.

It was true. We had had our first taste of impersonal love. It had so disarmed us that I felt the defenses I had built up over a lifetime suddenly fall away, leaving me empty and vulnerable—but also joyous.

He had seen what we needed, perhaps what everyone needs, and that had once been provided for him by Gurdjieff: a place of safety from where we could dare to be ourselves.

# · CHAPTER SIX ·

The Friday night meetings were for beginners. They were located in what we called the Gallery, a basement apartment in a brownstone in midtown Manhattan, near Lexington Avenue. It was also a training ground for those being prepared for leadership positions. The Foundation was composed of a definite hierarchical structure, as I would quickly learn. One had to pass muster at the Gallery before being allowed into the Foundation. This was the bottom rung of the ladder.

As we drove home from our first meeting, I mentioned to Nonny that it looked like we would have to begin our search with young people in their twenties, after all, as the adherents here were of the same generation as those at Claymont and Chardovogne Barn.

The two people sitting in front had been our age or older. One of them read while the other remained motionless and contained. I was impressed by his ability to sit, unmoving, throughout a half hour reading. Was this part of the training, I wondered, and quickly concluded that it was. This was not something I would have been capable of myself.

I had felt uneasy throughout the hour, but at the same time, I also felt exhilarated. I kept asking myself if our search had finally ended, and our quest begun. The reading was from P. D. Ouspensky's *In Search of the Miraculous*. This book, I would soon learn, was the Bible of the Foundation. The Foundation was comprised largely of Ouspensky people, who had gone over to Gurdjieff after Ouspensky's passing, and just one year before Gurdjieff's own death.

After the reading there had been a silence while those in the audience prepared themselves to ask questions. Both the questions and the answers seemed forced, without any urgency on the part of the questioners, or any feeling on the part of those who were replying. There was a palpable feeling of fear in the room that disturbed me, in part because I was aware of my own fear: an overriding feeling that I wouldn't measure up.

From the very first meeting I noticed two things about myself: I was envious of the two leaders in front, and I wanted to ask impressive questions and be noticed.

It was our third Friday meeting. I had told Nonny in advance that we would receive a message at that meeting concerning our wish to be placed in a group.

"Intuition or cockiness?" Nonny said.

"Both and neither. It's time."

"And if we don't?"

"I'll go back to Pentland and ask again."

At the close of the meeting, as we were filing out, the man we had first seen at the desk in Pentland's office came up to us and handed me a slip of paper. It contained a time and a date, and an address, that I would soon find out was the address of the Gurdjieff Foundation. I wasn't surprised, but I *was* pleased. "For a group meeting?" I asked the man, but he walked away without answering. Was I supposed to know, was I not supposed to ask? I had learned by now that no one said anything unnecessary, but still.... Maybe I was supposed to know. Perhaps, if I thought about it without speaking I would or could know. Pentland had mentioned at our first meeting with him that Gurdjieff rarely spoke. Maybe there was a reason for this, too.

Lord Pentland, as it turned out, was our Group Leader. It seemed an ignominious title for someone who was about to become our guru.

We rang the bell above the stoop, at the entry to the Foundation. The building was an old mansion on the Upper East Side of New York. The door was opened by a young man dressed in a suit and tie.

On the wall of the entryway was an alphabet unknown to us depicted in pictographs. There was a large oriental rug on the floor of the reception room to our left, where we could see a large bowl of flowers on an antique table that stood beside the office. Through its double doors we could hear the strains of oriental music filtering into the reception room and hallway. This, we later learned, was the music that accompanied the Movements. We were able to take all this in at a glance, before mounting the steps, as directed by the doorman, who contributed to the overall silence by motioning instead of speaking.

The chairs had already been set up in our meeting room, including the chair in front that faced a slightly arced row of seven other chairs. The first thing I noticed was a beautiful but worn Oriental rug on the floor.

The room was in silence. Fear, respect and awe seemed to emanate from the people in the room, as well as from the walls. We placed our wraps on one of the chairs in back, as the others had done, and took our seats.

I felt completely subdued, and I could feel Nonny drawing up inside herself. It was a strangely thrilling moment, unlike anything I had ever experienced before.

The room had filled, and from my end chair I studied the other faces. Only one man seemed reasonably comfortable inside himself. It turned out that he had been in groups before but had left for six years while dissolving one marriage and making another. His name, I was about to learn, was Philip, for he was the only one among us that Lord Pentland acknowledged by name.

Like the others, we had arrived early. Apparently this was the thing to do. The idea was to collect oneself, or remember oneself, while we waited for the leader to appear. Lord Pentland arrived several minutes late, as he would for every meeting we would ever attend. We would wait for the dreadfully thrilling moment when the tread of his shoes could be heard marching in our direction down the long corridor, carrying in their step doom, hope and the reckoning of time, all mysteriously rolled into one.

Our hunger, fear, and our shared uncertainty slowly made a bonding within the group, even though we never saw one another outside our group meetings. While we were there, together, we were like hungry birds, sharing a single nest, waiting with open mouths to have food dropped from on high by Lord Pentland.

Slowly, the training began.

I doubt that any of us knew what was happening to us.

We were told in one of the first meetings that without Magnetic Center—that may have been nurtured by music, literature or art—we may not have come into the work, as the Magnetic Center was really the property of essence. Magnetic Center was something everyone in the Work had, to a greater or lesser degree, because it was this alone—in the beginning at least—that could distinguish between ordinary life and the life of the spirit.

We chewed and pondered on all this as best we could.

Or that the only thing we can do in the beginning is to put ourselves under a higher influence, which it was clear we had done. But as for the rest of what was said, one day I half understood, the next day it had been completely forgotten. What I felt, what we all must have been feeling, in meeting after meeting, was that we were being taken to the stars. It was as if the life of the spirit were made palpable and real—and believable! We were hearing the truth for the first time, and it was almost too much for us. We had lived on half-truths, if that, for so long that we hadn't the muscle to take in anything else. Nor were we able to exercise even a tenth of what we were being given.

At one of our first meetings Lord Pentland spoke to us about essence and personality. Essence, he said, was what we were born with, whereas personality was acquired. "They cannot grow simultaneously. If the essence is passive, as must happen in contemporary life, the personality grows. Essence, as a rule, is stopped by the age of seven."

"What can we do?" one of the braver souls asked.

"Make personality passive, then essence will grow."

Can we do that, I thought, can we just *do* that? I began to make whatever feeble efforts I could, not realizing that by just taking it in, and understanding it to the best of my ability, I was already making a significant step.

I saw that my personality was who I thought I was. In my case, this sense of being David Kherdian was enough. Just that, without anything more, was the only identity I required. And I felt, unconsciously, that anything I might gain would be added to that. It was only in my poetry that I sometimes arrived at a deeper place in myself, but I didn't live in my poetry, as I *did* live in my personality. Nevertheless, I came to see that there was a difference, that although the personality could take over the act of creation (Lord Pentland had told us that the seat of the personality is in the ego), it could not itself create anything, except for an appearance, a *modus operandi*. It was necessary, it was even important, but it wasn't the point of our existence. It would die with the body. It had no life after this life. But the essence did.

"After all," Lord Pentland reasoned, "if you were born in China you would have had a Chinese personality." Looking at me, he said, "You wouldn't be David Kherdian, would you?"

Several weeks later, while talking to Philip in the corridor, I mentioned that my friends were beginning to find me boring. To my surprise, he later reported what I had told him during the meeting, and then said, "My wife said I should go back and tell all of you that I am *definitely* not improving." Everyone laughed, and the heaviness we had all been feeling was temporarily lifted. We had begun to see the humor in our situation. We were, after all, in the same boat, and I had begun to believe—as I knew Nonny believed—that our boat, however many leaks it might have, had become an ark.

But the school year was coming to an end. It was June and the Foundation was closing for the summer.

· C H A P T E R   S E V E N ·

It was evident from the very first meeting in September that Lord Pentland had upped the ante.

It had been a difficult summer. The work had provided a high that was more than counter-balanced by the low of seeing ourselves— *beginning* to see ourselves—in a truer light. I had begun to see aspects of my impatience and mechanicalness that disturbed me, but that I couldn't control. Until now I had simply moved from one desire to the next, calling each move "my choice," but now—by choosing at times in advance—I saw how quickly these desires asserted themselves and insisted on having their own way. All of this meant that I could not easily justify behavior that I was now beginning to feel uneasy about. I felt like I had been pried open and couldn't get myself shut again. I alternately yearned for and dreaded the return of meetings.

Our meetings took place in the same room but our tiny group had been combined with another group, and we now exceeded twenty in number. We were arranged into three parallel rows, facing the three chairs in front. Lord Pentland was flanked with question answerers, a man on his right and a woman on his left, both of whom were ten or more years younger than Nonny and I.

We could neither see our neighbors nor were we meant to. Eyes straight ahead and no fidgeting seemed to be the unspoken rule. I was aware, as I had not been the previous year, that there was a custom and a form to everything that occurred in the Foundation. And it was being followed—rigidly. Our warm room had suddenly turned cold.

Some of our members had been in groups for as long as ten years. It was little wonder that their questions and observations were often incomprehensible to me. At our third meeting one young man went on at great length, recreating a scene in which—it seemed to me—he exposed himself unmercifully.

My feelings for him slowly moved across my emotional landscape: from confusion, to surprise, to embarrassment, to outrage, to chagrin and finally disgust. How would Lord Pentland respond, especially since his observation contained neither a question for Lord Pentland, nor mercy for himself.

Lord Pentland was seemingly indifferent. I couldn't understand his matter-of-fact reply. Was he disgusted too, or was his response so personal that only the man himself could receive the instruction that was being hidden from the rest of us, for I assumed that everyone else was also in the dark, though from their unwrinkled stares and self-conscious composure I couldn't even be certain of that.

"Our star-gazing days are over," I whispered to Nonny, once we were safely on the sidewalk again.

"It's changed," Nonny agreed, "but if it stayed the same you wouldn't have liked that either. Remember how we read that Gurdjieff said it wasn't possible to teach directly, and how others said that he would answer them by speaking to someone else?"

"Also how his words were often incomprehensible to everyone but the one he was speaking to," I said. I assumed Nonny was speaking about the long-winded young man.

"Well, that happened to me tonight. I had this burning question that I was afraid to ask, but the more I put it off, the more I felt agitated inside. And then I heard him say, 'Don't ask your question.' Do you remember his saying that?"

"No."

"So right after that he answered me when he spoke to the redhead. He actually knew what my question was and he answered it! When he finished speaking to the redhead, he looked over at me, I guess to be certain I had known he was talking to me."

"What did he say?"

"I'll tell you later, after I've had a chance to digest it."

We drove home in silence, but we must have been thinking the same thing because as soon as we were home and settled in our chairs, and I had poured each of us a snifter of Armagnac, Nonny said, "Aside from some of the changes that probably trouble you more than me, the work is opening up for us in a way it hadn't last year. In addition to the Gallery talks, that we can still go to, there are the Wednesday lectures and the Thursday sittings."

"And I'm sure we'll be able to go to Armonk if we are active about what *has* been offered."

"We agree then," Nonny said, "that we need to take an apartment in the City."

"I guess we do," I said.

Nonny laughed. "Don't hang back." She was laughing because we were both so impetuous and quick to jump that neither of us were able to act as a restraining force for the other. At best, one of us sometimes hesitated for a few moments, and in most cases it was me. In this instance we had discussed it briefly before, and had decided that we couldn't consider selling our house, so it was only a matter of being able to afford both: a house in the country, and an apartment in the city. We didn't see how this could be managed until we realized that the only way we could pull it off was to rent our country house. We had agreed, reluctantly, that without the work nothing else mattered. Just as we knew that what we stood to gain on one end would have to be lost at the other. Our comfort and security would be the first two things to go.

We rented an apartment in the same complex that Nonny had been living in when we met. But this time we had a larger ground floor apartment, which was a decided improvement over her third floor walk-up. The superintendent was Maltese, and loved plants. He had turned the courtyard into a miniature botanical garden.

Our cat, Missak, slowly adjusted to being an indoor cat. Whenever we came home together he would be sitting on Nonny's work table, staring into the courtyard, waiting for us to come home.

More than sixty people attended the Thursday sittings. They took place in the main hall, where most of the activities took place: movements, lectures, concerts and even celebrations, such as Gurdjieff's birthday celebration, which was the major event of the year. I had never understood why our sittings were not called meditations, as they were in all other esoteric traditions, until I finally concluded that it was because we were not trying to get anywhere. We were trying to drop everything without gaining anything, an almost impossible feat, given our avidity and aggressiveness.

The cloakroom, toilets, workshop and dressing rooms were all downstairs, along with a tiny cafetèria where some people—the higher-ups, it appeared to me—had refreshments and snacks, and socialized. I later heard that it had been instituted for this purpose, since socializing by people in the work with others in the work *was* in fact work, and something that beginners, presumably, could not be invited to attempt.

There were also long benches in the basement, and after hanging up our coats and taking off our shoes, we sat on one or another of these, in silence, while waiting for the movements class taking place above our heads to end. The music of the movements provided the nirvana that I had thought the sittings were meant to provide. Before, that is, I actually began sitting and learned the bitter truth.

We ascended the stairs to the waiting cushions and, taking our seats—women on the right, men on the left (so as not to mix vibrations)—we loosened our belts, adjusted our privates, and prepared to lower our eyelids at the undeclared signal from up front, where a line of group leaders made long flanking rows on each side of the person conducting the sitting. Lord Pentland took most of the sittings, talking us through its early part, largely with exercises in sensing, though I didn't know yet what that term meant, neither its function nor its purpose. The important thing was to drop our thoughts and really be in our bodies. Relaxing occurred through sensing, and although we were encouraged to be in our centers, I did not realize for some time that this could not be possible if my body was rigid, and my thoughts out of control.

The sittings lasted forty-five minutes, an unbelievable length of time for anyone who had not sat before, and our ten minute chair sittings had been poor preparation for this.

I was disappointed but not very surprised to hear snoring in the room during each sitting, quite often from one or more of the people in the front row. If I was heartened by this I certainly wasn't encouraged.

No one told us what it was we were gaining from this arduous discipline, and I was not brave enough to ask. The spiritual benefits were never questioned, only our ability to meet this seemingly superhuman demand with an appropriate response.

Without wasting any time, we asked to be put in a movements class, even though we knew we would be refused. We had been in the work now for one year. We had heard of people waiting five years and even longer before they were assigned to a class. I found this incomprehensible. If you needed something it was yours, you took it. Nothing belonged to any of us: not the earth, not other people, not even our own lives. We had to take what we needed when we needed it, before the time passed. Even if it proved that what we wanted was not what we needed—for there was no other way to learn this, except by trial and error. Denial, if it could teach patience, had some merit. But I had no patience whatever, and if patience was something I needed to learn, it would have to be one of the last things, and I didn't think denial would be the teacher. Rather, it would have to come from a need that I would have to see for myself.

I had heard the Gurdjieff music for the first time at a special concert given at the Foundation just before the summer break. I had listened to music all my life, the range of my interest and evolving taste having traveled from pop to jazz to classics. I had also listened to Middle-Eastern music from the time I was a child. But nothing in my background had prepared me for Gurdjieff's music, which was a completely new and different experience. It engaged my emotions in an unaccustomed way, a way I was not able to define. His music was neither excited nor inflammatory, but understated, controlled, refined. It moved me—not to abandon or forgetting—but to remembering something that I had long forgotten. But above all, one sensed at once, even before its full effect had taken hold, that this music had been brought into being for the listener, not for the creator.

Now that I had heard the music for myself, I had no trouble understanding the stories of Gurdjieff evoking whatever feelings he wished in his listeners when he played his harmonium for small groups, or individuals, often at the end of a day of work.

I was certain now that the movements were also a form of objective art. Except for some of the simple exercises or warm-ups, the movements were always accompanied by music that was integral, since each movement had its own music. The scores for these had been composed by Gurdjieff, with his pupil Thomas de Hartmann. This music had the same haunting quality as the music Gurdjieff had composed for listening, which had a separate, though not so very different, purpose.

The movements were the most treasured part of the teaching. I had heard more than once that the last thing anyone was willing to give up, even after they had left group attendance, was the movements. I had even heard that many people had not understood the work until they took movements, or that they would not have stayed in the work if it weren't for the movements. And yet I knew that Gurdjieff had made movements available only for given periods. Even movements were not meant to go on forever. Once their purpose had been accomplished they needed to be dropped.

We went to the sittings at the Foundation earlier than we needed to in order to listen to the music from our bench seat in the basement. We were still sitting in the mornings, as Lord Pentland had advised us to do, except that we had gone out and bought special meditation cushions from East West Bookstore in Manhattan. At the group sittings my legs would fall asleep after fifteen minutes, by which time my back would begin to ache, causing my torso to feel like it had caved in on itself. My eyes, which were closed, were wide open inside my head, and dreaming. I didn't really think that anyone was getting anything exalted from any of this, but I did wonder if anyone was suffering as much as I was.

But Nonny's problems were even greater than mine. In addition to having all of the difficulties that I had, she also fidgeted. She said that on several occasions she had nearly fallen over part way through the sitting.

We must have assumed that there was no way out of our dilemma because after the second or third session we stopped complaining to one another. It had never occurred to us to ask for help.

When help finally came it did not appear in a form we would have wished for. At the conclusion of one of the sittings, while I was stretching out my legs and waiting for them to return to life, I heard a woman shout, "Stop your fidgeting. You're a disturbance to everyone around you."

For some reason, I knew the outburst had been directed at Nonny. When I reached the foyer I saw her standing red-faced in front of Cindy Tower, one of our question-answerers. I walked up and joined them, wondering who the woman was that had scolded Nonny, for I knew that it couldn't have been Cindy. "You need to sit with your hips above your legs," Cindy was saying. "Use as many cushions as necessary. This will keep your legs from falling to sleep. It's going to take longer before you'll be able to keep your spine straight, but try not to give in to your body, if it hurts, let it hurt. Incorporate the pain, don't try to remove it by fidgeting."

It would take a full year before I would be able to sit for an indefinite period without moving, without any aching in my body, and with my spine erect. I had learned the hard way that once something begins to ache no movement will improve it. Cindy had been right, only ignoring it helped. But Nonny's problems with sitting went on for a much longer time. She eventually saw that it was her resistance that made her legs fall to sleep. If she sat for ten minutes, her legs fell to sleep in five, if fifteen minutes, her legs fell to sleep in ten. We were beginning to see what Gurdjieff meant by sly man. One had to be sly with oneself. It was us, each and every one of us, who were the saboteurs of our own work.

·  CHAPTER  EIGHT  ·

Lord Pentland announced at the close of our third meeting, after group meetings resumed in the fall, that all those who wished Sunday work at Armonk had to sign up with our group secretary a minimum of five days in advance each week.

Named after the city in which it was located, Armonk was perched on a knoll, surrounded by wood lots and separated from the bordering land on the West by a ravine. Once a secluded seminary for women, the area had been built up over the years, although each individual plot preserved an inviolate privacy, and our own plot, which consisted of a mansion, three houses and outbuildings, was no exception. There were beautiful gardens everywhere, maintained by one of the landscape architects in the work along with a crew of workers, and an appropriate use had been found for each of the buildings. There was a children's house, a two family home where one of the movements instructors lived, and a caretaker's cottage. The garage had been converted to a tool shed, and the carriage house into a workshop. There was also a separate shed for pottery, as well as a row of single-story buildings whose original function was un-known, but that were now used for a lapidary, a forge, as well as various floating projects.

A long, wide hallway ran the length of the mansion, and led to a large room with fireplace that was a recent addition. This room served as a dining hall and movements room, as well as an alternate site for the Gurdjieff dinner and other celebrations. It was here that we gathered for our work day that began at 9 A.M. every Sunday.

One of the elders gave a theme or simple direction for the inner work, often preceded by a simple movements exercise, the purpose of which was to sharpen our attention, and possibly even to remind us why we were there.

Another hallway, running off, and perpendicular to the main hallway, led to other rooms that I never visited, though I sometimes heard the strains of Armenian music emanating from one of the hidden chambers, where it was rumored Madame de Salzmann and Peter Brook were working on the film, *Meetings with Remarkable Men*.

The library, where the translators worked on various "work texts," was located at the front of the mansion, across the hall from a room that was kept private for the major Group Leaders (called Group I), a weaving shop with several looms, a room for the clean-up crew, where I often saw women bent over their ironing, and another room where the "Form and Sequence" classes were held, that had something to do with art. Rug repairing went on in the attic, and there was a repair shop, as well as a print shop and batik work in the basement. And finally, the kitchen, the room second in size only to the main addition, where a crew of about ten prepared our lunches.

Although nearly all of the eighty to one hundred people who came for Sunday work were professionals in life, we were largely incompetent at the tasks we were selected to work at on Sundays. For each chore, the person who seemed most capable was the one who seemed to be doing the least, only occasionally stepping in and giving advice, and then backing away, or disappearing altogether. Those in charge took their work very seriously—though not always responsibly—as I imagined they believed that they were directing our inner work as well as our outer work. For this reason, they often seemed to be puzzled and serious. We all knew that physical work— or "practical work," as it was often called—was the key to the work. Gurdjieff had said, "I teach but two things, conscious labor and intentional suffering." We at least understood *our* beginning point: unconscious labor and *voluntary* suffering. We didn't *have* to go to Armonk, and so our choosing to go constituted voluntary suffering which, although a long way from intentional suffering, was at least a by-path leading to the main highway. As for conscious labor, about that we knew very little, except that it had to do with attention, that in turn led to a correct understanding of energics that we must learn to direct (the sittings were an aid in this), and finally, it had everything to do with identification—one of those keys that everyone recognized but for which no one could find the lock.

Gurdjieff said that when we were identified we were like a monkey that goes completely into the object in front of him at that moment. Change the object and the monkey disappears completely into the new object. But we were supposed to be men—and not men in quotation marks, as he liked to say—which meant that we had an inner world as well as an outer world. Our inner world needed to be kept separate from—or at least have the ability to separate itself from—our outer world. Conscious labor had to do with working with all three centers at the same time: moving-instinctive, mind and feelings.

Just how difficult that was I would prove to myself over and over again. I began to see my own resistance: I didn't want to take orders, I was proud and self-willed, I couldn't take an interest in work that seemed menial or unimportant and I could find no value in learning something that someone else could do better, or that I could hire someone else to do for me. And finally, I couldn't see the point of work itself, even though I knew that Gurdjieff had said, "I love him who loves work for its own sake."

But slowly, slowly, in all of these attitudes I began to see my work. I had wanted to impress everyone with my life achievements, but in this place our life achievements were checked at the door. Over and over again I had to face up to my own inertia, rebelliousness, laziness, stubbornness, incompetence and, finally, my lack of real interest. In this last I would eventually—after years of trial and error—find my way. I had to become interested: and if looked at the right way, the correct way, the only true way, everything *was* interesting. Only the boring are bored was a truism I would come to tack over my door.

But it wasn't only a matter of "change of mind," or *metanoia*, as Maurice Nicoll had said in his *Commentaries* on Gurdjieff's teachings. *Metanoia* had been incorrectly translated in the Bible as "repent." The greatest obstacle was my conditioning. Not only the conditioning that had been foisted on me, but also the conditioning I had put on myself.

I had to look back on my life to try and understand where and how my problem began. The Armenians of my hometown had been hired off the docks of New York for factories and foundries in the Midwest. They had literally died working, for few lived to draw more than one or two pension checks. None had hobbies, pastimes, or the necessary leisure to think and dream, plan and create. They had kept the race alive by transplanting it to a new land. I had assumed the burden of their sacrifice: having decided that I would make my life count by leaving that place, and not having children of my own because they might impede my aim, and not working for a wage only. I would be the master of my destiny.

Well, I had done my best, but with the result that although one end of my stick was very strong, the other end had become brittle and badly chipped.

I couldn't seem to make myself work at something I myself had not chosen. I didn't know how to work with other men—having always worked alone—and I had never learned the necessary physical skills that most boys learn from their fathers.

So how would I begin?

I often thought of Gurdjieff's response to the woman writer who had told him that she felt more conscious when she was writing. Gurdjieff had replied, "You live in dreams and you write about your dreams. Much better for you if you were to scrub one floor consciously than to write a hundred books as you do now."

I had been assigned to the forge. I was sure that Lord Pentland must have known that this would give me suffering. To learn blacksmithing was not the point; to stay on the job and not run away was all I asked of myself.

I noticed immediately that the two men I worked with in the forge were factory types, essentially no different from the kind of people I had grown up with in Racine. They were here in the forge because they fit in this place, they were comfortable here, they had found their niche—and they had never outgrown it. Being with them I was thrown back on myself, and felt many of the same feelings I had felt as a young man. I had believed that I had been born in the wrong place, to the wrong set of parents, in circumstances that had nothing to do with who I was. But here I was feeling those feelings again in a place I had chosen to come to. With the result that I saw for myself that there was no place to move on to from here. I was where I needed to be. But it was hard to accept that what I was seeing was the material I needed to look at if I were ever to be free of this limitation, this feeling of inferiority that the circumstances of my life had imposed upon me. My problem was not the forge. My problem, once again, was my attitude toward work. But it was my work in the forge that made me see this impulse, or drive, to prove who I was through my work—by doing work that would be special, outstanding, eye-catching—work that said *who I was*. But I was *not* my work! If this were true then who was I?

Some time before, during one of our group meetings, Lord Pentland had explained that there were three lines of work: work on oneself, work with others and work for the work. When he was asked to say more about work with others, he had replied, simply, that "...it might have something to do with external considering."

External considering, as I understood it, was more objective, while internal considering was subjective. In other words, what he seemed to be saying was that we should consider others more, ourselves less, and not judge by appearances. Was that it? And was this why we met in a controlled environment like Armonk, in order to practice on one another? That must have been at least one of the reasons.

I remembered as a teenager having seen a Christmas card with the formulation from many cultures, that in English was translated as, "Love thy neighbor as thyself." For some reason, this had made a deep impression on me. I had never completely forgotten it, and often, when it returned to me, I would try to fathom its meaning. Now, for the first time, I had been given a clue. Surely, I thought, external considering has to be a factor.

I felt at times that it was the work's intention to throw us a bone at a time. There was good reason for this. Knowledge, such as book learning, must not take the place of experience, but rather must become one ingredient to be used in our overall quest for understanding. Knowledge was encyclopedic—it could be acquired and it could also be lost—but what we had understood was ours and could not be taken from us. We were working for permanent being, individuation, the gradual emergence of Real I.

I would have to struggle and work and suffer for every drop of understanding I might acquire. Nothing would accrue to me by simply being here. I had to work for myself, harder than I had ever worked before, and differently, because I was living in a new and unfamiliar—and yet strangely familiar—world. Someone had said, and immediately I heard it I knew it was true, that once one starts on The Way time is counted. Our unlimited time is now limited. It would be better not to start out at all, than to start and do nothing, or to start and quit.

I began to watch my step. Gurdjieff had spoken often about the Law of Accident, which I now took very literally. I did not want to have a foolish accident and be snuffed out just when I had reached the doorstep of a real possibility—the first true and real possibility of my life. I knew that I had something important to attain, and even more important that it was attainable. There was no time to waste, just as there was no time for foolishness or game playing.

I was eventually transferred to the woodshop, and this was an improvement of a kind. I could at least look up from time to time and take in the surroundings. There was, after all, more to see than *just* my resistance. Working with wood was something I had wanted to do as a boy. Carpentry and printing were the two crafts I had always wanted to know more about. Making a chair or table didn't seem so different to me from making a poem. The basic difference was in the materials used. Words—their usage and their possibilities—were my first love, and I saw now for myself why carpentry was not. I was repelled by the smell of sawdust. Had I not known this, was I finding this out for the first time? Still, I was fascinated by what others could do with wood, even though the noise and the mess and the smell were a disturbance to me. But printing was different. I remembered wandering through print shops as a boy. I realized now that "printer's ink was in my veins," as the saying went. I am sure it had to do with writing, and that it was connected to other lifetimes.

I was several months at Armonk before I began to understand that the morning theme or talk was something we needed to work with while engaged in our task. This was the basis of the luncheon discussion, and I am sure that the two together were the compelling attraction for the great majority of those who made the long and expensive drive out to the country every Sunday. All of the fees at the Foundation seemed high. In addition there was the cost of Armonk, to which we had to add gas and tolls, or carpool fees.

The questions asked after lunch had to do with attention, energies, dividing one's attention, and so on, but when it came to resistance, confusion, anger and other forms of negativity, one had to be very careful in dressing one's question in a very modest work garment. It seemed important that both question and answer be very impersonal. As time went on I had greater and greater difficulty listening to these exchanges. I understood with my emotions first, and I pondered from there, thinking only after I had become committed to a subject or idea. The idea of asking a question with the mind for an answer for the mind, seemed to me pointless. Too often the answers seemed to be coming from some work memory. Undoubtedly, the question-answerers had had a few real experiences in their time, but they suppressed their feelings, and this was obvious to me because they always addressed the question and not the person. Over and over I saw how they were unable to connect with the question by relating it first to their own experience and then translating that experience into an understanding of where the question was coming from inside the person that had spoken. This was more than evident to me by the lack of compassion on the part of most of the people at the Head Table, as it was called. What disturbed me the most was that the answers seemed to have little to do with the person that had asked the question. It was as if the outer man, that had verbalized the question, did not have an inner world. Whether or not he did, it was not being taken into account here. This was more than baffling, it was infuriating, because we were not there to be knocked down and trampled upon, but to learn how to work. I knew that the abrupt, harsh answers, that were all too frequent, were made to reduce people to their rightful size, but I knew enough about psychology to understand that you could only help people to *see* that they were foolish, not show them *how* they were. And we could be opened to this seeing through love—that is, *real* caring.

As a result of what I had seen and the judgment I had made about it, I decided that this was an aspect of the work I would not participate in. I would keep my questions, if I had any, to myself, or else save them for my group meeting.

My problem with Armonk was further compounded by the fact that the practical work had no function or purpose—as far as I could tell—beyond the study of energies and attention. If identification was such an important aspect of the work then I felt that opportunities for identification should have been created at Armonk through the work we were doing. As far as I knew the forge was producing grill work that would eventually be sold at a craft sale. In the workshop we were making various things, perhaps for the same use. Was everyone quiet and subdued because they were busy remembering themselves, or were they deadened from the work they were doing?

## CHAPTER NINE

In the beginning I had been so in awe of the work that I saw the people who represented the work as *being* the work, and therefore above reproach. But as I began to see things in a more truthful light, I felt that either the work had been misunderstood, or those who were holding positions in the work had been misusing their privileges.

On the one hand the hierarchy was based on time-in-the-work, and yet this was not open to discussion. Of course it had really to do with one's advances-in-the-work, but this too could not be known, or not easily known. It was all rather confusing, especially since I did not see for some time that I was imposing life values on a situation that was—or hoped to be—above the ordinary level of life. This willingness to kowtow to the "elders," combined with the sense that we should have been above such shenanigans, made for a dithery atmosphere, in which one could not confess, even to one's self, just what it was one was after, and just what our business was in all this, and what it was not. Were we justified in being ambitious because those above us clearly were, or could we rise above the folly around us and really learn—through our own efforts—to become men?

It was a privilege to serve the work, not to serve the privileged of the work, which was clearly what was happening. And I could see that those a rung or two below were jockeying for position. Everyone seemed a great deal more eager to provide work for others than to attempt to work on themselves. For those of us on the bottom stoop, there was the feeling that the slightest slip would be perceived as a major gaffe and the cause for expulsion. But more than any of this, it was the long faces of everyone there—the newcomers and the elders alike—that most disturbed me.

In the way all of us adjust our faces before looking in a mirror, everyone adjusted his face before entering the Foundation. If palpable fear had a manifest look, it was here, engraved on our visages. We were intimidated and intimidating in turn, for one never knew if *his* face was good enough, and if his *look* would pass muster.

To one degree or another we all feared excommunication based on our unworthiness. We didn't have to look very deep inside to know the unfathomable depth of our unworthiness. But we were *all* equally unworthy—the highest and the lowest of us alike. We were in fact lucky to a man to be here.

So why this charade?

The problem was compounded by the custom or notion that the older adherents had the jurisdiction to correct the younger ones. It was the work that had opened us and made us vulnerable, it had nothing to do with the "elders," who thought or imagined or believed that they alone were capable of providing us with the work. At Armonk, where my work was directed, I expected to receive support and guidance, but felt instead that I was being encroached upon and violated, in that I was being watched without being guided. Perhaps I should have been more trusting, but it was an atmosphere that was not conducive to trust.

It is no secret that if too many buffers are removed at once a man will go mad. We are at home in our contradictions, which must be carefully unraveled one at a time. Gurdjieff had referred to us as broken-down machines. It was true. It was what all of us in the work had in common. But what we were in need of was repair, not disdain or humiliation. This only resulted in our putting on another false coat of armor, hence the work faces.

Although I was able to avoid direct contact with almost everyone in the Foundation, the atmosphere of the place alone was sufficient to open old wounds, and to return me to the same fearful boots I stood in when, as a boy in the Midwest, I had been discriminated against solely for being Armenian.

Wasn't it like this for everyone? Didn't this place remind each of us of our childhood and the dream we had lost or corrupted? Once again, as children, we were being driven back inside our own skins. But there was no reason to retreat again into that place, the very place we were trying to reappear from. It would be different, I knew, if we could get to know one another. Only that would provide an avenue out of our lonely, private corridors of fear and apprehension. We had in common our wish for development, and that alone might have made a bond that would be far more useful than being brought up short. I could see the result of this, because it had already begun to manifest in a particular way. Everyone wanted to get into a leadership slot because those that had apparently received the work were meant to be emulated. And how would it be revealed that one had received the work but by behaving precisely as the leaders were?

The teaching as presented in the Foundation worked, if it did at all, only because we had created a confidence in our teacher, who was our pipeline to the ideas, the teaching, the benevolent love we felt both in Gurdjieff and in the work he had labored to bring us.

It was important, always, to remember why I was there, what brought me there, and to never forget what I stood to gain by my efforts. Though a part of me was eager to accept this new challenge, I was nevertheless carried by my inertia along old grooves of complaining, fault-finding and the irrepressible urge to question everything and everyone—and by doing so, often shutting out the good with the bad. For all the elders who were apparently useless to themselves and the place, there were others who had been there for many years, and who *had* made something. Their example helped to sustain us. Christopher Freemantle, also English and a lord who had eschewed the title, was a man of character and humility, who seemed never to speak an unnecessary word or make an unnecessary gesture. That he loved the work and had benefitted from it was more than evident. He was a living testimony of the work's providence and beneficence.

One Sunday at Armonk, he came into the workshop to work on

a project with one of the people in his group. The still, quiet way in which he went at his work, which included both the project and the young man he was teaching, was an inspiration to me. Watching him work I learned that it is not what you do, but how you do it, and even more important, where one is in the process—scattered, identified, agitated—or quietly placed and centered. Watching him at his work I was reminded of Gurdjieff's statement that there were three ways to learn from another: example, magnetism and imitation. For me, Christopher Freemantle seemed to embody all three.

Despite the Foundation, and even in spite of myself, the work was beginning to take hold in me, but in ways so mysterious as to be beyond my comprehension. One evening I was standing before my kitchen chair when Nonny placed a plate of food on the table in front of me. I looked down at it and for the first time in my life I was aware of the life in the food: where it had come from, what had died and been transformed for my benefit, the toil of the workers... everything! I was overcome by remorse for having been given so much that I had always taken for granted.

In our first year the exercises had been relatively easy: such as remembering ourselves on the hour and to the minute, and when we failed to do so, to splash cold water on our face. I had gone out and purchased my first watch the day following the meeting in which this exercise was given. It was an exercise I was able to struggle with. It was specific and definite. One either remembered oneself or one did not. I didn't question if it would enlighten me, I just did it. But it wasn't always easy to find water on the street, and even harder while driving down the highway. We had to carry a jug of water in the car, which also acted as a reminding factor.

Although I remembered nearly half the time—and it was uncanny how, with attention as well as intuitive awareness, I could sense when the hour was up to the very minute. But if I was overly attentive and tried to keep track of the last five minutes, I would invariably forget, and remember a minute or two minutes after the hour. There were also stretches of several hours during each day of that week when I forgot completely.

This was beginning work at dividing our attention. It became increasingly important as time went on to do this without external reminders, such as an exercise. Our goal was to be able to divide ourselves into the observer and the thing observed, an almost impossible feat.

When we failed, as we did repeatedly, Lord Pentland would say, "If it were not possible, the work would not be possible—for this is the work, which has been placed before us to reveal to us that we are two. We must see this from our own observations. For if we do, then we will begin to move in the direction of one. One indivisible. The one that cannot be divided. The individual, hmn?"

More than once he broke the inevitable silence that followed a statement that was out of our grasp by saying, "I don't know how it is with you, but up here the weather is fine."

One evening, while walking home with Nonny, I tried to step around a frankfurter vendor, but I had apparently gotten in his way because he pushed me and started hollering. I turned and began hollering back at him, matching his volume and duplicating his anger. But as I did I felt myself becoming detached from the argument. It was as if I was watching two people having a fight. It was almost funny, in part because it was over nothing—as I could clearly see—and also because I was enjoying the confrontation, not as one caught in it, but as an actor performing a role.

When we left him and began crossing the street, Nonny remarked, "I've never seen you like that before. You seemed, I don't know how to put it, untouched, almost indifferent...." I hadn't put it into words myself, but from the moment I had turned away from the vendor and began walking, I felt like I was traveling on air. I saw, not only that something in me had separated from the event, but that my ordinary state was one of heaviness, a heaviness of spirit that had clearly affected my body, and that I had always taken for granted as being *how I was*. And now, suddenly, and out of nowhere, I saw that there was a new possibility: a possibility to not always be as I had always been.

That winter, at the close of our regular Tuesday group meeting,

Lord Pentland announced that it was time for us to work together as a group. "You may have noticed that our building is always clean and in good working order, yes? The various groups take turns at cleaning. It is a good opportunity for you to work with others, as well as being a practical way to keep the Foundation in good working order. There will be a sign-up sheet downstairs."

The work included scrubbing the kitchen and bathrooms, dusting, vacuuming and repairing carpets, repairing faulty wiring, as well as plumbing and general maintenance.

Nonny and I signed up to work half-days for the entire two week period. On the first day another man and I were given the roof to clean, while Nonny was assigned to clean one of the meeting rooms.

The first time I came down for clean water, I noticed Nonny out of the corner of my eye, and realized she was in a negative state. She was standing in front of the closet, staring in at the vacuum cleaners. Her very posture of stillness was uncharacteristic, because she was always in movement, never indecisive or confused about what she was doing, and she always thought on her feet while engaged in whatever she was doing at the moment. She was good at everything she did, and was almost always able to figure out how things worked. Nothing intimidated her and, unlike me, the very thought of idleness disturbed her.

She was not only standing and staring into the closet, she was fuming.

I didn't see her again until it was time to leave. On our way home we stopped for coffee at the cafe around the corner, where she told me what had happened. The rug in the meeting room had been made up of sample carpet pieces, and had been sewn together rather clumsily to make an area rug. Nonny explained, "The rug was filthy and the colors offended me, and my commentator was telling me that the rug wasn't worth the time it would take to give it a proper cleaning."

"Commentator" was a new word in our work vocabulary. We were told that we had a commentator inside of us who explained our life as it went along. We had not only verified for ourselves that this was true but we had become intrigued about just who this commentator was.

Nonny went on, "The closet was jammed with vacuum cleaners, as well as all kinds of parts, few of which fit, and many of which didn't even work. I'm sure they were worthless donations—all of them. And all those parts, I just couldn't understand it, because nothing would fit. After an hour of trying all the cleaners, I just threw them back inside, slammed the door and kicked it. I almost came to tell you I was leaving."

"I wasn't exactly having a great time myself."

Nonny sipped her coffee and looked out the window. "The strangest thing happened. I went back into the room, got down on my hands and knees, and picked that ugly rug clean...."

I waited for her to continue. "When it was over, I felt this incredible lightness of being. I don't know how else to put it. It's still with me, although it's beginning to fade."

When Nonny reported her experience at the next meeting, Lord Pentland seemed very pleased. After smiling at his assistants and looking at each of us, he began to tell us about forces. "On the one hand," he said, "was your wish to work, yes, and then, on the other hand, there was this...what would you call it?"

"Fury!" Nonny answered.

"Yes, thank you, fury, hmn?" He smiled and continued. "Two equal forces. You didn't express one, nor did you suppress the other, yes, do you follow?" He looked around the room to see if we had understood. "What happens when two equal forces meet: active and passive," he said, clenching his fists and bringing them together. "A third force appears, yes, transformation, yes. What happened?" he asked, looking at Nonny again.

"I felt as light as a feather."

"Did you ever have this feeling from reading any of the books, hmn?"

"Never!"

"Never," he repeated. "You see why we call this the work." He looked around the room, very pointedly not including Nonny in the challenge he was facing the rest of us with. For the moment she was excluded from our company, and this was her reward, a marked step in the long process of initiation.

As the week went on we got to work with other members of our group, and at noon a number of us went to lunch together. This slowly began to change things among us. We had begun to know one another as people, and not just as members of the group. It helped us to drop certain judgments we had made, and I was hoping it would make it easier for all of us to talk during group meetings.

Our group meeting had always been the most important event in our week. But as time went on, I began to have conflicting thoughts about their importance in my work. After the first year, when we had been carried on Lord Pentland's energy and love—for that was how it seemed—the meetings had turned cold and unfriendly, with long lapses between questions that sometimes lasted for nearly five minutes. Nonny, unable to bear both the silences and the wasted opportunities, would ask a question, just to break the spell that all of our fears had cast us into.

But in addition to feeling alienated and alone, I began to notice that my questions and observations were not being attended to as I felt they should have been. Also—although I hated to admit it to myself at first—Lord Pentland was often harsh, and even cruel to me. "If this is the work," I told Nonny, "it isn't working on me." I began to go silent, and it wasn't long before I stopped speaking altogether.

When I had reported on my observation with the vendor, Lord Pentland had looked to Cindy Tower and whispered something in her ear that I could see puzzled her. Her answer was not only meaningless, but I felt offended by what I took to be a put-down.

That same winter a new book of my poems had been published. Our house in the country was between tenants, and I read some of the poems again in the same chair where most of them had been written. As I did, I reflected again on whether writing could be a three-centered activity. It seemed doubtful to me that the body could have a significant role in the process.

On our long drive to our next meeting, I found myself thinking again about Beelzebub traveling through time in his space ship, and Gurdjieff (or Beelzebub) stating that air was our second food—the first being food and drink—and this air having come from the solar system, assists in the development of our kesdjan, or astral, body. I couldn't tell if he was saying that we needed to learn how to breathe consciously, with greater awareness, or simply understand the source of our food. Was everything done for us, or did we need to learn how to assist the process? I would have to go back and read that section again.

With these thoughts swirling in my head, it suddenly came to me that the body was the poem's breath. Music and measure, I thought, are determined by the poetic line, which in turn is directed by the breath. As we breath, so are we lived. We are the living breath, but each of us is breathed differently, and this is our individuality. It is the only individual thing about us. We are breathed into life, and we are each breathed differently.

When I excitedly reported my insight at the meeting, Lord Pentland said, "Oh, you've published a book of poems," the implication being that I was bragging. He turned to Wendell Kirt, the lawyer on his right, who had seemed intrigued by what I was saying but could think of nothing to say on his own, and could only stare the ball back into Lord Pentland's court, where it was dropped.

I was doubly offended because the insight had come out of my struggle to understand my work as a writer, and it was dismissed as if it were a manifestation of my ego, which he thought needed to be squelched.

· CHAPTER TEN ·

It was in the middle of our second year that Lord Pentland was hospitalized. According to rumor he had a serious infection that he had apparently contracted during a trip to India.

Madame de Salzmann had come to New York for the winter, as she had been doing for some years past. She came every Sunday to Armonk and often talked in the morning, sometimes giving a simple sensing exercise without leaving her chair. She was now eighty-five years old but looked no more than sixty-five or seventy. Her back was as straight as a board and I noticed that she always sat in an upright chair with a tiny pillow placed in the small of her back.

She never tired of talking about the movement of energies, as well as the body, that she pronounced *boodey*. She was without equal in the work, a kind of mystery figure that everyone seemed dependent on in some way or other, but someone that no one else could know or understand. Gurdjieff had said that we cannot see above our own level. She was certainly living proof of that for every one of us.

She never made an untimed gesture, or a false movement. I felt magnetically attracted to her, studying her every gesture and hanging onto her every word, although her words, despite her seemingly simple declarations, had a way of slipping out of my mind as soon as I thought they had adhered. She often took the questions at the luncheon discussion, and I very soon realized that her answers were given in the form of an exercise that all who wished could follow, as the thrust of her work was energies and sensation, as well as attention. She must have felt that our psychological growth would follow naturally from this, once we were grounded in our bodies.

For the first time the luncheon discussions meant something to me. Her formulations were especially meaningful because they came from her own personal and deeply entrenched experiences in the work. Only Lord Pentland had moved me as much, but her wisdom always embodied practical directions, whereas Lord Pentland, although he was witty, eloquent and brilliant, neither directed nor guided our work. I was made aware of this because of the sharp contrast between the two of them. It was obvious that there was a big difference between their levels of consciousness.

In a late obituary on Bennett in one of the New Age journals, it had been mentioned that Gurdjieff had known and probably studied with Armenia's famous composer, Gomidas.

Gomidas had rescued Armenia's folk music from oblivion, and had also composed its church music. As a result of the massacre of the Armenians during the First World War, he had lost his mind. As Armenia's greatest folk hero his name continued to be legendary among Armenians all over the world. It thrilled me to think that Gurdjieff and Gomidas had known each other.

Upon reading the article, I wished that there was someone I knew who could corroborate the story, someone who might even have been present at such an historic meeting, or who might have heard Gurdjieff speak about Gomidas. Walking down the corridor at Armonk the following Sunday, on my way to the dining room for lunch, I passed Madame de Salzmann standing in one of the doorways. Without giving it a second thought, I walked up to her and told her about the article. I had never spoken to her before, nor did I ever think I would. Although I didn't realize it at once, the experience had put me in shock. "Is it true?" I asked. "Did they know one another?"

"No," she replied, "they did not."

But I didn't believe her. It seemed perfectly sensible that they *would* have known one another—and besides, I *wanted* it to be true.

I asked again. She gave a slight shake of her head and looked at me, with a gaze I couldn't fathom. I neither knew what to say next, nor did I know how to extricate myself. Without excusing myself, I quickly turned and began marching, self-consciously, down the corridor.

The next thing I knew my name was being called. I turned and, peering through the flow of people heading toward me, I could see that the voice belonged to Lady Pentland, who was standing beside Madame de Salzmann.

When I approached her, she said, "You are Armenian. From where?"

"From here," I answered, "America."

"Oh, your *parents* are Armenian."

"Yes," I replied, suddenly feeling less Armenian than I wanted to be.

We were conversing now, but I was not so much aware of my words as I was my stance. My hands were thrust in my back pockets, and although my posture struck me as inappropriate, I was unable to make a change. I was also shouting which, I was able to observe, came from an attitude about older people that I had not previously been aware of. But what was most unusual was that I was even more aware of myself than I was of her. Instead of being aware of the impression I wanted to make, I was aware of the impression I *was* making, and I felt disturbed by this person making the impression because I could see that this person was me.

I was totally aware of myself and completely out of control. She merely looked at me and listened. But really listened, perhaps as a mirror would, if it had an apparatus for hearing. And like a mirror, clear and without predispositions, she was able to reflect me back, without criticism or judgment. Because I had nothing to react against, I was left completely to myself, and I was able to see myself exactly as I was. Of course I didn't realize any of this at the time.

"I am translating the poetry of Charentz," I said, as much to make myself interesting as to find something that might interest her. Charentz and Gurdjieff had both come from Kars, and Charentz was Armenia's greatest poet of this century. "Do you know the poetry of Charentz?" I asked.

"Yes," she said, "I have read him."

I remembered that Charentz had been translated into French, her native language.

I looked at her carefully. Was that an amused or wry smile on her face? I couldn't think of anything more to say. This time, when I turned to leave, I found myself bounding down the corridor.

The move to the city had placed an extra demand on us. It cost more to live in the city than the country, and our house was renting for less than the mortgage. We also had the added expense of the work. But our life had a direction now and a purpose.

We became aware that the city was charged with energies that were being released into the air because people did not know how to harness what they had and apply it intentionally. These energies could be collected and used through one's own efforts.

I was editing two and sometimes three poetry anthologies at once, while collecting material for what would be my first novel. In the midst of this, along with our normal work activities, I found myself beginning a new book of poems about my childhood. This book, that I would title *I Remember Root River*, was a complete departure from my earlier book of poems about childhood. It was concerned with my own, not my elder's, experiences, and my slow maturation into manhood. I sensed in the writing that at last I had begun to inherit my life: by taking my stand on my own existence, based on my experiences, and the pattern of those experiences that I now began to see. Through this book I was making a declaration for my life by authenticating all that I had seen and witnessed and observed.

I had been saying for years that I did not see how I could possibly resolve the first twelve years of my life. I felt that if I could have truly understood and come to terms with that much of my life, I might stand a chance to become a real man—and not, as Gurdjieff would have said, only a man in quotation marks. All of my searching, my writing, along with my hometown returns—when I would haunt the places I had earlier haunted as a youth, my meetings with old friends, as well as the long hours that I sat in front of the lake, and my wanderings down to the river that followed the veins of the city on its way to Lake Michigan—all of this had finally reached an apotheosis in this book, that poured out of me and onto the page in a period of two weeks. The opening epigraph had set the tone for the poems that would follow.

> At the bottom of Liberty Street
> the Island Park Bridge—
> (the hollow heart of the city);
> and I return there now for
> the soundings:
> pavilion dead, river dead,
> city all but dead,
> with only the breathless
> remains of the imitation
> rock-garden city in the yard
> almost touching the bridge
> it imitates (on which I stand)
> and there,
> on that spot,
> just beyond the heart
> but palpitating with it, the
> new city, the city that
> sings these poems
> is going up

Since meeting the Teaching, I had wanted to sacrifice my art, if necessary, in order to make something permanent in myself, and now I was being shown that one of the ways to this permanence—what the work called Real I—was in fact to be effected *through* my art provided I remained above it, did not become identified with it, and if I were able to sacrifice my personal ambitions for my art and allow it to be my teacher.

I had known to ask—for this was the truth of my journey—to have my life given back to me through my achieved understanding of my childhood. For this was the two-way passage I was on, and now this significant step, that felt so freeing and joyous, proved to me without a doubt that I had not been wrong in my assumptions. I also saw, unequivocally, that it was not enough to merely journey back on foot or through memory, but that a tool and a technique were needed, for without this only dreams and introspection were possible. But with my writing as a tool, and the work as a technique, true self-change was possible.

Immediately following the writing of the poems for *I Remember Root River*, I began a poetry cycle called *Taking the Soundings on Third Avenue* that was comprised of the scenes, sounds and smells that were a part of my life in the neighborhood where we had settled. It seemed that whenever my writing went back it also went forward. By correcting the past, I both earned and inherited the present. Gurdjieff had said, "Repair the past, prepare the future." I knew now what that meant.

Roses began to appear in my inner world, but as Gurdjieff had warned: When roses on inside, thorns on the outside; thorns on the inside, roses on the outside.

Our outside thorn, ironically, had become the Gurdjieff Foundation. Although I felt I owed everything to the work, I was now beginning to feel that I was receiving the work in spite of the Foundation. We had stopped attending the Wednesday night lectures, which consisted of two of the Group I people lecturing from a raised platform to an audience of over one hundred people, who followed the lecture with questions cast up to the platformed speakers. The questions, in proper conjunction, were as theoretical, mental and devoid of feeling as the lecture had been. In our last attendance I whispered to Nonny that I wondered if a well-placed explosive might not be the proper solution to the problem. I thought of Gurdjieff, and speculated to myself what he might have said and done if he had been there to see what had become of his work.

We were kept going by the hope that Lord Pentland would be returning soon. But there was no news and we knew there would never be an announcement. Unable to contain herself any longer, Nonny blurted out at our next meeting that she couldn't understand all the secrecy surrounding his illness. She wanted to know where he was and when he would be returning.

"That is none of your business," Cindy said, "and we will not engage in a discussion about this in a meeting, or at any other time."

"But he's my teacher," Nonny said, "I want to know how he is."

There was a deadly silence in the room. Cindy and Wendell Kirt, the other question-answerer, stared at Nonny without speaking. I could feel in the room a palpable support for Nonny, because each of us wanted to know what had happened to Lord Pentland, and only Nonny had been brave enough to ask. We were obviously all lost without our teacher, who was our connection with the Higher. Nonny began crying, and reached for her purse to find a handkerchief.

"Put it away," Cindy shouted. "There is no room for emotion here." But Nonny began to sob even more. When I looked over, her nose was running and tears were falling from her cheeks onto her blouse.

When we got home that evening Nonny took out the telephone book and started calling all the hospitals in Manhattan until she located the one at which he was staying. Before going to bed she baked a pan of choerag, an Armenian pastry that Gurdjieff had mentioned in one of his books. I took down a limited edition copy of *Homage to Adana* and inscribed it with a poem I had just written for my poetry cycle.

> the hidden foot
> dancing
> finds the earth
> that prays

The next morning we wrapped everything into a single package and took a taxi to the hospital, where we left our present with the receptionist.

Some time later we got a thank you card from Lord Pentland, but he did not say if he would be returning, or when. Although we felt much better from having heard from him, we were still in the dark, and feeling more alone than we had been since entering the work.

· CHAPTER ELEVEN ·

I didn't know there was another Armenian in the Foundation, until I was visited one Sunday at Armonk in the workshop by a woman who made her presence and her identity known by standing in the door, and shouting, "Where's the Armenian poet?" She was carrying a clipboard under her arm. She adjusted her glasses and looked down at the sheet. "Kherdian!" she said, raising her voice, "where are you?"

I walked up and led her to a quiet corner of the room. "So, an Armenian," I said in our language, but I could see she didn't understand. "You don't know the Armenian language?" I asked.

"My mother's American, so we never spoke it in our home. I used to know some curse words. We lived on a ranch, out in the country, by ourselves. I got out of Fresno as soon as I could."

"So tell me, what are you doing here? I thought my wife and I were the only Armenians in the work."

She laughed. "World-wide?"

"Well, America-wide."

"There have been one or two, ...some time back..."

"You've been in the work awhile?"

"Yes, I suppose, but what's long? I'm just back from Oregon. I was with a group out there but I started here, with Lord Pentland."

"Like us. Have you met Nonny yet?"

She looked down at the roster again. "Sure. Here she is, in the kitchen. But we couldn't talk for long."

"Where are you on the roster?"

"Here." She pointed to her name. "Rose Dohanian, rugs and

restoration. Type-casting, no?" she said, and laughed.

"A good name," I said. "What's its origin? What did your people do?"

"I don't know. How about you, what were your ancestors famous for?"

I laughed self-consciously. "We were carpenters."

"Really! More type-casting, ha."

"Actually, the origin of the name is Turkish. It means break and run. One of my ancestors built a door for a Turk and when the Turk wouldn't pay him, he broke the door in two and fled. *Kherda* (break), *khatchda* (run). It stuck."

"Could be karmic. You know what the work says."

"No, what does it say?"

"Well, some things have to be worked out. We may have one lesson to learn in this life. But one lesson is enough, no?"

"I like that. I've not heard it before."

"I learned that from my teacher in Oregon. But tell me more about your name."

"Well, it isn't my real name. I just learned that our Armenian name is Bakaian, and since David in Armenian is Tavit, I'm thinking of taking the *nom de plume* of Tavit Bakaian."

"Maybe David Kherdian should be your *nom de plume*. Or whichever one is the real you. Do you know which one that is?"

"That's why I'm here, to find out."

"That's good. And I think you will. What does Bakaian mean?"

"I don't know."

"There are only two ways to know things, from the outside and from the inside. Maybe when you change your pattern, if you do, you will know for yourself. And then again, it might not matter. Do you still break and run?"

"I think it might look that way from the outside, but it doesn't feel that way to me. Nevertheless, I think there is something to it. The Kherdians are certainly impetuous, suspicious, vengeful and slightly mad. And to the extent that I'm a Kherdian, I am at least all of those things, and a great deal more: some good, some bad."

"But you could say that about all Armenians, at least the ones I've met. I mean the suspicious, vengeful aspect."

"I suppose, but some of us have a greater talent for trouble. Let's change the subject. Tell me about the school in Oregon."

"Oh, that's a long story. It'll keep for another time."

Our second year was beginning to draw to a close. We decided not to rent our house in the country again. We had long ago stopped going to the Gallery talks, and now that we had also dropped the Wednesday lectures, all that remained was our group meeting and the sittings. We could drive down to one or both of these from the country, as well as to Armonk on Sundays. We still hoped that Lord Pentland would return and that, when he did, things would change for the better. In the one private talk we had with Cindy Tower we let her know how we felt. We told her that everything about the place; the people, the atmosphere, the conditions that had been set up to maintain control and order, had us strait-jacketed.

Several days after our talk, Cindy called us up in the country to tell us that we were being put in two different movements classes. The classes were at different hours but on the same day, mine at the Foundation, Nonny's at a school further uptown. She told us to get white tops and black bottoms: slacks for men, skirts for women, and pairs of Capezio exercise slippers. We drove down to New York at once, full of anticipation and hope. Three days later our movements classes began.

After several exercises that took place in a circle, we were given the basic movements march step: a simple forward-backward shuffle of the feet to maintain motion and rhythm. We were placed in rows and files and, under the guidance of the instructor and the pianist, we began moving forward together. As we did, slowly, slowly, a haunting melody from another realm moving our feet, strangely familiar, and reminding us of something nearly forgotten, we were suddenly stopped, just as we were about to touch, with our bodies sighing, trembling.

Paul Reynard, who was in charge of the movements in America, attended Nonny's class to train the instructor who was leading her first movements class.

During the winter we had seen one of the movements movies that Madame de Salzmann had made. Reynard, in the front right file, had the lead position, and it was at once clear that his mastery provided the heartbeat for the class. His precision, timing and flawless movement—as he seemed to glide effortlessly from position to position without any wasted motion—set him apart from all the others, although as a group they gave credence to the meaning of Sacred Dance, as the movements were called, and could only be called when brought to perfection.

Nonny arrived home more than an hour after her class was to have ended. I had been waiting for her, so we could share our experiences.

"What happened?" I asked, when she stepped in the door. She stood in the doorway, flushed and breathless. "It was incredible. I was so high that I just kept walking. I meant to catch the subway at 96th Street, and then again at 86th, but I kept walking. I couldn't stop myself. I was just too excited. Before I knew it I was in our neighborhood."

"I walked home, too."

"You did! Was it great?"

"More than great. I was waiting to tell you about it, but now that you're here I don't think I want to spoil it with words."

It had been rumored that Lord Pentland was well again and had been seen at the Foundation. Then one Sunday he walked into the main hall at Armonk and delivered the morning theme. His voice seemed very far away, and I was not aware of what he was saying at first. For some reason, the figure of Wilhem Nyland rose before my eyes. He was standing before the piano, hesitating, as if caught in a frieze, and then, looking up at us, he said that he could not see why a man should have to die. I was hearing the voice, not the words, and the voices of Pentland and Nyland had merged. I was trying to penetrate through the voices into the words that were being spoken. He was saying that his generation had come into the work from a need that had not been provided by their culture. But although this work had provided a spiritual life for them at the time, it seemed to him now that the work was *passe*, that perhaps its time was over.

What was he saying! He had been our savior, our beacon of hope, and now this ... this irresponsible ... this careless ... how could he say this to new people ... those just beginning ... was he mad!

His words had passed over me at first like a cloud, but now little by little they began to sink in. I sat there and, without turning my head, followed him out of the room with my eyes. He seemed smaller, frailer, almost shrunken. I wondered if he *were* mad. I had expected him to end his talk by saying he was leaving, but he hadn't done that. He had merely gotten up from his chair and left, as if it were just another Sunday morning theme.

I was dumbfounded. I looked around the room at all the faces. None of them seemed altered. Was it only me? But then I felt a slight disturbance in the air as we began to file out. I passed Jerry Needleman standing at the back of the room, who made a jocular remark as I walked by.

My head was in a whirl when I entered the woodwork shop. I was trying to think, but my emotions were too inflamed for that to be possible. I wondered to myself if anyone else was as disturbed as I was. The room was quieter than usual, and as the morning wore on I could feel the tension mount and then subside.

I didn't see Nonny until the late morning coffee break. She was sitting in a corner by herself. I knew, looking at her, that the talk had affected her in the same way it had affected me. She said, "There was a little mumbling in the kitchen at first, but that was about all. I don't understand, don't these people have any feelings? Can't they think for themselves? Do they just swallow everything whole, without question?"

"We'll stay through lunch," I said. "If he's challenged, we'll see, but if not, we're leaving. If he is against the work then he is unqualified to pass it on. And of course we can't go over his head within the Foundation and ask for a different Group Leader." I hesitated. "Maybe I should be the one to speak."

"No, don't do it. Let it come from some of the older people in the work. It won't come to anything unless one of them speaks."

I prayed during the luncheon discussion for something to happen. I picked on my food and looked at all the faces for signs. What would it mean if he wasn't challenged? I didn't want to think that far ahead.

I watched the clock and looked at the long row of faces at the head table. Slowly the questions and answers began. As always, questions from the head, answers from the head. I thought again that I should speak, but knew it would be a mistake. I was also overwhelmed with fear. I could never challenge Lord Pentland in these circumstances. I also knew that nothing would be gained. I could see only one thing happening: Lord Pentland would have to be overthrown. And if I had secretly, even unknowingly, harbored such a hope at first, I knew with certainty now that it would never happen.

The hour was up. The head table slowly filed out of the room. I looked over at Nonny, who was crying. She was seated next to Cindy Tower, who was not looking at her, although it was obvious from the expression on her face that she was aware of the state Nonny was in. I was also certain that she knew why, and that she had chosen to sit next to Nonny for that reason. Perhaps she thought she could save the situation somehow. But it was too late now. I walked to the row they were in and waited for Nonny to get up and leave with me.

On the long drive home it slowly sank in what we had done. I felt a pain in my solar plexus unlike anything I had ever experienced before. We could never go back. That much I knew, just as I knew that we were now without the work. I felt like an orphan, dispossessed of everything that really mattered, left by the side of the road, with no safe harbor in sight.

"I don't know if I would have had the courage to leave if I were by myself," Nonny said.

"You would have. If not today, then tomorrow. Inside, you feel the same way I do. And you know as I do that once a thing is over no power on earth can keep it alive. It may go on by momentum for a long time, but...."

"I think what explains it for me—his not being challenged, I mean—is that the place just never *has* been alive."

"Maybe once, a long time ago, but no one remembers anymore. No one with a real wish, who has the courage to see his wish through, would ever stay in such a place."

"I think somewhere along the line it turned into a church. But how can they be such sheep?

"Sheep move in a body, turn in a body, respond as a body. They want to make a body so they can be carried, so they won't have to think for themselves.

"But where is the work? It must still exist somewhere?"

"If it does, we'll find it. Maybe it's gone into hiding, the way the Essenes went into hiding when Christianity became crystallized."

As soon as we got home I called Cindy to tell her we were leaving groups. I didn't want our decision to fester. If anything might abate the pain it would be to make a clean break, final and irreversible. There would be time enough to think of the consequences and alternatives.

The following Friday Cindy called and asked if she could visit us in the country, or if we could come and see her in Westchester. We agreed to meet her. She named a coffee shop and we settled on an hour.

There was an awkward moment while we found a table and ordered coffee. It was an assignment for her and we needed to respect her effort. If communication had been difficult for us before, it seemed impossible now. I told her again why we had left, but repressed the wish to ask if she had told Lord Pentland. "Maybe," she said, "there was some confusion about what you heard."

"Didn't you hear what he said!" I tried not to raise my voice.

"It's hard enough to be certain of that, without trying to guess what you heard—or thought you heard. I don't think we can discuss it. Lord Pentland said that he is going to give a new exercise at the next meeting. It would be good if you could come to the meeting."

I had forced her hand early. I could see that this was the temptation she had hoped would draw us back. We hadn't been given a new exercise in a very long time.

I stared back at her. "No," I said, "we won't be coming to the next meeting." I had been tempted, because I knew that we couldn't work on our own. But I also knew that we could never again work with Lord Pentland. I thought again that had he not been the head of the Foundation we could have asked to be in another group, but of course that could never be.

"I think we should tell Lord Pentland ourselves," Nonny said.

"That would be a good idea,"Cindy said.

"Thank you for seeing us." I could see she was uneasy and I felt sorry for her. The only important thing about this meeting was the effort she had made. Because she had, and I suppose because we had also made a small effort, some real feeling had passed between us for the first time since we had known her.

We stayed in the city over the weekend and met with Lord Pentland on Tuesday afternoon.

Although he was obviously weak and tired, he was once again open and affable, just as he had been at our first meeting. But this time I was much more aware that he was at home in the role he was playing, and that it *was* a role. We took our chairs, as we had once before—so long ago. In one way or another, we had all changed a great deal in that time.

"Our last Sunday at Armonk," I said, "you spoke against the work. I want to know why."

"That's a very interesting question," he said. "I was in California just after that, where we had a weekend work session. I wasn't able to participate in the work, but for that very reason, perhaps, I was even more aware of everything that was going on. As I looked on it was apparent to me that this ability we have to work with others toward a common aim is our greatest possibility as men. Wouldn't you agree?"

The picture he made with his words called up something from deep in my psyche. I had to agree that although I had never had that experience, as he portrayed it, I knew it to be true, and in that moment it did seem as if that could be the whole work, complete and entire of itself.

We sat in silence for a time. I felt mesmerized, as I often was in his presence. But it was not what he said that made me feel this way, but what I had remembered for myself. As I reflected on this I became aware that this often happened at our group meetings, when I would feel that it was my experience I was having, even when it was not.

What was my experience?

I looked over at Lord Pentland. "But you never came and observed me at my work place in Armonk. Not once!"

He smiled, and I heard for the first time, the clicking of his pace-maker. He had begun to slump just slightly in his chair, a movement so uncharacteristic that it alarmed me. We had tired him. His smile, I saw now, was a sign of discomfort, not pleasure. He had always used it to disarm, and also to stall for time. He nodded agreement now, as if to say, Yes, I might have done that—but he offered no explanation. I had always taken his inscrutability as a sign of elevated being, but I wondered now if it wasn't simple duplicity, simple in that it fitted a predictable design, to be used when needed.

He turned to Nonny. "You wanted to say something about the Foundation?"

She said, "It's stuffy."

He looked amused, almost pleased, but affected instead a look of confusion. He turned to me. "What did she say?"

I raised my voice. "She said it's stuffy."

The smile slowly slid from his face. It was time to leave. When he rose from his chair he looked serene again. "I'll see you tonight, then, at our meeting."

We didn't answer, but said good-bye with finality, not for his benefit, but for our own.

"Let's go straight to the Foundation," Nonny said. "I want to pick up our movements clothes and pay our dues through the month. I want a clean break."

"It just now hit me," I said, "that he never answered my question."

"Isn't that funny, I hadn't noticed either. I was too taken by the story he was telling, and I could see that you were too, and then I forgot about it. I'm just never myself when I'm around him. Strange, isn't it, we come here because we don't know who we are, or what we want—and I know Gurdjieff is trying to help me—but I don't feel that anyone else is."

"We'll feel better when we pay our dues. You know what my mother always says, 'God never closes every door.'"

II


THE GURDJIEFF WORK

# · CHAPTER TWELVE ·

Although I couldn't have seen it at the time, our leaving the Foundation, and thereby temporarily losing the work, opened the door to an opportunity for work that I had believed I was too busy to engage in while in groups. It is a paradox of work that in finding the form we very often forget that the work is about our life, not about some system that purports to save us, but that can just as easily lead us away from some essential truth that we would more likely face if we were outside the illusory safety of a teaching. The secret that eludes nearly everyone hinges on the need to bring the two into balance; to use the work without losing one's life.

Long before I ever began to think of myself as a writer, I can remember my mother asking me to grow up and tell her story. I am sure that her lament was one that ran through all the other Armenian households in our community and, for that matter, throughout the entire diaspora.

By the time I became a writer no one else had taken up the burden, and so one day I made a commitment to my mother to write her story. All through my life she had wanted to tell me about her life during the time of the Armenian Massacres. It had occurred so long ago—now nearly a lifetime ago—for she was five when it began, and her trials continued until she left her homeland at sixteen. Her life during those years had been a living hell. She had wanted to unburden herself on her children, who had now become a part of her history, for they were her token of hope, that would help balance the tortured past, and partially redeem the loss of her own family. It was understandable that when I was young I had refused to listen. In fact, I had refused her life, and so this book was my penance: it was also my door to the past, for if I were to refuse this passage my knowledge of myself would never be complete.

The summer previous to our leaving the Foundation, I had flown my mother to New York, asking her on the phone to write her story in Armenian, so I could record her reading of it and transcribe and translate the tape I would make of it. It had seemed to me that the time had finally come to go to work. But that fall and winter I had done little more than research the period and the events that were the historical setting for the book.

When we returned from our final meeting with Lord Pentland I began to intensify my work on my mother's book. At the same time we began our search for another group. The first person we called was Rose Dohanian. Since she had been to a school in Oregon, perhaps she knew of other groups in the East.

She wasn't surprised to hear that we had left the Foundation. When we had inquired about other groups over the phone, and made an appointment to see her, she had said only, "Don't do anything until you see me."

She greeted us at the door with a big hug. After looking us up and down, she said, "The last time I saw you two, I knew. You looked cold and hungry. But I didn't want to bring it up until you did. Now you can tell me what happened."

We told her about the Sunday at Armonk, and our subsequent meetings with Cindy Tower and Lord Pentland, as well as the problems I'd had with Lord Pentland earlier when he wouldn't speak to my questions, and how I felt stifled by him, and also that he took no interest in the practical work I was doing at Armonk.

"You can forget about all that now, it's over. Anyhow, you two are too hot-blooded for the Foundation. I didn't know myself that I was starving there until one day Mrs. Staveley sat in on our meeting and took questions."

"Mrs. Staveley?"

"Annie Lou Staveley from Oregon, my teacher. She's still my

teacher, but I'm here now, and the Foundation no longer troubles me. I get what I need, and I ignore the parts that are harmful."

"Could you know from one meeting?" Nonny asked. "What did she say or do that convinced you so quickly?"

"It wasn't only what she said, but how she was. For one thing, I had this feeling that I could ask her anything. Not like the Foundation, where it's all theory, and the response is based on *how* you ask your question. I could see at once that she was able to perceive what I needed, and it was to my need that she spoke. She believes that our lives are our material. It seems obvious now, but when I first met her I was knocked over by just that. She was listening to *me*—and my question. I used to feel like you, that Lord Pentland could take me to the stars, but when I told Madame de Salzmann about my work with Mrs. Staveley, she knew at once what I was talking about. She said, 'Yes, you are here,' indicating a spot on her palm, 'and Annie Lou is here,' and she pointed to imaginary spots with two fingers, to indicate a proximity and relationship. "You move here—where she was—then she moves here, always she is in sight, watching, yes.'"

I looked over at Nonny and winked. I could see that her spirit was also being lifted by Rose's words.

"She's coming next month," Rose said. "You can wait that long."

"Why is she coming to New York?" Nonny asked.

"She comes with a few of her people every winter, to talk to Madame de Salzmann, to receive exercises, to maintain contacts."

"But you're here," I said, "you left Oregon. Why?"

"There's no work in my field out there, for one thing, and for another, they bought a farm out in the country two years ago, and I'm a city person. I missed New York, my friends, making money. Mrs. Staveley thought it would be good for me to come back here for awhile."

Rose got up and went into the kitchen to pour us each a glass of wine and bring in the hors d'oeuvres she had prepared. When she returned to the living room with her tray, she said, "I want you to think about something. I have to find an apartment for some of the people Mrs. Staveley is bringing. She'll be staying with me, and I thought, since your apartment is just a few blocks away—providing that you are willing to hold onto it for another month—the group can rent it from you while they are here. That'll be a good way for you to meet everyone, and I know they will be very thankful."

"It sounds good," I said. "We need to be here for awhile, so I can do some work at the public library for the book I've begun."

"I no longer feel so desperate," Nonny said. "The time will go fast. I hope we like her."

"It's settled then," Rose said, "and while you're here we'll get together once a week and work on the Sunday theme that Mrs. Staveley always sends me. We can meet in the morning before I go to work. I'll read it and then we'll have dinner together in the evening and discuss our questions and observations. This will be a good introduction for you into her work. And in the meantime you can be thinking about your interview with Mrs. Staveley."

In the month that had elapsed we had taken stock of our situation, had reassessed our work and our needs, and knew a little better what we required for the future.

As I pondered our situation I came to the conclusion that what we needed was a small group, a group without visibility or reputation, and—most importantly—a group that was not under the Foundation's ubiquitous umbrella.

The interview with Mrs. Staveley took place in Rose's apartment in the winter of 1976. She answered the door wearing a Pendleton pant suit, with comfortable walking shoes. Her gray hair was tied up in a bun in back, and cut into bangs over her forehead. She was small, aged and very clearly in bad health. Unlike Lord Pentland, she looked her age. She was plain, the kind of person that one might not notice in a crowd. But her eyes gave her away. She had penetrating eyes that took everything in, but without intruding, and even, it seemed, without judgement. Although she was at home in herself, I had the strong impression that she was not at home in the world. Why that should have been so I was not able to tell.

We were seated on the couch, where she faced us in a straight-backed chair. To help us overcome our nervousness she asked, casually, where we grew up and how we liked living in New York. It turned out that she had grown up on a farm in Washington, where her father owned the local newspaper. At sixteen, apparently because she was too bright for her class, she was graduated from high school and sent off to live with an aunt in St. Louis. From there she was enrolled at Reed College in Portland, where she met her husband, an English professor from London, who soon took her to England, where she had lived until just recently, when she had returned to Washington to be with her parents, who were both in ill health. After their deaths she moved to Portland, because, as she explained, something told her that that was where she needed to be, and very soon after that she began a small reading group that, in a few short years, became a work center of more than fifty people. Her husband, I was to find out later, had died many years before, but the work had always been a point of contention between them.

On the surface she appeared to be a sweet old lady. She was even ingratiating, but without condescension or self-consciousness. She was intentional, deliberate and self-contained, and I knew this was the result of work.

"You come to New York once a year?" I asked.

"Yes, so far I've been able to manage it, in the beginning years alone, now with some of my people."

"Are you part of the Foundation then, under their umbrella, as they like to say."

"Heavens no. I'm not sure they'd even have me," she laughed. I could see from her affected lightness that it was not a casual subject. She had known that we had left the Foundation, but it hadn't yet come up in our discussion. "We are all related, of course. I feel that we are like a big tree, the trunk of which is Gurdjieff. Each branch is separate, but each is connected from being a part of the one trunk. There is only *one* trunk.

"Of course there are changes from branch to branch, but I have always been interested in our commonality, not our differences. After all, God did not make any two of us alike, and we are each of us only trying to become ourselves. Wouldn't you agree?"

"That's a pretty big *only*, isn't it?"

"Yes, but we needn't get heavy about it. What man has done, man can do. We all start from the same place, and we all have the same chance."

"But not the same possibility."

"Even Gurdjieff was not able to be certain about that. No one can predict that. For myself, I have to believe that each new person will go beyond where I am, and to allow them the space they will need. Only Jane, my teacher, seemed to know each of our possibilities, and she would say that she wished she hadn't. I think it caused her great suffering."

"That was Jane Heap?" Nonny asked. "What can you tell us about her?"

"After Gurdjieff, she was the most amazing—I guess one would say advanced—person I had met. I first met Ouspensky just before the war and I was to be in his next group, starting in the fall. But everything was blown apart by then, and then he left England and went to America. Of course I was forever grateful, because then I met Jane. She was an American."

"I know," I said, "she edited The Little Review with Margaret Anderson. Her name was familiar to me before Gurdjieff's."

"How interesting. Hardly anyone knows her anymore in that light. She always said that when she met Gurdjieff she locked her studio door and never went back. You may not know that she was a painter first, and a writer second—and of course an outstanding editor. But I'm getting ahead of myself. She had studied with Orage and Gurdjieff, and after just seven years, Gurdjieff sent her to England to start her own work. 'From you,' he told her, 'I want quality, not quantity.' She was an artist, you see, but I don't have to tell you two. She often said, 'when you meet this work, you must leave the bride at the altar and the dead disinterred.' She was as tough as she was sensitive."

"In her pictures." I said, "she looked more like a man than a woman."

"She once said that even Nature makes mistakes, and that she was a mistake of Nature. Gurdjieff was very fond of her. He called her Miss Keep because she was so possessive of us, her brood. Gurdjieff once told her that she had become a priest, a real priest, and that her tail had begun to grow. When Jane told this story, she said, 'When I got home, I sat down very gingerly.'"

"You come from a very different line than Lord Pentland then. He was with Ouspensky until the last year of Gurdjieff's life."

"Yes, he went to Gurdjieff after Ouspensky's death. I first saw Lord Pentland at Gurdjieff's table in Paris, after the war. Jane took us over from England whenever she could. It was very different then. We had to make great sacrifices. Now everyone wants things to be handed over on a platter.

"There were other groups in England, but Jane always kept us separate. We were given the work, pure. Jane was a stickler about that. Of course she gave it in her own way, but it was *the* teaching, not her teaching. She was very definite about that. Just as I try to be now. For example, we read *Beelzebub* before every meeting."

I said, "The only time we heard *Beelzebub* read at the Foundation was a short reading at the Gurdjieff dinner our first year."

"It's a great pity, because the teaching is all there, but one must dig for it. Of course that was Gurdjieff's intention. You know, don't you, that Ouspensky never read *Beelzebub's Tales*."

"I didn't know that," Nonny said, "but it doesn't surprise me. I've never been able to read *In Search of the Miraculous*, and yet I don't have any trouble reading Gurdjieff."

Mrs Staveley thought a moment and then said, "Wait five years before you try to read Ouspensky again."

My nervousness had disappeared. I felt relaxed in her presence, in a way I never had with Lord Pentland. The contrast reminded me of the conflicts I had always had with men, beginning with my father, and then the Armenian community at large. I knew that a great part of the problem was mine, because I couldn't accept authority, and I had always refused to work *under* any man. Even though Saroyan had been my mentor, the minute I began to find my own way our relationship came to an end.

It was my mother who had nurtured me, and who was really responsible for keeping me out of harm's way. All the friends of our family knew this to be true; that it was my mother's care, love and patience that had gotten me through so many difficulties. And now here was another woman, also a nurturing type, and I felt I could trust her enough to begin to open myself. It would still be a risk, perhaps, but for the moment at least I did not feel threatened. It seemed so obvious that I wondered that I hadn't thought of it before. My teacher in the work would have to be a woman.

"There is one thing that worries me," I found myself saying. "I have never learned to work with my hands. If we were to come out … the idea of working on a farm … with my hands … I don't know if I could do it. It really scares me, and yet I know how important practical work is. I don't like the way I am about work, but I don't think it's in me to change."

Mrs. Staveley had not taken her eyes from me while I spoke. It seemed at first that she was not speaking to my question. She began, "In the work we throw whatever we have into the pot. We bring our skills and, for the moment, that's our money in the bank. While you teach what you know, you learn from another what he or she knows. There are many ways to pay for the work, the least interesting of which is money. In fact, we never seem to have any money, and yet the necessary money always turns up. We've had to do a great deal of rebuilding. We bought a broken-down farm on thirty acres, with nothing but part-time city people to work on it. We're a very motley crew. I have slides with me of the work we've done so far, thanks to one of the men who takes pictures. Perhaps you'd like to see them. It is quite amazing what can be done if one sets one's mind to it."

"I can see that it could be different with an objective that connects everyone without interfering with the special needs of each individual. There was no outer purpose to the work we did at Armonk, and as a result I couldn't find an inner purpose for my work either."

"It is very difficult to combine the two, and maybe we are lucky, just because we are impecunious, and also starting from scratch. The urgency we feel is both real and imperative. You know, Gurdjieff spoke often about the terror of the situation. Young people today are born knowing that we are running out of time."

"But how I am about physical work goes so deep."

"Yes," she said, "but we don't always have to do what 'it' likes." She looked away from me towards Nonny, "And you don't always have to say 'yes.'"

She had given each of us something to chew on, and before we left she invited us to have dinner with her group that evening. "They would like you to stay with them tonight, in your old bedroom."

"But where will they sleep?" Nonny asked.

"There are two other rooms, one for the men and the other for the women. We're used to that kind of thing. Besides, we're not that many, only eight, and two of them—we have two sisters who are older—are staying with a couple from the Foundation. Wouldn't you like to meet the rest of us?" she said, and smiled ingratiatingly.

"Yes, of course."

"Good! Come at six then, and after dinner we'll show you some slides of the farm."

Mrs. Staveley's people were quite young, and somewhat unworldly. But we liked them immediately. They were robust—perhaps from working on the farm—and they made a striking and favorable contrast to the pallid, sunken forms at the Foundation. The two older women, Bea and Alice, were sisters, and a little older than us. Because they were divorced, they were referred to as the Taylor girls, after the maiden names they had lost. Bea was quiet and reserved, and Alice was a bit eccentric. They couldn't have been less alike, but they were both very likeable.

The meal was a simple stew, with a baked potato and salad on the side. I felt it made a declaration about their life. Simple, straightforward and hearty.

Mrs. Staveley indicated that I was to sit beside her. Since she was the focal point of attention, I felt that I was too, and it made me a bit uncomfortable. The dinner had just begun when she told the group the story of our parting from the Foundation, and how on our leaving, we had paid our final dues for the month, even though the month had not expired. "Gurdjieff would have said, 'simple, honorable,'" she declared, letting the import of his words—and hers—sink in.

It seemed important to her to impress this story on her group, and I noticed how she used every opportunity to make a point.

After dinner, as promised, we went into the living room and watched the slides. They showed first the barn, where the major renovations had taken place: from a broken-down building it had been transformed into a kitchen, canning and storage room on the first floor, a combination dining room and movements hall on the second floor, with the attic space used for storage of crops. In some ways it was still primitive because everything was in a state of partial completion.

I was impressed by the work they had done, and even mildly interested. Although it was difficult for me to be wholly interested in the slides when I was not yet involved with their work, I had to respect the enthusiasm and dedication of her people. They were working for something, but of course that ineffable something could not be captured on film. Mrs. Staveley was in many of the pictures, but she was always just standing and watching, or talking to a circle of people. Although everyone in the room was identified, including Rose, none of them were as identified as Mrs. Staveley. If the building and renovating was the project of the people, then those people and the construction of the farm was *her* project. It was obvious that she was experiencing something more than simple pleasure and satisfaction in watching her charges at work, though it didn't occur to me what that could be.

We spent the night in our old apartment as guests. They insisted that we have our old bedroom, so the four women camped out in my study, while the men slept in the living room. We took a liking to them at once.

They were simple and open and seemed to take joy in being alive. We felt refreshed by their enthusiasm for the work and, despite certain misgivings about their lack of worldliness, they were more to our liking than the people at the Foundation.

By the time we reached New Concord we had decided to rent our home and move to Oregon. The following month we flew out for the Gurdjieff dinner, staying one week, which was long enough to convince us that we had made the right decision. On our return we began making preparations, and by March we were ready for the drive across country with our cat, Missak.

## CHAPTER THIRTEEN

Shhh... baby chicks inside
QUIET PLEASE

I was standing, reading the carefully scripted words tacked to the ramshackle chicken house just beyond the main barn. I was standing by myself in the misty Oregon rain, feeling the quiet of the words in the expanding stillness. All around me people were moving in opposite directions at once, each dressed in white tops and black bottoms.

I moved a step closer to the door of the chicken shed, in an atmosphere so light it held my thoughts without intruding on the changes occurring inside of me. I felt myself expanding inside, and I was aware of everything around me, not with my senses, but from some other place for which I had no name. I had never before experienced such lightness, or this feeling that sensitivity had a place, that it could be held and entered into. That it could support me.

When we had toured the farm in January it had not felt like this. We were not a part of the place then, and so its true meaning was sealed from us. We could only experience what we had participated in, what we had learned to value because of our own work and understanding. This was my first day of movements on the farm, and I was now a part of the energy field that we had created collectively from our work.

The movements here were very different from the Foundation. It seemed at first that the only similarity was the white tops and black bottoms. The Foundation had been equipped with professional musicians and instructors, and the farm had neither. Even the movements seemed quite primitive to us here. But I realized later that it was because of our own inadequacies—which caused us to work twice as hard—that something else was made; an atmosphere that was palpable in its vibrant yearning.

The music was meant to both lead and accompany the movements, even though the actual directions had to come from the movements instructor. It was this symbiosis that was indispensable to a correctly functioning movements class. This meant that the instructor had to know music, while the musician had to know the form, meaning and purpose of each movement. With all of this in place, a class was able to work at the movements as they were meant to be worked at, and at such times everyone in the room was aware that something was being made from the collective effort that was far greater in its totality than the sum of its parts. We had had a taste of this at the Foundation, but it would be some time before we would experience it at the farm.

Alice London, one of the musicians, had been told some time back that she needed to develop a skill. She had chosen the piano. Not being a natural musician, she had to make a greater effort than any of the others to learn the Gurdjieff music. In time she would become our best musician. No one could have suspected this at the time because she was over forty when she began playing. Her progression was a good example to me of what someone could do in the work, and with the help of the work. All of us were operating in a magic circle, and to some degree we understood this, and were open enough to receive more than we had earned.

We were staying with Alice London and Wendy Parker in a small house they had rented in one of the villages surrounding the farm. We had taken a liking to both of them when we first became acquainted in New York. In time they would become our closest friends on the farm. Within two weeks we had found a smaller house of our own to rent in a neighboring town. We were just two miles from the highway that led to Portland, a short half-hour away.

I had insisted, upon our arrival in Oregon, that we rent in Portland, which seemed the closest thing to civilization in what I was convinced was the most backward state in America. I didn't think the frontier mentality still existed in America, but it did, and it was flourishing here. The Oregonian idea of civilization was a boat in every garage, and a trailer camp with running water alongside every good fishing lake in the state. The state seemed equally divided between water and trees, with people an afterthought. I had lived in or visited every state but South Dakota, and this was the only place I had seen were they hung their wash on the front porch, and where every driveway held a broken-down car or truck that would obviously never run again.

Nonny was appalled. "I don't understand you," she said, "you're willing to travel three thousand miles for the work, and then you want to live away from the farm, to be near parks and libraries and bookstores, instead of what you came out here to be near—the work! It doesn't make sense."

"We don't have many friends out here, and I can't abide the people in the towns around the farm, so why not move to Portland, where we can disappear into our own lives, and go to the work from there?"

"You're just being resistant and negative!"

As usual, Nonny was right, and she dragged her feet just long enough for me to come to my senses. Our low-rent corner bungalow, just ten minutes from the farm, was in fact the perfect place from which to begin our Oregon sojourn.

I was getting ready to begin the actual writing of my mother's biography, and the loneliness I was feeling was nothing new. It meant it was time again to write.

I didn't see how my dislike of Oregon and my ambivalence about some of the people on the farm would ever change. I would simply do what I needed to do in spite of all this. It never occurred to me that this was what Gurdjieff called second force—resisting force—and that without it nothing was possible. I had a strong "yes," and I therefore needed a strong "no," which Mrs. Staveley probably would have found a way to provide, if I hadn't already provided it myself. As much as I cared for Patrick Murphy, who was Mrs. Staveley's right hand man, as well as Alice and Bea and most of the people in my own group, my dislike of others on the farm provided all the resistance I needed. It helped me to overcome my reservations about Mrs. Staveley, because without her no movement would have been possible. Later I saw the reasons for this, just as I was able to understand why she complained about the chummy chatter at the coffee breaks, and at other times. "We are turning into a social club," she would say, in her most disgusted tone of voice.

Lord Pentland's organizational bent was administrative, whereas Mrs. Staveley had organized the teaching and her life around her people. In the same way that I had felt neglected and harmed by the system at the Foundation, I now felt helped and protected under the method instituted on the farm.

Nonny and I elected to be in a beginning group, feeling that we needed to start again from scratch. I didn't know at the time that I would always feel like a beginner in the work.

Mrs. Staveley had evolved a definite program of work that included not only sittings, movements and readings, but also the teaching of the work's cosmology. Even more important, she knew how to speak to each of us individually, according to our understanding. There were no pat answers, and therefore no pat questions. We could speak from ourselves, assured that we would receive an answer for ourselves. The work was individual and personal, as I had known all along, but here for the first time was someone who not only understood this, but knew how to implement it.

We were told from the first meeting that what was said in the meeting room was *sub rosa*, that we were never to repeat anything said, "under the rose" to anyone outside this room. Mrs. Staveley explained, "Gurdjieff said it is stupid to be sincere with everyone. Here, in this room, we can be and must be sincere with each other, and about ourselves and the work, but to be sincere with everyone is pathological.

"And we need to know what it is we are being sincere about! For this to be possible, we must have an aim. That is the first thing for each of us. To know why we are here, what brought us here and what we *wish* to find here. There is no stronger force than wish, but without an aim what good is wish? Otherwise, we'll end up like the person in the parable who was granted three wishes and, having foolishly used the first two, needed the third to return to the place he started from." She laughed. "In any case, that's the wrong kind of magic. The real magic comes from doing." She stopped speaking and took a drink from the glass of water placed on the end table beside her chair.

Someone exclaimed, "But Gurdjieff said man cannot do!"

"That is true—as we are. But to be able to do, isn't that what we are working for? Wasn't that Gurdjieff's definition of a real man? To have an aim is the first step. This is where we begin. Remember, tiny steps for tiny feet."

"It is my aim to become free," I said.

"That's a good aim," Mrs. Staveley said.

"What do you mean by that?" someone asked.

"I can't define it very clearly. It's more of a feeling of knowing I'm not free. But because I know I'm not free, it means to me that freedom is possible."

"You mean if you thought you were free, you wouldn't be."

"That's another way of putting it, I suppose."

Mrs. Staveley asked if anyone else had an aim.

Nonny said, "I want to be myself."

"That's an excellent aim," Mrs. Staveley said. "This should be everyone's aim in the work because this is where the work is leading us. But this of course doesn't mean that it cannot also be your personal aim."

At the beginning of our first hour we were given a seemingly simple exercise to do concerning gesture, posture, expression, carriage and tone of voice, and we were advised to draw stick figures of ourselves that typified our carriage and posture.

We were reminded again of the statement Mrs. Staveley had made at the beginning of the hour, that we were "toddlers." "Tiny steps for tiny feet," she said again, and neatly folding her sweater, that had been draped over her lap and legs, she walked out of the room and into her kitchen.

The meeting room was in the Main House where she lived by herself. We filed out the door at the opposite end of the room that led to the cloakroom and the outside porch.

In one of the letters Mrs. Staveley sent us, between our visit to the farm for the Gurdjieff dinner and our move out, she had enclosed a piece of handmade paper that they had produced some time back. Owen Hammond, the farm's chief benefactor, as well as its oldest member after Mrs. Staveley, was also interested in becoming its resident papermaker. Owen owned a factory in Portland that made chemicals for papermaking, and had evolved the method of acid free solutions that would extend the lifetime of paper for two hundred years. His interest in paper making by hand had evolved into a hobby, and over the years he had collected all of the necessary equipment. Owen was living on the farm, with his son, in a portion of the abandoned hop barn—hops being a once popular crop in Oregon— that he had renovated for his personal use.

Without telling me any of this in her letter, Mrs. Staveley had said simply that it was a project they had one day planned to actualize on the farm. I wrote back saying that perhaps I was her man. I had already sent her the limited edition of *Homage to Adana*, published by The Perishable Press, and she had written back saying that she didn't know things of this quality were still being produced in life.

The Perishable Press consisted of a husband and wife team that set their own type and printed letterpress on a Vandercook proof press. They also made their own paper in their basement. On one of my visits to their home I helped with the papermaking used for a broadside poem of mine they printed for the occasion. They let me handfeed one of the sheets through the press, and the total experience had instilled in me a desire to one day own my own press. I felt now that perhaps the opportunity and the possibility had arrived.

It was an opportunity as fortuitous for Mrs. Staveley as it was for me. She was a farmer first, but her father had been a newspaper man who printed his own paper, and she had always had a secret ambition to write, in part from being an intellectual, but also because of Jane's influence, for Jane had introduced her to people like Marc Chagall, James Joyce, Ernest Hemingway and many other writers and artists. Her second son's godfather was E. Powys Mathers, a poet whose translation of *The Thousand and One Nights* is still considered the preeminent translation of that work.

Her real calling was teaching children. She had been a pre-school teacher at a famous private school in Portland, from which she retired when she began her groups. She and Patrick Murphy—who had also been a teacher at that school—were planning to begin a school at the farm. The ground breaking had taken place shortly after our arrival.

Papermaking was not one of the ongoing projects on the farm. All the current projects were posted after Sunday breakfast in the hallway outside the dining room, with the head of each project at the top of the list. Patrick Murphy made out the list under Mrs. Staveley's supervision and, although anyone could request working on a special project, the list was made according to the needs of the farm. The work was practical and real, but it was not done under compulsion, which meant that nothing could be counted on. Nevertheless, all of the necessary work seemed to get done, after a fashion.

Until I found my own work I decided that I would not question any assignment I was given. At our first Sunday discussion Mrs. Staveley talked about the meaning of disciple as one who puts themselves under a discipline. The truth of this seemed self-evident. It was one thing to be a rebel, as I was, providing one kept to oneself, as I had, but if I had come here to learn, then I needed to recognize that I needed guidance.

The first Sunday I chopped wood with a crew. This, along with the gathering of wood, was a constant task on the farm, since all cooking and heating was done with wood. The other major projects were cooking, which included preservation, as well as building and farming. When Patrick asked me what I would like to work on—and

I was sure Mrs. Staveley had warned him of my problem—I replied that I had never cooked, nor had I ever attempted to build or construct anything. This left only farming and odd jobs, which I felt I could handle.

It seemed there was only one way to work on my fear of physical work, and that was to challenge it head on. Although I was able to do this only sporadically, it did seem to make a difference in my attitude. That there were periods when I was overcome with nausea in the face of what seemed an impossible effort, made me wonder if any kind of improvement in my condition would ever be possible.

It took me a while to see that my first or primary fear was not physical work, but a feeling that I couldn't learn, a legacy from my grade school days. The combination of these two fears, when they conjoined, was enough to overwhelm me, and so I finally decided on a course of action I would never abandon: whenever work was available I went to it, without question, and without let-off. Even if I could do little more than stand there and refuse to run.

On one occasion my persistence paid off in a totally unexpected way. In addition to Sunday work, there were two Farm Nights a week during the times when crops were being sown, cultivated, or harvested. One evening, working alongside Ted Peters, who was our head farmer, I was digging out potatoes, working on my hands and knees. We were engaged in conversation, which had kept my mind occupied, but I soon saw that I was having difficulty keeping Ted's pace. I had a pain in my side and I had become short of breath. Instead of stopping, I increased my pace and, to my great astonishment, I was suddenly suspended over my body. All pain and tiredness had vanished. The work had not only become effortless, but it had become enjoyable. I not only felt that I could have worked indefinitely, I actually *wanted* to work. I realized that my body was happy, as an animal would be that has been let out of a cage it had been locked-up in for most of its life.

I never forgot this experience and, although it never repeated itself again in this way, I had been given infallible proof that our limitations are not in our bodies, but in our heads. However buried

I might be in my neurosis, and whatever the reasons for my entombment, extrication was possible if I was willing, as the Bible had said, to pay to the last farthing.

I became an unlikely member of the rotating and floating farming crew. Nonny, in turn, had decided to take on the kitchen garden, under Ted Peters' supervision. Mrs. Staveley complained that we were always planting the same crops, that we needed to be a little more daring and experimental. Something new was needed. The year before we had had to sell our shallots to a fancy restaurant in Portland because none of the cooks would use them on Sundays.

We were told that Mrs. Staveley had been an excellent cook, and because she was, or had been, she was able to see a natural bent for cooking in Wendy. She told her one day to take up cooking. Wendy quickly became an expert, with her specialties being bread, cakes and candies, as well as the simple, wholesome foods that were the mainstay on Sundays, because Mrs. Staveley had insisted that hardworking men needed to be well-fed. There were several excellent cooks on the Farm and Nonny, who also loved to cook, often took her turn in the kitchen.

Nonny had become a capable gardener in the few short years of our marriage, in part because of the legacy she had inherited from her childhood summers in the Catskills, but also because of the thorough way she went at things.

I seldom worked in the kitchen garden, but I enjoyed watching the women from a distance, their bent forms and invisible faces, shielded by green-hooded, floppy parkas. They seemed to belong to the misty rain and black earth, their presences blending quietly with the elements and the growing crops. During the heaviest showers their numbers would quickly shrink, and occasionally, while passing by, I would see Nonny working by herself. One day, when she came into the downstairs cloakroom just before lunch, dripping water and oozing mud, Mrs. Staveley remarked—loud enough for everyone to hear—that Nonny must have a very strong wish. It took me some time to realize that there was a connection between Nonny's refusing to quit, and her wish for being. I had for so many years separated mind and body in my thought, but I was slowly beginning to see that the body is our instrument for actualizing, that without it nothing is possible; without it we couldn't be and wouldn't be here. It was no wonder that Gurdjieff had said that our first striving should be to take care of the body, stating that we should have in our being existence everything satisfying and really necessary for our planetary body. By satisfying I was sure he meant that we should keep our bodies both well-tuned and in tone. If the body was not harmonious, how could anything else in our lives flow correctly?

One Sunday I was allowed to get on the tractor and disc the front five acres, between the road and the hop barn. Although I had grown up in Wisconsin, in a city surrounded by farms, I had never been on a tractor before. The moment my buttocks fell onto the metal seat, I felt that I had entered a private, ancient world, with its own laws and meanings, and inviolable truth. As I churned the earth, various birds came and went, hopping ahead of me or behind, or circling as I circled, chirping, and then falling on the insects and grubs that the freshly-turned earth had revealed.

I felt that I was mediating between levels, simultaneously conjoined to earth and sky, and mysteriously participating in the life of both. To my surprise, people walking along the road, or passing in their cars, waved to me, their smiles telling me that I was connected to them as well, for I was a man engaged in farming, planting crops and producing food: the common substance of all our lives.

When I reported on my experience during the luncheon discussion, I said—after explaining what I had been doing—"I couldn't get over it, here were people I hardly knew waving to me. I mean, nobody thanks me for writing a poem, but here were people acknowledging my work *while* I was doing it ... not waiting until it was published ..."

"Now you begin to have a taste of what I mean by service," Mrs. Staveley said. "It's in the giving that we receive. And in being connected to others, instead of our usual way of thinking we are the center of the universe."

"I felt connected on so many levels," I said, "to the earth, the sky, the animals, the people. I really saw that this was a function of man, as a guardian of the lower animals, and also as an intermediary."

"Would you say that we are agents for forces that harness us, as we must in turn harness other energies?"

"That's how it felt."

"We are the planet's nerve endings," Mrs. Staveley said. "It is our hope—and our possibility—to one day become a cell in the brain of God."

From that day on I felt a little less estranged from the rest of the people on the farm. There was a meaning to their work, just as there was a meaning to my work as a writer. I was intrigued by what Mrs. Staveley had said about service. The writing of my mother's story was going to be a real test for me. I prayed that I would be equal to the challenge.

## CHAPTER FOURTEEN

It was a strange feeling, a feeling like falling in love. It was a love that didn't seem to be directed at anything, but rather as if it were something that was both swirling and growing inside of me. A connection had been made with God by the very act of my coming in touch with the innermost part of myself—my spirit in infancy—whose hunger was being fed by Annie Lou Staveley. And so I fell in love with her, too, as an infant falls in love with its mother. Nonny and I, both separately and together, went to her for almost everything: our questions, our hurts, our observations, our joys and our despair, and she fed us, and nursed our hurts, and shared our joy, and cut away at the despair, and urged us forward toward our aims.

She was everything and more than we could have ever hoped for in a teacher.

A question had been raised in our group meeting. It had to do with where the work fit into our lives; what was it more important than, and what was more important than it. Nonny had always assumed, and I had always assumed, that our marriage was the most important thing in our lives. We had both felt threatened by this question because in pondering it separately we had come to the realization that it was our spirit—our wish for being—that we called for convenience sake "the work," that was the most important thing for each of us. For several days we were afraid to confess to one another the truth of our finding. But when we were finally able to speak about our feelings, it became evident that this realization only deepened our bond and strengthened our marriage, because we knew, as we had not known before, that the values we shared were even deeper than we had believed.

I was beginning to see that my capacity for work was equivalent to the measure of my wish. I could not improve my wish, I could only be faithful to it. Over and over again, my wish would appear and direct me. I felt certain that the work had brought me before a collective memory that I could not have known existed as such if I had not found a discipline that would help me to reconnect with what was already there in me.

I felt the time had come to intensify my work. We were now in our second year in Oregon.

Of the three lines of work that Gurdjieff had spoken of, the third and last was undoubtedly the hardest. Although I understood very little, I did know that since there were three lines of work, I needed to participate in each of them. To serve the work—for that was the third line—seemed therefore to be imperative.

The Law of Reciprocal Maintenance, that Gurdjieff stated was the maintaining equilibrium for the planet, certainly applied to one's psychological life. Everything, he said, is either eating, being eaten, or preparing to eat or be eaten. Payment, or food, had to be exacted in one form or another and voluntary payment meant voluntary suffering, a step up from the mechanical suffering of ordinary life. If I elected to serve I stood to suffer, and if I elected to suffer I stood to gain. That seemed as ineluctable as the law it followed, which I felt explained perfectly life on this planet. Just as one had to prepare to eat, one had to be prepared to be eaten, and one was no more important than the other, since what ate me would be determined by what I had prepared in myself to be eaten.

I saw that the only way I could serve was through my skill, or perhaps from an extension of my skill. As a writer, I felt I had little to offer, but as a printer and publisher I could introduce a new factor into the work. For the Gurdjieff work, with few exceptions, had never taken responsibility for the publication, design and distribution of its own material—whether Gurdjieff's own writing, or that of his followers—and this material therefore stood dependent on the whims and fancies of commercial publishing. The material of the work was too important for the work itself not to be responsible for its publication and dissemination. If I—or we—could do this it would be a service for the work, and therefore life.

I had always wanted to learn how to print, and Nonny, who was already a professional illustrator and book designer, wanted to learn bookbinding and other related bookmaking arts. Owen, in turn, wanted to revive his papermaking project, that had long been in abeyance.

I also had a trick up my sleeve. If I started this project I would need to be on the farm, and therefore in the thick of things. It had taken me a long time to find a real work center. I was now forty-seven years old. There was no time to waste. Mrs. Staveley was old and not well. Our region of Oregon was flat, rainy and unpleasant, and I had little in common with most of the people on the farm. Like Beelzebub I felt in exile. Under the circumstances, it was imperative that I make good use of my time.

When we proposed our idea to Mrs. Staveley she acted surprised. "You do!" she exclaimed. "But David, how could we ever do that *here*? It sounds so grand, printing, publishing, bookbinding. Are you really prepared to take on something like this?"

"I've thought it out," I said, "I know I can see it through. I had a small press in the 60s, and so I know something about distribution. All I need to do is to learn how to print."

"I can do the designing and illustrating," Nonny said, "and I would like to teach others. I've always wanted to have an etching press. I'd also like to work with wood and linoleum blocks. It's always been one of my dreams to have my woodcuts printed directly on a letterpress."

"You know, of course, that it has to be work or it will go bad in the end. We're always starting projects on the farm, and most of them are short-lived, and that's all right because they provide new opportunities for inner work. But publishing! It seems to me that you would be all alone, and that would not be good. The people here think that because we own a farm that farming is all we should do.

"Well, Jane would certainly be amused—and pleased. She always wanted to have a press, and she made us study type faces at one point, I remember."

"It's all hand work," I said, "and so it would be perfect for work on attention."

"Wouldn't the press be automated?"

"Not the kind I want to get. Each sheet will be fed and turned by hand."

"Well, I like that. We use too much electricity here as it is, and we never know when the time might come that we'll be without all these modern conveniences, and then where will we be."

"I want to get a stamping machine for binding, but we could also print our own title labels, if we had to."

"But could you just pick it up and leave it, week to week? And remember, you have commitments in life. You're also so new in the work...."

"The only way it can work," I said, "is if we live on the farm. It would have to be a farm project, and that means that we need to be here, to tend to the business end of it, as well as the practical work, because we'll want to work at it whenever we have time."

"But you can't live here, David. You know the zoning laws. We're only supposed to be one family on this property, and already there are five of us living here—four illegally, if it comes to that."

"I had the hop barn in mind. It would be perfect. Nearly half of it is lying empty, and the only thing we're using it for now is to dry flowers, with the sole entrance being that second story window that can only be reached by ladder. Nonny and I have a rough sketch. If we can move the machinery out of the hovel on the ground floor, that would be our press room, and there is enough space for us on the two floors above, which would be tight, but I think adequate for our needs."

"But David, where would we get the money?"

"Nonny and I have discussed that also. We've decided to sell our house, which means we'd have the money for the conversion, plus the equipment we'd need."

"That's a big step. I really think you should give it some more thought."

"We've decided," Nonny said. "It's what we wish."

"I'll need to discuss it with the planning committee then. It's going to come as a surprise ... it's certainly come as a surprise to me ... but I like challenges. Still, we wouldn't want to bite off more than we can chew. You're sure this is what you want?"

We nodded our heads.

"Let's have a drink to mark it then."

The "planning committee" that Mrs. Staveley had spoken of came down to the securing of Owen's permission for us to convert the unused portion of the hop barn. Owen was not only agreeable, but was happy to have us as neighbors. But an outcry came from the younger members of her inner circle, for, besides Owen, only two families and Patrick lived on the farm, and our move onto the farm both seemed unfair to them and meant that we had come into favor with Mrs. Staveley. They also saw publishing as something threatening to their dreams of living from the land, uncorrupted and in defiance of the American status quo.

Being a rebel and something of an outcast myself, I tried very hard to understand why I felt so set apart from the young people on the farm. Apart from the usual, predictable animosities that came from our difference in age, vocation and background, it seemed to me that our approach to the work was also divisive. The work for me meant a possibility to be delivered from all the accumulated errors of my life, both the conditioned and the self-inflicted. The work was not an end itself, but a method. But I had the overwhelming feeling that the great majority of the young people on the farm were seeking to find, simultaneously, a spiritual truth for their existence, along with a counter culture to replace all that they had despised—and in large part rejected—in the lives they had been given. They were content to be part of an organization, that is, the Farm, since they had chosen it for themselves, and even more importantly had participated in its making. For all of this to be true and valid, it had to remain what they said it was: a farm, that was definitely outside the approval of their parents, and their parents' generation.

From our point of view, we had made our own third line of work, for which we would take complete responsibility, and from their point of view we had bought our way onto the farm.

The situation was saved, as all such situations were, by its being a work project. We had all of us a common aim, and it was clear we could not travel toward our destination alone: we needed each other, and our personal feelings or opinions were of no importance. What mattered was our work, and as Mrs. Staveley had impressed on us—over and over again—it is always harder to work in a situation where one is right. And of course both sides felt they were right.

The work was not democratic, and although Mrs. Staveley worked for a consensus, the purpose of all her meetings—and we heard there was a special, heated discussion over our project—was to bring everyone around to the one inevitable conclusion.

There was something here that none of us could see. It had to do with the breaking down of our own self-will in order to make Real Will. When this happened, if it did, the group, or "work" would no longer be needed. In the meantime, it was important that we feel our situation was one of life or death, just as one would in ordinary life, because if the stakes weren't pitched that high the necessary energy would not be there for our personal transformation. The situation, for all of us, was far more precarious than we could have known at the time, and it was our ignorance alone that saved us—for in believing it was all real, we had the chance, however slim, of one day seeing the truth, *if* we could also see the illusion.

Sunday work was now divided into three basic crews: farming, the school and "Printing and Publishing," as our project had been dubbed.

Our first job was to move the heavy, rusted machinery out of the ground floor. Just beside the sliding door entrance stood the farm's only holly tree, in the exact spot where the stairwell entrance would have to go, connecting our upper dwelling to the print shop below.

I elected to dig it out myself, and I was joined by a Scotsman who thought of himself as an artist. Even before we began, while sharpening our shovels, he let me know that this lone holly tree was, like me, young and taking root in new soil, and that we were about to sacrifice it for my wish. "Something has to die for something to be born, isn't that right, Kherdian? It makes a man think about his life, doesn't it? What if your project fails, what if it never comes off, then the death of this lone holly tree will have been in vain. Have you thought about that? Well, you can be thinking about that while you dig it out, me boy."

His banter and seeming insensitivity did not make the task any easier. But as I watched him out of the corner of my eye, I wondered if his lightness wasn't really a mask for feelings he couldn't risk to bring out in the open, and into some kind of constructive use. He had the make-up of an artist, but was lacking the tough hide that I felt was a necessary ingredient, and without which no artist could succeed. I became aware, as we worked, that our feelings for the holly tree were very similar, however different in perception. He had not placed a sentence on the holly tree for his goal, as I had. It didn't need to be on his conscience, but it *did* need to be on mine. I would have to justify its death, and I was determined that I would.

·  CHAPTER  FIFTEEN  ·

The conversion of the hop barn would take two years to complete. Given my impatience, overweening ambition and general anxiety about time, this slowing down was probably just the medicine I needed.

We were settled into our rented house, and now, with the work on the hop barn securely under way, I was ready to begin my mother's book. I knew from the teaching how important it was to strike the right opening note. I had felt, even before the work, that how a thing begins determines how it will go. Since I hated to do anything over again, it was especially important that I make a correct beginning. Except for Franz Werfel's *The Forty Days of Musa Dagh*, no one had ever written a successful book about the attempted genocide of the Armenian nation. The tale was simply too horrific, and the few eyewitness accounts that resulted in composed books had not reached a general audience.

The historical books on the subject seemed incapable of an objective assessment. Each writer was interested in advancing his or her own theory about the meaning of the events, but the faces of the characters in the drama were missing. History had missed the living story, just as the eye-witness accounts had missed the large-scale picture in which their personal stories had been held captive. I realized that any two families, living side by side, would have a very different experience from one another within the same historical context. The reasons for this had to do with more than just circumstance, luck and chance. It had to do with the person experiencing the event. Just as Gurdjieff had said that our way to understanding our work was through personal experiences personally experienced, I saw now that the only way I could make sense of my mother's story was by entering into her in such a way that I would inhabit her experience, which meant in turn the sufferings she had endured. It was the only way I could understand what motivated her, and why she was a survivor. For the others were not, they had not survived, and she had.

She was a survivor. And my book would be first of all the story of someone—an individual—who had come through. The genocide would be the backdrop, the dramatic stage on which her fate would be played out against her destiny. Only in this way could I keep the drama alive for the reader. I could restrict "history" to what she saw and felt and overheard. Even at that the pacing would be crucial. I decided to write the book in the first person.

From the very start, I noticed that the book gave my life a rhythm it had never had before. As a poet I was at the mercy of the Muse, and as an anthologist my work consisted mainly of research and reading, neither of which required scheduling. But now I was working every morning from 7:30 to noon, and spending the afternoons researching, ruminating and simply storing energy for the next day's writing. I saw how important it was to have a flexible program and that, without a plan, an intention and a resolve, very little could be accomplished. The space between my inner work and my outer life was beginning to narrow as I found ways to put into practice what the work was attempting to teach.

While one half of the crew was moving all the outer boards on our section of the hop barn, in order to reverse the weathered sides, as well as to place a steel girder around our section to keep it from swaying, the other half of the crew was roofing the new section of the recently constructed foyer with wooden shakes. Two of us were working from the top rungs of our ladders, at opposite ends of the roof. I called across for a tool I was missing, and when I reached for the wide toss to my right, I upset the balance of the ladder and fell ten feet to the ground.

The only pain I felt at first was in my wrist, which began to swell at once, and was quite obviously broken.

I was walked to the middle bay of the barn, while a car was brought around to drive me to the nearest hospital. I stood at the glassed double-doors, that looked out at the courtyard, where several people were busy at their tasks. There was a total clarity to the scene, as if all existence had stopped except the very moment I was standing in front of. For once, my feelings, thoughts and opinions were unrequired—and I was able to see what I was looking at for what it was. The truth was so simple it needed neither commentator nor judge, but only something that could see. If I needed to break my hand to know this, I wondered if I would have to break my head to understand and not forget it.

That was the second ladder I had fallen from, and I would fall from three more before an edict came down that I was not to mount another ladder.

As I reflected on my accident, I remembered that my father had fallen off a ladder when he was the same age as I was now. It had nearly crippled him. Were the sins of the father being visited on the son, I wondered? Mrs. Staveley explained that it probably had more to do with my animal nature than my karma. But I didn't know what my animal was. According to the teaching, our planetary bodies were comprised of the substances formed on this earth, the animals being the emotional center, with each of our natures corresponding to a particular animal.

My arm was in a sling for one month. I quickly learned to scribble with my left hand, and continued with my book. Instead of carpentry, I became the project's gopher, running down equipment and supplies for the Sunday crews.

The problem I had had with Lord Pentland in group meetings continued to repeat itself on the farm. Although I often spoke in meetings, I was careful to make a separation between myself and the material I was discussing. I kept a guard around my own experiences, fearful that I would be slammed-down, though it was clear that Mrs. Staveley was not out to get me. On the contrary, she had taken a personal interest in both Nonny and me, and she encouraged us to see her privately.

There was always a constant stream of people in and out of her library, that overlooked the courtyard, the barn and the site of the school, that had recently been erected, all of which she faced, while her visitors faced her and the wall of books at her back.

She was obviously and openly interested in every aspect of my work. It wasn't long before I found myself going to her, like an excited child, whenever I had an insight or had made a new observation. I also went to her whenever I got stuck. After hearing me out, and placing me back on my path—or simply charging my battery—she would say, when I tried to thank her, "Don't put your thanks on my shoulders. Thank Gurdjieff, his shoulders are bigger than mine."

The work was clearly her life, and although she enjoyed talking about life matters—and part of her interest in us was that we reminded her of the days she spent among artists in London—she always came back to the work, applying every situation to a work principle or idea. This often had the effect of deflating the fantasies, illusions and dreams I had about life, and I'm sure this was her intention. However strong my wish for work, I was still in the grip of life. I had to see for myself how they were separated and how they were conjoined, for Gurdjieff had said that the Fourth Way had to do with work in life, which had meant to Jane Heap that we had to keep our life going, but even better than before. This made sense to me. I could see that if we traded one in for the other we would eventually lose both. But how to keep the balance: that was the question. And this was one of the questions Mrs. Staveley would never be able to help me with.

My inner contention with the young people on the farm was that they had traded their lives for the work, with the result that they took their life ambitions out on the work. She was willing to hear me out on this subject, and would even agree with me, but she had a deep attachment to these people, in part because they were the great majority, although to mollify me she would often say, "They've thrown the baby out with the bath-water."

Although the farm was not in any sense a commune, it *was* a community, aligned with a common interest and need. Because of the inherently—perhaps inevitably—limited social sphere we moved in, we had rapidly become both insular and ingrown. Affairs were rampant, as they would be in any community or commune, and the parents were forever embroiled over the issue of the school. There was also a constant round of competition and comparing that went with people wanting a place in the established order—and of course a position, however much the work preached that there was no place for such things.

Although Nonny and I each taught one class in the school—one hour a week for me, two for her—we had only a passing interest in the school beyond our interest in the importance of educating the children properly, and seeing that they learned the value of physical work. On Sundays most of the men, by taking turns, took part in "Boy Care," which meant taking the boys off the farm and participating in various activities. Something similar was arranged for the girls, but neither Nonny nor I ever got involved with child care, partly because we didn't have children of our own, but for the most part because we had the responsibility of publishing.

Alice London, with whom we had felt a kinship from the beginning, continued to be our close friend, and later we made a bond with Alice's sister, Bea Greer. Wendy and Patrick Murphy, who were now married, were the only permanent tenants on the Farm besides Mrs. Staveley and ourselves. Although we referred to them as friends, they were really like work kin. Often when Nonny and I were working on a deadline in the pressroom, Wendy would suddenly appear in the doorway and ask us to join their family for supper. We also shared our worries when Mrs. Staveley was ill, and we met for drinks after special work sessions to share our experiences. But neither Nonny nor I was socially aggressive and, aside from the prescribed farm functions, all of which we attended, we never got involved with the general partying and meeting at the local tavern, which was the only place in town to gather outside of people's houses.

I remained embroiled in my own dilemma: I wanted the work, but

I also wanted everything I had always wanted from life. I didn't see—and I would not see for a very long time—that this was the very material that had to be transformed, and that my passions and aggressive ambitions created the friction and fire that would make this transformation possible.

Although Mrs. Staveley gave out life advice as readily as work instruction—and it was clear that many of the young people had found in her a surrogate parent—I rarely, if ever, took my personal problems to her unless they were work-related. On the one hand, I didn't want to tax her unnecessarily and, on the other hand, I had always been very private, even secretive about my personal life.

I had told her soon after we arrived on the farm that I had always felt that the most important thing for me was to understand my childhood. I had been unable to feel free as a man because I hadn't yet understood the meaning of my earliest years. This seemed crucial to me, and I had found the opening to speak about it when a young woman I had felt a deep sympathy for, said during the Sunday lunch discussion that she had noticed that she got older every year, but only chronologically; that nothing else was changing. "I had always been waiting as a child to grow up, to become twenty-one, or whatever, so I could become an adult. But it didn't happen. And last week I turned thirty, and it still hasn't happened!"

We all laughed, because we were virtually all in the same boat. Aside from our comic predicament, I'm sure Gurdjieff would have had something to say about this, but Mrs. Staveley had not spoken to her question.

And now, when I explained to her what I thought my work was, she also had nothing to say. Although she seemed puzzled—possibly even dismayed—she talked for some time about the importance of knowing our own work, but that the work was constructed in such a way that by following the indications given, primarily through the exercises, that in time everything would be seen for what it was. I was only mildly disappointed by her response, because no one had ever understood my compulsion to go back over my childhood years, not my mother, sister, or even Nonny. And yet I knew I was right, that my own instincts were superior to everyone else's judgments. From now on, I would simply keep it to myself. I would use the work, but I would not discuss my obsession, if that was what it was, within the boundaries of the work.

Combined with this another thing happened that made me see that both Nonny and I needed to keep our private lives to ourselves. The summer break—the second for us—was approaching and we began discussing the possibilities of taking a vacation, primarily because we needed a break from Oregon, if only for a couple of weeks. Mrs. Staveley's immediate suggestion was that we take separate vacations. Neither of us could understand the meaning of her advice. We tried to see it as some kind of work assignment, that was meant to benefit us. But no matter how we turned it over, it just didn't make sense.

"I'm not going to do it," Nonny said. "I didn't wait nearly forty years to get married to spend time *away* from my husband. If she only knew how many holidays I spent alone."

We had decided to go to Mexico City, where neither of us had ever been, but Mrs. Staveley suggested we go to San Francisco instead. In part because we had rejected her advice about separate vacations, we decided against Mexico City in favor of California.

Several of the most important years of my life had been lived in the North Beach district of San Francisco, where I wrote my first book, *Six Poets of the San Francisco Renaissance*. The Beat poets were then in vogue, and working at Discovery Book Store, next door to Lawrence Ferlinghetti's City Lights bookstore, I came to know most of them. Nonny was curious to see some of my old haunts, including the derelict hotel where I lived while writing my book on unemployment checks. We drove slowly down the coast, and stopped in Bolinas—where many of the poets were now living—to pay Aram Saroyan and his family a visit.

After driving around the city for an hour, we drove to North Beach and parked our car and began walking through the parks and neighborhoods, and by the bookstores, cafes and bars I had frequented ten years before. I couldn't believe that there was not a single person in the streets that I knew.

We got back in our car and drove across the bridge to Marin County. After driving through Sausalito and Tiburon, we meandered over the highway and headed for downtown Mill Valley. All at once a man stepped off the sidewalk, and without looking in either direction, began crossing the street.

"Stop!" Nonny shouted. "Oh, my God, it's Lord Pentland." I rolled down my window and called his name. He stopped, hesitated, and only then did he recognize us. He was as baffled as we were. "What are you doing here?" he asked, peering down at us from the street.

"We're on holiday," I said.

"On holiday," he repeated, and almost laughed at my use of the English term. He had already begun to recoil, but all at once he checked himself and turned back. "Why don't you come to my place for tea at two o'clock?" Nonny jotted down the address and, as quickly as he had appeared, he was gone. Although it wasn't visibly obvious, I was at once aware that he was making work for himself by asking to see us.

His secretary answered the door. We recognized her from the Foundation. She led us through the house to the back yard and sat with us until Lord Pentland appeared. After he had been seated, she got up to make the tea.

He hadn't known that we had moved to Oregon to be with Mrs. Staveley. Nor did he ask any questions about her or our work. On a one to one basis, outside the teacher-student format, we had little to say to one another. I brought up the subject of translation, and expressed some of the difficulties I was having. He answered me as if I needed instruction, when what I was hoping for was a give and take discussion.

After a short, polite half-hour, we got up to leave. In spite of everything, I knew that it had been an important meeting. We had cleared the air between us, and this was important, not only for us, but for Mrs. Staveley as well, since she needed to maintain a friendly relationship with the Foundation.

"You'll want to see Jerry Needleman, I'm sure," he said, as we were leaving.

"I had hoped to run into someone I knew from my San Francisco days," I said, "but we hadn't, until we almost ran you down."

As we headed back to the city, Nonny said, "Do you want to call him?"

"Why not? We were friends once, and this is the city we were friends in." I stopped at a pay phone and made the call. Jerry was his old self on the phone. It was as if the years had not passed, and the unpleasant—at least for us—times in the work had never existed. Lord Pentland, in his last attempt to hang onto us, before we had left the Foundation, had Jerry call us for a luncheon date. I knew of course that it wasn't friendship, because Jerry had been cold and distant the times we had seen him at Armonk. "Are you calling for the work, or out of friendship?" I had asked.

He had hesitated. "Let's say for both."

"I don't feel like obliging you in your duty, Jerry," I had answered. "Maybe some day when we *want* to see each other, as friends."

I hadn't thought that day would ever come again. As I dialed his number, I remembered that I had mentioned his name to Lord Pentland the day I had called for our first appointment. It occurred to me now that Jerry must have told him I was a writer. I wondered now if he hadn't also seen Nonny's mother's *Armenian Cookbook*, that Nonny had illustrated—and hadn't also mentioned this to Lord Pentland. That would have explained the seeming clairvoyance of Lord Pentland, when he advised us at our first meeting to do what we of course had always done. But for all that, our running into him in the street was certainly a strange, and even mysterious occurrence.

"Hello," Jerry had said into the phone.

"I'm in San Francisco," I answered, waiting for him to recognize my voice, "in a pay phone across the way from the Legion of Honor."

He had seemed genuinely pleased. "Can you come and have drinks with us tonight, say around eight o'clock?"

Carla answered the door, warm, shy, ill at ease, but welcoming. She led us into the living room. "Jerry and Don Hoyt are in the library, working on the magazine our group puts out, 'Material for Thought.'"

"We know the magazine *and* Don Hoyt," Nonny said. "He comes up for movements."

"That's right," Carla said, "he's told me that Annie Lou's people work very hard at the movements."

"We gear up for his visits," I said. "I've dubbed him the Rembrandt of Movements."

"In the work it goes both ways. A teacher is only as good as his or her pupils."

"That makes sense," Nonny said, "but it's hard to see what they get from us."

"Food," Carla said. "Just as you are fed by them, they are fed by you."

Jerry and Don appeared in the doorway. Don said good-night to Carla, and hello to us, without being introduced.

Jerry came into the room and shook our hands, as if we were long lost companions, and asked what we would like—coffee, a drink, a sandwich—he seemed to want to serve us. I couldn't understand why he was making such a point of it.

"Whatever you're having," I said.

"You used to drink scotch," Jerry said, "when you could afford it."

I laughed. "I still do—we both do."

"Good, I'll be right back."

When he returned with the drinks, he said, "Now tell me about your career."

"Poets don't have careers," I said, "at least not in America."

"You'd probably say that poets aren't successes, either, but to my way of thinking, to write a poem is to be a success." Jerry was a great talker, and I enjoyed listening to him rattle on. As he continued talking about the trials of being a serious artist in America, I remembered the day we were standing in line at Armonk, when a woman came up to him and began gushing about his latest "spiritual book." He turned away, embarrassed, and nodding in my direction, said, "Here's the writer." The woman gave me a vague smile and walked away.

Nonny said, "David's finishing a book about his mother." "How exciting," Carla said. They knew my mother, and had heard about her life from my sister.

"What will you call it?" Jerry asked.

"*The Autobiography of My Mother*," I said. "That's the working title."

Jerry looked over at Carla. "A genius title!" He looked up at the ceiling, calculating my triumph.

"It kills me," he said, "that the *New York Times* will not review my books. They've put a taboo on sacred literature, and I don't think they'll ever change their point of view."

"It's too new, the West needs another ten or twenty years to adjust to the changing climate. But why should you be discouraged, I see your books in all the metaphysical bookstores, and the Penguin series you are editing is a great service. It's a privilege to serve the work, and that's something you've earned. That must fill you with a sense of purpose, if not triumph."

Jerry accepted the compliment in silence. "But there is all this new work begging to be born—and also to be recognized. It's not enough to bring things back, the news has to be carried forward from where we are, right here."

"I think that has been every writer's lament, since the beginning of recorded time, regardless of the genre."

"All thinkers, too," Carla added, "not to mention mystics."

"I just don't think we should get too far outside the market place," Jerry said. "The tip of the iceberg needs to be seen before anyone can be drawn to its depths."

"I think the people at the farm would argue with that," I said. "They don't want anyone to know where they are, or what they are doing."

Jerry looked at me from under his drink before speaking. "You're happy there?"

"We're getting the teaching. It's the pure, straight stuff, and from an American. We couldn't stand the stuffy English atmosphere at the Foundation. Do you know Michael Arlen's books?"

"Only that they were drawing room dramas about English society in the 20s."

"His real name was Dickran Kouymjian. He was Armenian. Isn't that ironic? I never read him, either, but someone reported—it might have been Evelyn Waugh—that Arlen said the English were the opposite of the Armenians."

"He said that?"

"Yes, I never forgot it. It helped me during our hard times at the Foundation. We were never comfortable there, you know."

"Lord Pentland's the fastest gun in the West," Carla said.

"Yes," Jerry assented, "the fastest gun, the best mind—and that's just the surface. You need to know him as we do, from years of real work."

"He always impressed us," Nonny said, "but we weren't always learning. I don't think he really helped us to see what our own effort needed to be. There's more to teaching than speaking the truth. The truth is needed, but so is guidance. What he said never stayed with us. I felt inspired in the moment, but it soon vanished. You know Gurdjieff's parable of the two monastic brothers, Brother Sez and Brother Ahl? Their names standing for what they do and are."

"Are you saying that Annie Lou is your Brother Ahl?" Carla said.

"No, I didn't mean that. What it comes down to for me, is that the work is accessible for me on the farm in the way it never was at the Foundation. What she says goes deeper, and stays with me, and little by little I find what I need to work on for my being."

On our way to the car Nonny apologized. "I talked too much again, I'm sorry. I think Lord Pentland told Jerry to have us over. He probably even thought we came looking for him, or something, and that we want to come back. That's just conjecture, but one thing is certain, Jerry was leading you on. And you didn't know it, did you?"

"No, well ...."

"I didn't want to spoil the evening, and I knew you were enjoying all that literary talk ... and I know there's nobody in Oregon to talk to except Mrs. Staveley about these things ..."

"You're sure of that?"

"Yes, David, I'm positive."

"Uhm, well ... I'm glad we saw Lord Pentland, anyhow, and I *did* enjoy the evening, didn't you?"

"Yes, I did. And I agree, it was important we met with Lord Pentland. In fact, I can't wait to tell Mrs. Staveley about it."

· CHAPTER SIXTEEN ·

The trip to California had confirmed something. By the time we returned home we knew the farm was our place of work, and that Mrs. Staveley was our teacher. We were certain she had a crystal ball, and had foretold our meeting with Lord Pentland, and further, that we would return home with our tails tightly drawn up between our legs.

From that day forward we never questioned her again. Whatever doubts or misgivings we may have still had, or that we would have in the future, we set aside as being unimportant to our work, and therefore outside our business. We had come for the work, and we felt certain now that we could receive it here.

I was glad now that I hadn't spoken out at the luncheon discussion when Lord Pentland had denounced the work. Mrs. Staveley had let me know at our first meeting that she would not have been able to take us into her group if I had, for I would have been considered a pariah and a threat to the established order. Our meeting with him in California was therefore important to Mrs. Staveley, as well as to us.

It had not only cleared the air, but it had showed me that he *could* work and *did* work on himself—something that I could not say in honesty I had begun to do, at least not in an intentional, self motivated, and purposeful way.

Every teacher taught from their own brand of special expertise. In the Foundation we were slammed-down, on the theory—more or less correct, *as theory*—that we had to be broken down before we could be rebuilt. Mrs. Staveley had begun her teaching from this premise also, but after losing many of the people in her first groups, she had the wisdom to begin again, simply and quietly from herself.

Although I was reasonably relaxed and able to be myself when I was with her privately, and by now our visits were social as well—I was still rigid and ill at ease in group meetings. The dynamics of the group meeting—and for me the group meeting, not movements or Sunday work, was the crux of the teaching—were such that everyone was on edge at all times. This was the place where we dared to speak the truth, where we were revealed to ourselves, and where the work was parceled out, both in its general outline and form, and even more importantly for us, in exercises which, if practiced, would increase our consciousness.

We each had a way of dodging the issue, of avoiding the truth of our actual situation. Some, in what seemed like unabashed sincerity, were really indulging a camouflaged self-pity. Others perfected the art of misunderstanding, while the majority agreed vociferously with the teacher's pronouncements, thereby pretending to the same un-derstanding, if by no other means than by being on the side of the accepted truth.

Nonny, as Mrs. Staveley had warned, was always saying yes, attempting to be right, and therefore acceptable, by doing good. I, in my superior wisdom and disdain, spoke of books, as well as tales I remembered from the experiences of Bennett, Nott, Hulme, Hartmann and other of Gurdjieff's pupils, as well as from theories, ideas and other concoctions. This had gone on into the second year, until one day Mrs. Staveley said, in what seemed her severest tone of voice, "When are you going to begin to speak from your own experiences?"

Just that one statement delivered, obviously, at the perfect mo-ment, changed something in me forever. I never again spoke from my head, or someone else's experience, although for more than a year I had to constantly check this impulse, which I began to see, little by little, was a deeply entrenched personality trait in the service of the ego. I did not think of this as being an observation—and a useful one—probably because all of my energy had gone into checking this impulse whenever it surfaced. Instead, I disciplined myself to be straightforward, sincere and honest whenever I spoke, which by itself kept me from rambling and getting off the track. I had to constantly fight the machine from taking over. The result was that I was always embarrassed and self-conscious, and painfully aware of "its" dishonesty.

But my failures helped me to understand, at least, what I was working for, and at moments I was able to see myself as I was, which was in itself a very useful observation, though again I did not understand this. Just as I did not see that every time I spoke I had to remember myself, and this also began to make a strength that I was also unaware of.

We were all variations on a theme, so different and so alike. The insensitive had to be battered to feel anything. The intellectuals were led down an intellectual impasse. And the do-gooders were given more good work to do than they had bargained for, and intentionally shunned in the process, so they could see the degree to which they worked for praise and approval. One young woman was told to take a cold shower every time she let herself off from a particular exercise. This she was able to do. I shuddered at the thought, remembering all the perforated-tin-can cold showers I had taken in Korea. Life was the cold shower I was trying to awaken from. I didn't need an additional reminder in order to work. The great obstacle for me was the insidious, deeply-ingrained feeling that I already knew. Mrs. Staveley called me an enlightened idiot, and explained that I would have to go back to scratch and start over again. "To know is not 'to do.' Gurdjieff's definition of a Real Man is one who can *do*, not one who can *know*."

We were each of us different, and that there was someone who could see this, and *speak* to each of us differently, and *handle* each of us differently, seemed—and in fact was—miraculous.

In the beginning we were given simple exercises but, as Mrs. Staveley often reminded us, they were forgotten even before we left the porch outside the meeting room. The written exercises were harder to forget, or to get out of. Of all these, the Questionnaire was the most memorable and telling. I never learned where it came from, but I did know that it had appeared in the last issue of The Little Review, that Jane Heap and Margaret Anderson had edited.

The questions were:

1. What would you like most to be? To Know? To do?
2. Why wouldn't you change places with any other human being?
3. What do you look forward to?
4. What do you fear most for the future?
5. What has been the unhappiest moment of your life? The happiest?
6. What do you consider your weakest characteristic? Your strongest?
7. What do you like most about yourself? Dislike most?
8. Make a list of your (a) likes; (b) dislikes.
9. What is your attitude to Art today?
10. What is your world view?
11. Why do you go on living?
12. If you died tonight what would you feel most cut off from?

The Questionnaire was certainly not devised for the review, and in fact its presumed author, A.R. Orage, was one of the people whose responses were solicited for the magazine. Not surprisingly, his was the one sincere answer. But as he himself had said, these questions, together with the answers they were meant to elicit, were the very province of art, and why should an artist give his secrets or his working energy away to another, gratis. Perhaps the editors were out to prove a point, and the response to the Questionnaire was their reason and excuse for ending the magazine.

The point Orage had made was interesting: who *was* one to work for? One's life self, or the Higher Self?

I had made a conscious decision soon after I arrived on the farm that I would not keep a notebook. I did not want to write about my work. It would have been too easy, and I knew that without trying, even without knowing it, I would have cheated and cheapened my efforts. I wouldn't have had to struggle in the same way as others to formulate my experiences. Mrs. Staveley would often say that the left hand must not know what the right hand is doing, and I began to see more and more what that meant.

The ego will feed from the garbage can or the pulpit. It will process whatever comes its way. Only by removing the platform, plank by plank, on which it stands, did I have a chance of dismantling it. Mrs. Staveley often said that we must chip away at it, but I couldn't agree with this. In my own experience, it grew back at the same rate at which it was being chipped away. I had to begin to make new alignments in my inner world.

The work on the hop barn continued. I was working on the chimney with Kevin Landry, who was something of a mason. He had the same gung ho approach to the work as those of his generation, but there was something about him that set him apart from all the others. Like me he was a loner, and a quiet fighter.

We were now in the same group, as the two youngest groups had combined at the start of our second year on the farm. His wife, Julia, had been in our group the previous year. They had lived on the farm in one of the two apartments, and it was Julia who had written the cautionary note over the chicken shed, that I had read after my first movements class. She was artistically inclined and had expressed an interest in our publishing venture.

Another of Kevin's attributes proved to be a benefit for our entire group. In meeting after meeting, he would break the ice by asking the first question. It was apparent to me that he had the courage to be himself, right or wrong, and he was willing to risk his self-esteem in order to learn what he needed. This quality seemed to come from a deep, unperturbable honesty, that I had guessed had been produced from suffering in childhood.

His chimney work had proved to be fairly scandalous. The living room chimney he had constructed for the Main House had backed up the first time it was used. The brick ovens he had built for the barn kitchen had presented even bigger problems, although they were very beautiful. Mrs. Staveley made him tear them out and reconstruct a new chimney, brick by brick. He had done this, not only willingly, but with aplomb. Of all of us, he seemed best to understand that the work was an opportunity, that the farm was an experiment, and that it had been put into place for the benefit of those individuals who could learn to use it.

He was extremely forbearing with me, and I was sure it was for this very reason. He was there to work on himself, not on me, and he never interfered with my suffering or tried to lighten it.

Working with water, cement powder, trowels and mortar, not to mention measuring lines for determining plumb, and God knows what else, all of it alien and repugnant to me, and all of it calling up latent fears of incompetence, feelings of stupidity, as well as the apprehension that I could not learn, combined with my contempt for physical work—also based on fear (for hadn't it literally killed my father's generation)—began to take its toll on me physically. The body, of course, must pay for everything, and once again I was up against it. But I refused to quit, and hour after hour, on Sunday after Sunday, we slowly erected the chimney, from the ground floor, up through two stories, and finally up through the roof. It was only at that point that I was made to leave the job—which I was more than happy to do.

I was aware that Mrs. Staveley knew of my anguish. When I made some excuse or apology for not being able to be at the job for the finish because of my problems with ladders, she said something to the effect that I needn't expect to become conscious in my second year on the farm. I hadn't any idea what she was talking about. I had certainly not valued my resistance, nor my teeth-gritting ability to stand up to the work in the face of my psychological problems.

I simply didn't understand second force and its value. It was through the friction created by my resistance that third force, unseen by me, could appear. There had to be a strong yes *and* a strong no. One without the other was of no use. I had heard this so many times, but it was very difficult to take it down from the blackboard and both see it and apply it to myself.

It was difficult to understand second force, and even more so to appreciate it. It would take years before I would be able to see that it was not a negative force. It was my conditioning that made me think of the active force as positive and good, and the second force as negative or bad.

What I needed to do was to rid myself of the notion of good and bad, right and wrong, and this was almost impossible for me to do. Owen liked to refer to second force as the good adversary, and this should have helped, as certainly Gurdjieff's definition of the two forces as Holy Affirming and Holy Denying should have done. Both were needed, for without them, third force, or Holy Reconciling, could not appear.

But a child will affirm his individuality with a No, as in "No, I won't," by which he means, "Yes, I am!" And I was that child.

For the first year or more I would forget that movements were on Saturday and Nonny would have to remind me, week after week, to change my clothes and get ready. When I looked befuddled, she would shout, "You can't have forgotten *again!*"

This, more or less, was how I responded to every work activity. Group meeting night was the worst of all. Nearly everyone dressed for their meeting, and since I had always hated changing clothes during the day, this only accentuated my pain. Nor would I prepare for the meeting night in one of the number of ways that everyone else seemed to do. Some ate less, or differently, or not at all; or wrote out their questions and observations during that week, or even memorized what they were going to say; had a second sitting, and so on. I tried to forget that the meeting was coming up, and found ways to kill time so I wouldn't have to think about it. I never wrote down the weekly exercise at the conclusion of the meeting, as nearly everyone else did, keeping special notebooks or ledgers for that purpose. Although I did often write down my observations during the week, it was always on a scrap of paper, or on the back of a receipt that I would either lose or, if I did reread what I had written before the meeting, it made little or no sense to me, and I would crumple it up and throw it away.

In short, the work was never something I looked forward to. It was torture. I can see the benefits of this only now. For had it been otherwise, it would have become mechanical and comfortable. I was inadvertently making it almost impossible for the ego to invest an interest in this area of my life, and this was a great help in allowing my spiritual life to develop. Had I known this then, it would have been ego that would have known it, and hence it would have usurped my efforts for its own ends. In this case, at least, the light was being produced in the dark, or in Mrs. Staveley's words, the left hand didn't know what the right hand was up to.

"What the body weeps to lose, the spirit rejoices to gain," says the Arab proverb.

I began now to see why a strong emotional center was necessary. Mrs. Staveley had said that the purpose of the work was to awaken our emotional center. Obviously, it was the quickest of the three centers, and in my own experience I could trust the knowing that came from it the way I could not trust the logic of the ordinary mind. So often I had seen women waiting patiently for men to work something out with their minds, that they had understood at once with their feelings. Women were also informed by Nature. They were closer to the Earth. But men could not trust themselves, and hence, they could not trust one another.

But we each had one lazy center, if not two, and, in general, women had to learn how to think, and men, to feel.

My donkey was the moving center, and I understood now why I had been ineffective in my writing before the age of thirty-five. I remembered very distinctly the day that I began to say things in my poetry—to voice opinions, to express thoughts; in short, to possess ideas, and to dare to express them. The two centers, emotional and mental, had finally combined, producing a voice.

## CHAPTER SEVENTEEN

Work Week was thought to be the highlight of the year. It always fell during the Fourth of July weekend, which made it possible for those who could not take their vacations at that time to at least have three consecutive work days. For everyone else it lasted eight days, but ending on Saturday, it meant that the following day was treated like a regular Sunday work day.

Nine days of intensive work under controlled conditions made things possible that were not possible otherwise. As such, it was useful. Perhaps what it gave all of us was a promise for the future, if we were able to work and change our being. In reality, it produced highs that, for all their exhilaration, had no lasting results. Perhaps it was enough that we could see that life might be different than we had known it to be. But the work was for life—*as life was*—and not as we had artificially constructed it. We needed to understand that the community was a training ground, and temporary. It needed therefore to be tough and unsentimental, not gushy and chummy. How difficult that was to learn, and how easy to forget.

It was no wonder that when the time came for someone to leave the group nearly everyone considered it a betrayal of the work, instead of as a function of the work, for the work was not the end but the means. It was meant to throw you out, not enfold you.

Our first Work Week was a high we hated to come down from. We were therefore determined to move into the hop barn for the start of our second work week. The sheet rocking had been completed, but the windows weren't in, and the flooring had not been laid. We lasted two nights before Owen rescued us, offering to share his quarters with us until our apartment was ready.

The winter before, Nonny and I had accompanied Mrs. Staveley to New York for her annual visit. We had gone as a crew, with Patrick Murphy the only repeat from the year before. Lord Pentland had begun a program of eliciting memoirs from all the people who had known Gurdjieff. He had no intention of publishing these, but wished to preserve them instead in the newly-constructed vaults of his archives at the Foundation. Mrs. Staveley had produced a small book of her own at his urging, and had taken the original manuscript to New York to present to Lord Pentland. On several evenings, at Rose Dohanian's apartment, where she was again staying, she read us chapters from her book.

Our party had returned home a week ahead of Mrs. Staveley, and by the time we had flown back I had decided that her little book was to be the first from our press. It had a different flavor than all the other books on Gurdjieff I had read. She presented the teaching as it had registered in her: personal, intimate, and real. Her love of Gurdjieff and the work shone through.

When I phoned her with my decision she was nonplused, but also secretly pleased. The problem, as I knew, was that she would have to somehow get around Lord Pentland. By the time she returned to Oregon she had come up with a solution: she would dedicate her book to him, placing much of the credit for its creation on his shoulders.

In addition to her interest in binding, Nonny was also beginning her first experiments with marbling. I was determined to produce a limited handbound edition of Mrs. Staveley's book, that we had titled, *Memories of Gurdjieff*. Nonny had done the design, and for the jacket she had produced a pencil sketch of Gurdjieff from our favorite photograph of him. We had hoped that this would be the only book we would have to do with commercial printers and binders.

Lord Pentland's group in San Francisco did their Sunday work at a house on St. Elmo Street that, like Armonk, was named after its location. Bookbinding was one of their projects, and also letterpress printing. Their bookbinder was known to our group and someone suggested we ask him to come up for our Work Week and teach us hand bookbinding. When Nonny phoned him he seemed very agreeable, if a little guarded. Arrangements were made, and we bought the supplies he said we would need.

A few days before our Work Week began we got a card from him saying he would not be able to attend. He did not tell us, as we later learned, that it was Lord Pentland's decision. The reason was all too clear.

Nonny decided she would teach herself, and began searching for books that would help her. Although "P & P," as Printing and Publishing was now called, was a legitimate project, no one wanted to work with us. The sole exception was a young girl named Ava, who was the daughter of a woman in our group. Ava wanted to be an artist, and she was eager to apprentice herself to Nonny. She also had a curious interest in the work—curious in that she was only fifteen years of age. Between them they practiced binding until they had learned the craft, while I continued my search for the perfect Vandercook proof press, as well as all the other equipment we would need once the ground floor was ready to accommodate us.

It had always bothered me that the Gurdjieff organization had been so desultory about publishing work material. Gurdjieff had deliberately not copyrighted *All and Everything* and *Herald of the Coming Good*. What this meant to me was that he wanted his work to go out into life. Now was the time for manuscripts such as *Memories of Gurdjieff* to be produced and forwarded into the marketplace, instead of being locked up in somebody's vault, where they would vanish without a trace.

Later that summer, on a trip to St. Elmo for Pentland's work week, Mrs. Staveley took her book along, at my insistence. It sold well—in great part, I was sure, because of the dedication. But behind the scenes there was disapproval, and it wasn't long before they presented their worked-up case to Mrs. Staveley. They were unhappy about the publishing project at the Farm, and they made sure that Mrs. Staveley was made aware of their feelings.

I had always refused to live by the rules. I had also refused to learn what they were. But I certainly wasn't trying to make trouble in this situation. I had to know for myself that my motives were pure. That I wasn't simply taking the baton in my own hand because I knew that no one would hand it to me. But it had always been like this for me. I was sure there was something in this that I needed to look at.

I did not, I had not, I would not fit into life as most people thought it should be lived. Why did I expect that life would be arranged differently in the work? The only thing that could change in this situation was me. That was my chance. And little by little I began to detect a flaw in my reasoning—as well as in my being—that I had not seen before, and could not see in my current situation now, but which nevertheless helped to point me into the past and into a puzzle that I was beginning at last to fit together.

Short of joining-up, I had tried in many ways to break in as a poet with other poets. Since readership—as best I could tell—followed recognition by one's peers, their sanction seemed necessary. It was extremely painful to me that this was the case, because there was nothing rarefied about my poetry, and I believed that anyone who could read *anything* could read and understand my work. But there was no perceivable audience for poetry. I had not chosen poetry, poetry had chosen me, but I *had* become a willing medium. I had also used it for my own search and quest and, I believed that whoever was searching to understand *their* experience and *their* life would, very likely, find my work useful. But I also felt, and it was beginning to have a destructive effect on me, that I could not get my work out into the world unless it was recognized first by some imaginary establishment that was also effectively real. And yet because of its very reality, that I couldn't discern or come to grips with, I was unable to approach this established order with my work.

And then one day I realized what it was: everyone—everyone but me—knew that I didn't belong. They hadn't rejected me, it was simply that they *couldn't* accept me. My truth—the real truth of my life—lay somewhere else.

And wasn't my current situation a repetition of all this? The work was not my life, just as poetry was not my life. They were a means. They were my material. It had to appear to be life and death while it was happening. And the time had come for me to see this. For it was this very thing, my so-called life, that I had to be delivered from. I—or rather, me—was my problem. but it was only through *me* that I could be delivered to that other shore, where my Real I awaited.

*Memories of Gurdjieff* sold reasonably well, and we heard that there were groups in the States and England—outside the Foundation, of course—where it was read aloud. Just as important, our efforts found favor on the farm, and now, for the first time, we were able to garner a small work group on Sundays in P & P.

We followed this book with the first of three volumes of *Themes* by Mrs. Staveley, with the result that we began to be known to other groups, both in the States and abroad. New opportunities began to open to us that we slowly prepared for, as we began to make connections and alignments with other groups that were struggling as we were.

## CHAPTER EIGHTEEN

God help us! Why are we always looking into places where what we are seeking for cannot be found. Forever like the character, Mulla Nassredin, searching for his key under the street light, even though he knows he lost it in front of his door. When a neighbor asks him what he is doing, he says he is looking for the key to his home. "Do you know where you lost it?" "Oh yes," the Mullah answers, "I know where I lost it. By my door." "But then why are you looking here," the neighbor asks. "Because the light is good here, and it is dark by the door."

Our task is obvious, and yet near impossible. We have to bring light to darkness. But with us the situation is much more dire than it was for the smiling mulla.

*Light in the darkness*, the ancient canticle intones. Gurdjieff knew long before the scientists did that the thing examined changes while under examination. It changes by *being* examined. The light does this, and what is light but consciousness. To see the truth about oneself is to be changed, if even slightly. And we are so constructed that even a slight change inherently changes the entire inner construction.

The best way for us to assist ourselves in this process of self-change is through questioning. We must have questions. And we must bring questions. For questions open us, permitting something new to enter.

Questions are the very bedrock of the Gurdjieff teaching.

The exercises we were given were meant to open us to a new inner world—a world of questions. And the response to these questions, from one who had been over the course, and knew *from experience* where the question inside the question had come from, could provide the shock—or truth—that could temporarily awaken us.

Our group meetings, and more importantly—at least in the beginning—the Sunday luncheon discussions, because of our greater numbers, and the intensity generated by physical work and a common working theme, helped me to see more and more where this work was leading me. For a long time I was satisfied to simply have the truth of the ideas wash over me. I had observed to Alice London one Sunday that if we were to pay what these discussions were worth, we would be out of pocket several thousand dollars each week, but fortunately we only had to pay in the coin of our understanding: $2.50. And that included breakfast, lunch and the cost of supplies.

But now and then I did have a question, or even more importantly, it seemed, I would hear something that would go straight to the core of my being. One Sunday the question of superiority came up. Someone was speaking about this attitude they had about themselves, and it took a moment for it to sink in that this person, clearly very ordinary in my eyes, thought she was superior. But that was not what had upset me: all at once I saw that this belief I had in my own superiority was common to everyone.

And I saw what an affliction this was. Apart from not being objectively true in *anyone's* case, it separated us and alienated us from one another. "But I thought I had taken the copyright out on that one," I said, in the direction of Mrs. Staveley, trying to free my foot from the floorboard it had just been nailed to.

"Go to the Bowery," Mrs. Staveley said, "and ask any bum. Apart from their excuse for being there, you will see that each feels he is superior."

One of us said, "I've begun to notice that when I approach people I am saying with my face and expression that I know I am lowly. I mean, I make them *see* that."

"We all have our way," Mrs. Staveley said. "It comes from the same place."

But the part of me that wanted to do something about my life, that wanted to improve, get better, get ahead, get famous, get the work—gave me no peace. "What should I do now?" I was forever asking Mrs. Staveley. One day, in private, I told her that I needed more intensity in my work, greater opportunities, *something*. "I need to up the ante," I concluded.

She looked at me for a long moment, and then presented me with an exercise that I saw instantly I could not do. I willingly backed down, and actually felt relieved. What I really needed was to be put in my place, so I could begin from where I was, not where I thought I should have already been. Mrs. Staveley said, "We all think we are already nearly perfect. 'Just this one little defect perhaps, but as soon as I get that straightened out...'" She let her voice trail off so it would sink in that it was me she was imitating. But it wasn't personal—she was simply able to place herself immediately inside the various psychic attitudes and postures we all take. She undoubtedly had seen all these things in herself from years of inner work.

After a long silence, she said, "Don't work under compulsion. This is why you sometimes get mad at Owen. You're alike in this. We can't abide in others what we won't look at in ourselves. You've heard me say this many times."

"What can I do?" I asked. "I'm not changing."

She smiled again. I knew what her answer would be. I'd heard it so many times before. "Throw everything you have—or think you have—away. What is not yours you don't want anyway. And what belongs to you cannot be taken away."

I lowered my head, knowing that this too was an exercise that was beyond me. What if there wasn't anything left, I thought. Then what? I couldn't risk it—I couldn't even entertain the notion of risking it. But it sounded good, all right. It was undoubtedly the work.

"I don't get it," I said to Alice one day. We were on wash-up together. It was the day the question of superiority had come up.

"If I could make an observation, or remember myself as often as you say, 'I don't get it,' I'd be enlightened by now," Alice answered.

"Also 'uh huh,'" I laughed.

"In that case I'd be conscious."

"Nevertheless, I feel lost all the time," I said. "No joke."

Alice thought for a moment. "It's so hard to believe that all we have to do is *see* ourselves. And yet I *know* it's true. Seeing changes everything. That *is* the one thing I have been able to observe over and over. And yet I don't—or can't—trust it."

"So why *are* we always trying to *do* something? Gurdjieff says we can't *do*, as we are, and Mrs. Staveley says that wanting *to do something* comes from our conditioning, as well as our avidity."

"Because we think we're alone. We don't really—or at least not very often—believe in the help that is available. Tell me, do you know why *you* think you're superior?"

"I know all the false reasons, but what I think they are sitting on—really banking on—is the conviction that I am a son of the Father."

"Really?"

"Yes, really."

"But if we are all related in this way..." she let her voice intentionally fade.

But the next Sunday I was back working on my project, thinking of the effect my books were going to have on the world, immersed again in fantasy, in plans, improvements.

Yet I knew there were changes occurring in me. Real changes. I *knew* there were. If only I could relax and have faith.

Faith and Hope have been lost to man, Gurdjieff had written. Conscience, he had said, was our only possibility now. I asked Mrs. Staveley if she would write her next Sunday theme on this subject. She advised me to read again the chapter on Ashiata Shiemash in *All and Everything*. I knew what she was thinking: work with what is given. There is no need to ask for more than that. Be patient!

Part of my problem, I knew, was that the history of my ancestors tormented me; they were virtually all dead and gone, and their histories, with our fortunes (spiritual and material) had blown like sand across the vast desert that was once our home. I hadn't even a photo of my grandparents, or their village, nor did I have any early photos of either of my parents.

But I did have my hometown, which was all the history that fate had allowed me. Somehow, in that place, I would have to find the source of my life and its meaning. From the age of ten, when I realized my destiny, I also knew it would not be enacted in that place. I had already begun to move away in my thoughts. But when the time had come, at last, to leave, I had felt wrenched from the womb that had protected and nourished me, and had given me whatever meaning my life possessed up to that time.

I would have to return again, physically and in memory. For this was my taproot, the soul's material, my capture and release.

For years I had traveled back to Racine, sometimes as often as once a year, staying for a few days or a week, haunting the places where I had invested my dreams and seeing the people, mostly childhood friends, who had played an instrumental part in my life. I knew, without knowing that I knew, that until an act is repeated intentionally, it cannot be incorporated, it cannot belong to us.

It would take the work—years and years later—to put my experience into a formulation: what you do unconsciously you are doomed to repeat; what you do consciously does not need to be done again. This then was the meaning of eternal retribution.

At first it had surprised me that even Mrs. Staveley did not understand that I had to return to my childhood to find my balance. This only deepened my curiosity about her life. How could anyone let their childhood go unexamined, I wondered. She had always said that she believed she had to get the early part of her life over with because she knew her real life and work would not begin until certain responsibilities had been absolved. She often spoke of a recurrent dream of an inner courtyard where all of us dwelt. I suspected that she had been in such a school in a former life and wanted to return to it again in this life. Perhaps she believed that she was meant to recreate such a place here on the farm.

How different we are. How different and yet the same. I couldn't speculate about her life. It was enough to work to understand the meaning of my own existence. This search was my work, and in my own way I was repairing the past and preparing the future.

The work was so powerful that if merely given straight, which I knew she was doing, I would receive all that I needed—provided I worked. Which meant to work every day, at every given or stolen or captured opportunity. Once we had begun living on the farm the opportunities for work were endless, for here there were people. Working together we made an energy that each of us benefitted from, for alone we could have made nothing, alone we could have seen nothing, alone we were lost.

One Sunday evening, after a day of shelling corn with others on the third floor of the barn, I found myself writing my first poem in nearly two years. I gave it the title, "The Farm."

> Looking out the window
> > top of the barn—
> The wet, burnished green
> > and empty fields—
> The summer days come back
> > in a flush—
> > work week, its color and climate of talk—
> I quietly return to the
> > Indian corn
> > the working men
> > the women's voices drifting up—
> Together we are bringing in the sheaves
> > the music and mysticism of the work
> > concealed in our hearts.

I was so in awe of the teaching that the act of writing this poem *about* the teaching made me feel delirious. I didn't know what the poem meant, or if it meant anything. I rushed off to show it to Mrs. Staveley. Her obvious pleasure and satisfaction was all the encouragement and support I needed. I decided to write others on the theme of the farm, and our common aim in the work.

Apart from my first book of poems—a tentative selection of twenty four poems, extracted from a sheaf of two hundred poems that were largely exercises and experiments—I had always set myself to turn each of my collections into a book, in the sense that a novel or biography is a book. Writing always in spurts, I was able to trace my poems to the experience that gave them birth. Each book became a mined vein.

These work poems would be no exception. I set to work to record the farm, not only from past experiences, but just as importantly, from each day's activities and events.

Years before, after completing *Looking Over Hills*, I began to wonder if it would not be possible for art to move into the current stream of life's activities, investing the lived moment with its own meaning—the meaning inherent in its form—that had to be seen and then revealed by the invisible observer. Not just reflections in tranquility, but a commitment, and not to some abstract principle, but to one's own life. I had set myself this challenge with *The Nonny Poems*, and I would do this again now, with these poems about the farm.

On January 13, 1978, we celebrated Gurdjieff's one hundredth birthday. That afternoon I wrote a poem about the evening to come.

> The fog lifts, falls,
>     is penetrated by invading
>     lights of cars.
> I imagine candles in procession
>     walkers in Asian mountains,
>     chanting as they come to prayers.
> Here their descendants arrive
>     in shields of tin and glass
>     over mended gravel roads.
> O brothers, our Fathers
>     in the distant firmament,
>     with our drum the silent wheel
>     that turns
>     and our prayer beads rattling
>     in the engine

that hums under the hood
We　Affirming　Come

I brought the poem to Mrs. Staveley in a quiet moment just before
dusk, when everyone else had gone to their homes to change for the
evening's activities and festivities. This time she was more than
pleased, she was deeply moved. For a long time she didn't speak, and
then at last, she said, "We need to have Sol Rubin do this in
calligraphy on a large poster board. I'll have Patrick call him."

I began to turn towards the door. Her voice stopped me. "There
are people I wish could see this," she said. I thought I knew what she
was feeling. This poem had made a link with the past, and I could
see that she was traveling back in time, holding in her mind's eye the
faces of people she had known. I was sure that one of them, the one
she missed the most, and would have liked most to have shared this
moment with, was Jane Heap.

## · CHAPTER NINETEEN ·

To my surprise, Mrs. Staveley's next paper was on conscience. But I was not surprised when the theme and the discussion that followed began to stir some very old material inside myself, material that I had been carrying around for much of my life. Being an only child until I was nearly in my teens, I had been spoiled—not only for this reason but because my mother, having lost everyone in her family, had only me as her link to the past, as well as the future.

One evening, as my mother was preparing to go out, leaving me alone with my father, she was cut by the scissors I was holding while sprawled out on the floor, pasting clippings into my scrapbook.

I could never picture that scene without seeing the blood spurting from her ankle. Although it was treated as an accident, I knew that I was to blame. This was my first experience of remorse of conscience, but I would add to it as time went on.

Conscience did not judge, nor could it be bribed. It saw things exactly as they were. That seeing was the truth. Gurdjieff had called our conscience a particle of the emanation of the sorrow of our Endlessness. This was God seeing, this was God feeling, this was God bringing Real Life back into us.

This was undoubtedly the case, because those moments were distinctly different from all our other experiences. And it wasn't just that one was more conscious at these times, and saw things *as they were*, but one knew, and for a moment—a moment that was eternal—one had escaped the world of duality.

We all had the same question: How can conscience be awakened?

There was no answer to this. I was sure there couldn't be. It would come about as the result of long, arduous work on oneself.

One of the men began to relate an experience he had had with the children on a recent excursion to California. They had met an old, crusty character, whom they had thought at first was a bum. The children were intrigued by him, and one of them had asked him how he lived. "By my conscience," the old man had replied.

"What do you mean?" the children enquired.

"Well, for instance, if I go into a store and see some foodstuffs in a can, my conscience tells me if I should buy it or not."

Everyone enjoyed this story, but no one more than Mrs. Staveley. "It can be that way with us one day," she said.

I remembered that at the last Gurdjieff dinner Mrs. Staveley had read a transcript of a meeting with the French group where Gurdjieff had taken the questions. It must have been the group he was working with in Paris just after the war. The emphasis for the meeting seemed to be concentrated around remorse of conscience. It struck me at the time that this subject had never come up before, neither at the Foundation nor at the farm. I had been sitting between Alice London and her sister, Bea Greer. After the reading I asked them if there were other printed accounts of these meetings, and if so, had Gurdjieff spoken at other times on the subject of remorse. They hadn't thought of it before, but now that I brought it up they both seemed to remember that there were.

"How did he work with it?" I asked

"I suppose as you heard," Bea replied, "with exercises. By putting one in front of those times when one should have felt remorse."

"I can see what he's saying," I said, "in writing I can sometimes bring forward an event from the past that causes all kinds of feelings I must not have experienced then, or forgotten I had felt, or that I had simply not understood at the time."

"He certainly knew how to help his people work in this way," Alice said.

"And the others that came after him?"

No one said anything. By now nearly everyone had left the room.

Jay Oppen, seated in the aisle in front of us, turned in his chair and said, "Do you remember the questions Ouspensky's people asked Gurdjieff when they came to him after their teacher's death? One asked, 'Mr. Gurdjieff, can you explain the Law of Hydrogens,' to which Gurdjieff replied, 'First I want to ask you a question: what kind of a son were you?' And to someone else, who wanted to know about the Law of Octaves, he said, 'How did you treat your mother?'"

Jay Oppen was a rug dealer. We had our differences but he was good company because he was always questioning, and was able to poke fun at himself as freely and easily as he was able to poke fun at everyone else. He was never properly reverential toward Mrs. Staveley, and this had earned him his share of detractors.

He was forever running off to Afghanistan and other exotic places in search of rugs, and he felt—and I was sure he was right—that he must have been an Afghan in a former life. His parents were both of mixed European descent, but his mother had learned, after her husband's death, that his grandfather may have been a Sephardic Jew. Jay's wife, Carmen, was also of German parentage, but she looked Creole. They were an odd, inflammable couple, and the only couple besides ourselves who enjoyed putting on dinner parties. In my own mind, they had always been intimately connected with my first big experience on the farm; my first experience with super-effort. Super-effort was one of those terms that carried great weight in the work, even by those without a direct experience, who had nonetheless read about it in Ouspensky.

I had taken on the project of painting the movements hall and dining room for the Gurdjieff dinner. It was our second birthday dinner at the farm. Not counting Printing and Publishing, this was the first time I had taken on a project as its head. Responsibility was one of Mrs. Staveley's pet topics. She was always finding new ways to make us "respond-able," as she sometimes put it. She often said, "Responsibility must be taken, it cannot be given."

It is astonishing, when I think of it now, how often we must hear the ideas before they begin to penetrate. She had said, over and over again, that mental types almost never progress in the work—perhaps as a warning against those who could formulate, who knew in theory all there was to know, but had not begun to actually apply the ideas to themselves. As she often said, "The object of the work is to awaken the emotions."

And yet the mind had to take in the ideas. It had to begin there. Without this as our grounding, we would miss the experiences that were sure to follow, if we made efforts. Our greatest obstacle in this was to free our mind of all its old associations, and it was for this reason that Gurdjieff had constructed a new language, stating that for an exact study, an exact language was needed.

Taking responsibility in the work was very different from taking responsibility in life, as we were all aware. In life there were the expected rewards: fame, money, prestige, notoriety. But in the work the reward was suffering. There was an inference, never quite stated, that there might be other rewards, but suffering was the first and certain reward of taking responsibility. This did not prevent any of us—as far as I could tell—from not expecting all the usual life rewards, as well, in addition to anything else that might come our way. Most of the fights, arguments and contentions seemed to rise out of this very misunderstanding, which was also a result of our inability to be pure about our work.

I took on the painting of the movements hall. I was ready to take on a responsibility, provided that it was in an area where I had a skill: in this case, painting. The second story of the barn was about eighty by one hundred feet, five windows, three doors—two coats of paint on everything.

I began on a Monday, all alone. Two of the zealots were there, working on carpentry. "What's the matter, Kherdian, aren't you writing today?" Smirks and grins.

I turned back to my work without answering.

The days dragged on. People came for an hour or two, occasionally longer, but few returned. I worked from morning till night, with occasional breaks for food. Apart from having a bright and shiny hall for the dinner, it was hard to see the point of what I was doing. But of course I was not "supposed" to be working for results. Mrs. Staveley never came out of her house at such times, so as not to interfere with our work, although sitting by the hour in the library window, meeting those who needed to see her in private, she was able in her own way to monitor our work. But she couldn't see me at *my* work, and there was no one to talk to, and I was neglecting my "real" work in life. I also hated smelling the paint all the time, and feeling dirty, and no one seemed to be noticing me.

The dinner was on Friday, which meant the hall had to be completely painted by Thursday night, as the decorators needed all day Friday to prepare the room for the evening's festivities. I hadn't even completed the first coat by Thursday morning, but then, slowly, more and more workers began to appear, and the tempo of the work increased. Except for picking at some food in the kitchen, where Nonny had been working most of the week, I hadn't sat down to eat all day. By six o'clock I was exhausted, and in need of both food and rest. Jay and Carmen had invited us, along with the other workers, to a buffet supper, that they said would be available to us whenever we could get away.

They had a fire going when Nonny and I arrived, and Carmen, who was an excellent cook, had prepared some of her specialties. We sat in front of the fire with our drinks and food. I couldn't remember an evening so comfortable and luxurious and convivial since moving to Oregon. When Jay got up to take our plates, he asked if we would like another cognac.

I stared into the fire while I tried to decide. The work would probably get done, and it was clear the project no longer needed a head, since everyone knew what they were doing and what had to be accomplished. I slowly rose from my chair and walked to the hallway, where our coats were hanging.

By the time we got back the room had filled with people. It was hard to find either brush or roller to work with. I slipped into a spot and began working, unnoticed, and quickly got into the rhythm of the work. The exchanges between people were becoming lighter and friendlier, and there was none of the usual banter. There was also a feeling of cooperation in the room, a sense of sharing, and a willingness to be helpful and of use.

I could sense a mysterious change occurring in me. It happened slowly, as if my body were being warmed from the inside out, with this warmth slowly turning into a lightness that I felt was buoying me, and while it did it filled me with joy, that I knew was the result of the love I was feeling for everyone in the room.

We were connected, and this connection was real, and it caused me to drop all of my old associations and attitudes about these people, that had estranged me from them.

There was no name for what I was experiencing. For once my mind and my heart were in accord, and my body was free and relaxed. I didn't need to name my experience, I was in it and with it, and the experience wasn't mine, nor anyone else's. It was a field of energy that, because it was from somewhere higher, impinged on a quality of love that did not belong to us, but that we were able to share in, and this truth made us realize we were one, and not separate, as we had always assumed.

So this was what super-effort was. I could talk about it, and would talk about it for some time to come, theorizing how a buffer had been removed, and how I had tapped into an accumulator, but talk, or "ideas," as Madame de Salzmann liked to say, could not recapture the experience, only work could do that. But I would not easily forget what I had learned during that experience.

Only when work is raised to the "magical evocative," in Jane Heap's words, could it bring something lasting. But the work had a technique and, in fact, it was the technique of techniques, but it had to be fueled with our own sweat, given freely, with no promises, no guarantees, and above all with no deals, either coming or going.

## · CHAPTER TWENTY ·

The book about my mother, that I had retitled, *The Road From Home*, had by now been published. It was given several awards, and nominated for the National Book Award, with the result that I was invited to speak to various schools and institutions. Nonny and I were often asked to speak together. But if I imagined that I was out of the woods as regards my lust for fame, future events would correct that perception. For the moment, at least, I was being called out, and I began to enjoy the celebrity. It may have been just another experience, but it was a good experience and, I felt, long overdue.

I had never written anything about the work before, but now, in my speeches, it began to appear in a natural, inevitable way, and of course the same was true for Nonny. The work was in us and it was beginning to come out of us, not only in our formal talks, but in the question and answer sessions that followed. We were surprised at first by the effect this had on our audiences, until it became evident that nearly everyone was looking for some meaning and sense and truth in their lives, and they were therefore able to hear the work through us.

The work was meant to go out into life as an influence, as a food, as a helpmate and guide, for the Fourth Way work only came along in parlous times, when it was urgently needed.

The truth of this had overwhelmed me because I knew that it was in answer to the troubled state I had been put in by Mrs. Staveley's attitude about her work center. She would often say, "Sometimes I feel like we're the only ones who are working."

I didn't feel she was being competitive—at least not consciously—but that she believed, really believed, that our center was *the* work center. She had not only never seen another center she thought was on a par with hers, but didn't even seem to believe that one existed. Although I too wanted to believe that ours was *the* authentic work, the thought of belonging to the one and only place of real work had a depressing effect on me. If we were the only ones—and we were clearly very small and little—then it seemed to me the world was doomed. I not only did not want to believe that we were not the only ones in the Gurdjieff work, but I wanted to believe, and did believe, that there were many others, all over the world, in countless disciplines and teachings that I didn't even need to know the names of, that were also working, who were also raising their consciousness, and assisting the poor world and themselves to come to a better place, for the sake of the living and the dead.

Nonny felt as strongly as I did about this, and whenever Mrs. Staveley went into one of her tirades on the subject, Nonny would say, "But Mrs. Staveley, if we are here, and nobody knows we're here, then there must be others, unknown to us, all over the planet, who are working too." Mrs. Staveley would condescendingly agree that that must be so, but the next time it came up, it was as if what we believed, and what we had said, had never been heard by her.

It was obvious to me now, given my recent experiences in front of large audiences, that the work could not be taken personally, for the reason that its purpose was different from our purpose, and its aim was, and had to be, different from our own personal aims. Although I had had this thought before it had never really sunk in. But I was overwhelmed now by the sudden and obvious truth of it.

I rushed off to Mrs. Staveley's house, anxious to tell her of my insight. Patrick Murphy was with her and I joined them for drinks. After giving them some of the background from which I had drawn my conclusions, I said, "It's not for us. The work has appeared now, in all its varied forms—just as it has in the past—because it is needed by life. It is an incredible opportunity for us, but we are really besides the point. The work does not care about us, we—those of us who have this great chance—are not the point. The point is life."

Patrick looked puzzled. Mrs. Staveley smiled without speaking, which was a mannerism I had noted in her that meant she agreed, but not completely, and she had to be careful what she said, because it might disturb a balance she was maintaining, or possibly reveal a secret program she did not care to divulge. At last she said, "That is right, we have to make ourselves indispensable to the work."

Patrick, his puzzled look now grown anxious, said, "But how can we do that?"

"There is only one way, by working on ourselves."

"With our inner work, not with our functions, is that right?" Patrick asked.

"That's right, our functions don't count. Only our inner work matters."

Patrick's thoughts, that he obviously didn't want exposed, were not so different from mine. Obviously, Mrs. Staveley's work had brought her into her present function as a teacher. She was the only one of us who was secure, who could not be dislodged and cast into outer darkness. I had seen plenty of people come and go, their departures as mysterious as their arrivals. No one wanted to lose this work who really cared about it. Patrick liked to say that no one had left the farm for the right reasons. At this moment he must have felt as I did, that our work for the work—and we were not only the two most active and responsible men on the farm, but the two closest to Mrs. Staveley—should have secured us a place here. For myself, I desperately needed the work more than ever, now that it had taken permanent root in me, and I therefore felt desperate about not losing it. My insight into the greater meaning of the work made my position even more tenuous and real. This was an opportunity—the greatest opportunity of my life—but I alone needed to care for my work, to protect it and shield it. No one could do my work for me. But I needed the form, this school and my teacher. My trips off the farm had proven to me that I couldn't last a week without the work, because I was incapable of working longer than that on my own.

One of my greatest obstacles in the work, that followed a pattern from my life, was this need, not so much to have a place, but to be respected, to be held in regard, to be valued for the work I did. In life it had taken the simple form of needing approval. Again, all of this harkened back to childhood. But there is a difference between a child and a man. A man has the capacity to be responsible, and it was becoming clear to me that it was only by being completely responsible for myself that I could achieve the freedom I had always longed for.

I had no trouble acknowledging that I was temporarily dependent on a teacher and the work, and that my marriage had given a quality to my life that I could not have achieved without it. Although I had chosen my life and had worked for it, I needed to know for myself that I would and could function if everything was suddenly taken from me. I was not *only* my life. There was a life in me that was separate from what I called "my life," and the person inside that cocoon had to grow in strength regardless of the circumstances— good or bad—of his outer life. This was something I was working for. I had a great deal yet to learn about the reasons for my psychological dependence.

But the need for respect, of which the old craving for fame was merely a particle, was something I could not come to grips with. Why did I want to be in a position to instruct, to tell others how it was, to be the one who could point to the truth, and why did I need to have my example followed? I knew just enough to know that this need of mine did not make sense.

During a Sunday discussion, Mrs. Staveley had used her teacher, Jane Heap, as an example of someone who could work, not only with intensity, but by herself and for herself. Gurdjieff had given Jane an exercise to help her to separate from something in herself that was standing in her way. "So Jane went off by herself," Mrs. Staveley explained, "and she didn't come back until she had accomplished this."

"What did Gurdjieff say?" I asked.

"He didn't say anything. Jane said that she thought he might have been a little let down. He no longer—at least for the moment—had anything to teach."

The penny dropped. All at once I saw that this wish to teach, and to straighten others out, which was certainly this lawful impulse carried to its lowest denominator, was a common defect that we all shared. I had always thought that being conscious was to be totally pure, free of any human blemish, perfect. I had never taken this assumption out into the open and looked at it. But I saw now that consciousness is *to know oneself*. That is all. The fact that Gurdjieff also had this defect, said to me that this was a human attribute, and one that was perhaps inescapable. It had merely to be accepted. From childhood I had wanted to be perfect, thinking perfection was possible, and childish dreams die hard.

I had let go of something. And I saw now for myself what Mrs. Staveley had always meant when she said, about ourselves, "Let go," or about others, "Let existence exist." We really didn't have to either avoid what we are, or carry around what we are not.

We had come to love our small apartment in the hop barn. Although the staircase took a big bite out of each of the two tiny floors, there was a sense of space on the third floor created by the deeply set dormer windows, that jutted out of the angled walls leading to the cupola, where the huge winnowing fans had been replaced by circular leaded windows.

The hop barn towered over the surrounding buildings, and being set back from the road by nearly three hundred yards, the window in our cupola lit up the sky with a second moon, that was always full.

Mrs. Staveley had the idea, unnecessarily paranoid, I thought, that the farm was attracting too much attention. Instead of setting up a defense structure, it was my idea to become friendly with our neighbors and invite them to the farm for a special—or specially manufactured—occasion. I set out to make friends with the neighbor closest to us, a farmer that no one else had been able to get along with. Another neighbor, who had, with her husband, been an itinerant salmon fisherman in Alaska, was writing a book about their experiences. She asked for my help, which I was pleased to give.

Encouraged by my results, Mrs. Staveley had some of the neighboring wives over for tea.

Just when I thought she had gotten over her worries about our neighbors, she announced that she wanted me to put a bamboo shade over the window facing the road we lived on. Nonny and I both felt that it would destroy the beauty of the window, both from outside and inside, and I was therefore dead-set against it. But I couldn't tell Mrs. Staveley this, not only because she was my teacher, and her word was law, but also because my objections had to do with esthetics, and I didn't think she would understand. Although she had always been attracted to artists, she was by no stretch of the imagination an artist herself.

Sol Rubin was assigned to work with me on the window shutter. Neither of us were carpenters, although Sol, a computer analyst, seemed to enjoy working with wood. I was careful not to tell him how I felt, although it was soon evident that he had read my state. On our second Sunday together, he said, "Have you ever looked at your self-pity?"

My first impulse was confusion, quickly followed by outrage. Instead of answering, I changed the subject. But in spite of myself, I soon found that I was interested in what he had said. Did I suffer from self-pity? I asked myself in the days that followed. Little by little, I saw—and had to admit—that I did. "Watch it," Sol had cautioned, and it wasn't long before I began to observe it with growing frequency, until I began to wonder how many other things there were in me that I had never seen before, but that had always been there.

Three weeks later, in an expansive mood—because we were unable to make a shutter that we could control from the floor below, and were therefore about to abandon our project, I confessed to Sol that I had begun to see my self-pity.

"Which of your buffers was it hiding behind?" Sol asked.

"Would it be too easy to say self-love?" I answered.

"A bit too obvious, although maybe not in your case."

After that, I began to wonder if self-pity wasn't my Chief Feature. In time I concluded that it wasn't, but that it *was* the Chief Feature of both the Armenians and the Jews. So there it was again, our famous inheritance. How could we get out of these things that we had had no hand in making, but that were ours just the same? Gurdjieff had said that we inherit the good as well as the bad. In the past his statement had made me focus optimistically on the good things and, perhaps because Gurdjieff was Armenian, it was easy for me to identify with him and to ascribe certain of his qualities to myself by calling them racial. But now I was beginning to look, reluctantly, at the flip side of the coin.

Thanks to the success of my book, I had become a fleeting news item. The Portland and Salem papers had sent reporters out to the farm to interview me, and this inspired me to phone the young female reporter at the local paper and ask if she would like to do an article on the farm. She jumped at the chance, which seemed proof enough that the farm was a local item, and also that we needed to come out into the open. Mrs. Staveley had been saying for some time that we needed to find a way to get good publicity for the farm, and since Nonny and I were known in our fields, we should be the ones to make the appropriate arrangements.

After separate interviews with Nonny and me, and Mrs. Staveley, the reporter asked if she could visit on a Sunday to get the flavor of the place "in action," as she put it. Now that we had gone this far we couldn't pull back. Mrs. Staveley agreed, but with an indifference that puzzled me.

As I took the reporter around the farm, I watched in disbelief as people hooded their faces, pretended not to see her by burying themselves in their tasks, or scurried off when they saw us approaching, while making faces for my benefit when they thought she wasn't looking. Finally, a group of "men" marched off to Mrs. Staveley's to complain, officially, at this disturbance, this outrage, this violation of our sacred privacy. The news filtered back to me. By now I was feeling undermined enough to begin to question what I had done, and I was feeling not only outrage over the reaction, but fear about the consequences.

By the time I had marched across the orchard to Mrs. Staveley's, the entire experience had settled in me, and I understood something I would never forget: *No one will support someone else's effort, even for something done for the common good.* When I told this to Mrs. Staveley she smiled and said, so softly I had to strain to hear her, "Now you know what it means to be responsible."

A moment before, when I had entered her kitchen, she began railing at me about having this woman disturb our work, which I knew now—that I had stood up to her—was simply an act to make me squirm and see myself. But I *had* seen myself. And her face, when she saw this, changed. She had turned, without another word, and gone back to her dishes. I wondered in that moment if the whole thing hadn't been set up for just this experience. And not necessarily by her, because hadn't she always said that life brings us just what we need for our work.

She cared about work, and she didn't really care about anything else. I was probably the only person who had learned anything from this experience. But for her, one was everything.

## CHAPTER TWENTY ONE

From the earliest days on the farm a Men's Group had been formed, consisting of a select group chosen by Mrs. Staveley and headed by Bobby Skoulis, who had been in the work for twenty years or more. Like us he had begun in the Gurdjieff Foundation in New York, where he had been in groups for ten years. For the next ten years he lived in Oregon, where he had worked on his own—and it was clear that he *had* worked. We had a lot in common: our age, similar heritage (his father was Greek), and an interest in the written word. The Skoulis' had originally moved to New York from Colorado, their home state, for the work, and so Bobby's wife, Jeanette, an opera singer, could further her career.

Once a month, on Sunday mornings, the Men's Group had begun to give themes which preceded the work day, both to spell Mrs. Staveley and as work for their own inner development. Together they made a force that we all benefitted from. It was important to Mrs. Staveley to have a strong male presence on the farm and to clearly define and separate the roles of men and women. She felt this way, in part, because she believed that one inherits one's teacher's weaknesses, and she believed that Jane's failure was in her work with men. Mrs. Staveley was also interpreting this aspect of Gurdjieff's teaching. Her methods for doing this were dead-set against the changing social structure, that saw the two sexes moving toward one another in equality and conjoined in their humanity, not separated by their functions, roles and biology. It may have simply been that the men in Jane Heap's group were not strong.

I felt, if I thought about it at all, that the *modus operandi* was justified because, according to Gurdjieff, men were an example of the active force, while women were the passive force. Once, when Jane Heap had been asked by one of her pupil's to give an example of passive force, she replied, "Nature!" Clearly, one force was not superior to the other. But for Mrs. Staveley it meant that the men had to initiate, take the lead, and that anything that undermined this would take away from their "activity." Although there were exceptions, the roles were generally divided on the farm. The women did the serving and cleaning, and worked in the kitchen, with the children and in the gardens, while the men worked at building, farming, caring for the larger animals and so on. In the first years at the farm I assumed there were good reasons for all these rules, although in our own home the two forces were clearly equal. We shared the work in a practical way. Nonny did the cooking because she loved to cook and I didn't, and I took care of the paper work, bills and taxes because I was better organized than she. We cleaned house together and did the dishes together. It seemed more efficient that way, and it gave us each equal time for our own individual work.

In my third year Bobby Skoulis organized another men's group comprised of the men who were younger in the work. This proved to be a great boost for me personally, as well as for all the other men who became involved. Bobby gave us exercises to work with as we did our tasks, that were followed by discussions and, on some occasions, a sitting. The greatest benefit for me was the give and take involved in working with other men, something I had managed to avoid most of my life. At such times I had a good look at my willfulness; working at the other end of a saw, planting crops, moving bricks, washing walls and chopping wood. With all of these tasks, and others, I was brought up short over and over again, and I had the truth of myself rubbed up against my picture of myself.

There were moments when all of it seemed unbearable, and no doubt these were the best moments, but there were moments, just as valuable, when one became flooded with an inner joy from seeing at once the immensity of our need, and the equally great opportunity that had been provided for this impossible—and yet somehow possible—dream of self-development.

"What are you thinking?" Bobby said to me one day, as I leaned on my hoe, staring at the setting sun. "This work," I said. "I'm a lifer!" He smiled and turned away. It was the only way I knew to describe my gratitude.

Hospitality was a part of Gurdjieff's teaching, as Mrs. Staveley alone seemed to understand of all the people in the work that I had met. She would often say, "Gurdjieff would shop for us, and then cook for us, and then feed our other centers as well." As a result of her talks on this subject, the other people on the farm began to take an interest in service, and it became their aim to learn how to become serviceable. She kept insisting that caring was the key, along with a greater and greater interest in the process. Underlining the point, she would often say, "The product should be a by-product. Give up the idea of working for results, the results of work are inevitable."

Selfishly, Nonny and I were grateful to be among the handful chosen to do the entertaining. The guest quarters were cleaned and polished and there were always home-made cookies or candies and fruit to welcome the guests in their rooms. And we always had a large dinner celebration for visitors, so that in our far-off corner of the country we could gather impressions from the visitors and have an exchange about our work.

Gurdjieff had always used alcohol in his teaching. Mrs. Staveley insisted we call it "spirits," because it was a substance that had been transformed to a higher level. I doubt that anyone in the Foundation had dared to use spirits as Gurdjieff had, but this was a method—although beyond imitation—that had not been lost on Mrs. Staveley.

I had considered the drinking we did with her in private as social, a mark of our growing friendship. It wasn't until our fourth year at the farm, when we began to be invited to the Sunday evening gatherings in her living room, that I saw a side of her that she reserved for these occasions with her "inner circle," as she liked to call us. We gathered at the close of the day, after everyone who needed to had gone home and arranged for baby-sitters, and also prepared a platter of food for the evening's repast.

The special atmosphere, the talk, our tired bodies and the alcohol, all combined to open us to one another and to our teacher, and—whether we knew it or not—ourselves. Things were said and *heard* at these discussions that were not accessible at any other time. The spirits not only neutralized our animus toward one another, but opened our hearts to our teacher, who was able to create an atmosphere of openness and trust in which we all shared.

I knew that Jane Heap had held such evenings with members of her group, and of course we all knew about Gurdjieff's famous gatherings at his apartment in Paris after the war, when groups and individuals came from all over the globe to be with him and receive his personal instruction, his food, his music and his Armagnac. These Sunday evenings, I felt, were a continuation of that tradition, and for each of us the highlight of the week.

Now that we had a crew in Publishing, my role as its head began to present new problems and meanings. I had been a loner all my life, and my life work as a writer only reinforced this inclination. I liked working alone. I wanted neither to boss nor to be bossed. I preferred silence to speech, and listening to talking. I knew what I knew, and how little that was, whereas the talk of others was always grist for the mill. The hubbub of publishing, the noise, the talk, the confusion, was therefore very disturbing to me. I reacted at first by *wanting* to be taken out of myself, transferring the controlled and slow excitement of working alone, to the high pitched, short-lived thrill of being looked to for directions and answers. It was a new responsibility and one for which I wasn't ready. For this reason alone it proved to be invaluable. I had to learn how to give directions without losing my own work, and also to turn my task as the head into a role. In all of this I began to have my first real taste of power, and it seemed to me that power was acquired at the sacrifice of one's own personal work and privacy. It no longer surprised me now when Mrs. Staveley said, as she often did, that everyone had a job but her. It was a hollow complaint, of course, and I knew now where it came from.

In time I became comfortable and relaxed enough to be able to do my own work, which was typesetting and printing, as Nonny's work was designing, binding and illustrating. But working with others never became entirely natural or easy. None of the men who worked with me on the press were able to work with the kind of intensity and dedication that I brought to my work. At the same time, being even more hopeless with machinery than I was with wood, I was dependent on others to keep the press running, or just to make simple adjustments and changes when necessary. I became paralyzed by fear and anxiety whenever anything went wrong. I also knew that I had to learn to run the press by myself, and by fits and starts I began to do this. The marvel was that I was able to print at all.

Nonny had simply taught herself to bind, but I needed help before I could get started at the press. Faye Hammond, Owen's bride, had recently arrived from St. Elmo, the work center in San Francisco, where she had worked at printing. She stayed with me long enough to teach me the ropes. Working with her I saw an age-old pattern that had formed in me in grade school: as long as I could imitate someone, I would; but if thrown back on myself, I was capable of learning as well as anyone else. Because my grade school teachers had discriminated against me, they had instilled in me a distrust of teachers, which in turn made learning from others nearly impossible. On the one hand, I had found my own way to work with my disability, and through sheer will-power and stubbornness I somehow got the press to bend to my purposes. The first book we printed, at which I assisted, was by my standards a disaster. But it was just as well that it was, because it became my point of reference for all future work.

One day, after I had been printing for more than a year, Sol Rubin stopped by the press and asked, "What is the difference between what you are doing and fine printing?"

I knew we had arrived. Sol did not give out unearned compliments. "It's never good enough," I replied, which was both the truth and how I felt.

I began to acquire the reputation of being a difficult taskmaster. I was never satisfied with anyone's work, including my own. My reputation was earned in that I was, or could be, overly picky about the details of everyone's work, but I was not out of bounds when it came to my insistence that everyone who worked in publishing bring to it the highest standard of performance they were capable of. Everyone's best, anyone's best, was all that anyone had a right to demand. Compromise and acceptance of inferior work had been impossible for me.

As with all situations that came up in the work, there was something to be learned in this. Mrs. Staveley lectured on team effort, pointing out how one either suffered or caused suffering if one's part was better, or less good than the other parts of the whole. There was more to working with others than upholding one's personal standard. Everyone had a right to be, to work and to be a part of the whole. In this give and take we were working for our own maturity, as well as tolerance and acceptance, which were its instruments.

Nonny was not a perfectionist in the same way that I was. I believed that one had to work uncompromisingly for perfection, acknowledging *after* the work was done that perfection was not possible, or even, for that matter, desirable. Nonny incorporated this understanding into the process itself, and would often say, "We can only do our best." Her best in bookmaking was higher than most could reach, and that few—at least on the farm—could even see.

For a long time none of the men would come into publishing, while the two women who showed the most interest had literary or artistic aspirations. They had some vague, indefinable idea or notion that by coming into publishing they would be connected to their dream of becoming artists or writers. When it turned out to be tedious, uncompromising work, they soon lost interest. But instead of leaving, they hung around and turned their negativity into low-level defiance. I let all this slide. after all, this was the work. But the work days in publishing became difficult and strained because of their presence. After some time, the women themselves called for a meeting with Mrs. Staveley in the Main House. Their grievances were met by mine and Nonny's. Each person was asked to speak and give their version or picture of the situation, or simply state their grievance, as the case might be. "Let's put our cards on the table," Mrs. Staveley said. "We need to know where everyone stands."

As I listened, two things became clear: one, the issue was publishing, not personalities; and two, I was not going to let *anything* interfere with my work.

After everyone had spoken, Mrs. Staveley encouraged the two women who instigated the meeting to find replacements for themselves, since it was clear that they did not wish to work in publishing any longer. "In the work," Mrs. Staveley said, "when you are ready to leave something, you need to find your own replacement."

She had offered a positive way out of the situation, which was well accepted, and the air began to clear. I was happy it was over, and after I walked out of the room and began heading back to publishing, I suddenly felt an upsurge of energy, and I knew—as I had never known before—that *nothing* could keep me from doing my work and living my life. This power, this determination, this clear sight and sense of purpose came from my depths, and was so clearly true and right that it didn't need to be questioned, merely followed. If this was essence I had touched the central core.

Was this my first demonstrable experience of what we call Real I? I'm sure it didn't or wouldn't have occurred to me at the time. Whatever it was, it became my touchstone, and I knew that right or wrong had nothing to do with anything: I would henceforth do what I had to do, and I would let the chips fall as they may.

## · CHAPTER TWENTY TWO ·

After *The Road From Home* was completed and before it was published, I read the finished script to my mother on one of our trips to Fresno. When I had finished, my mother gave me her approval, as well as words of praise and encouragement. Until that moment, I hadn't thought that I might write other novels or books of prose. I had thought of my mother's biography as a non-fiction novel.

The next book I wrote was an autobiographical adventure novel about two boys who become marooned in the wilderness during a storm and have to be rescued. I began with the ending in mind and wrote my way to the destined conclusion, but I wasn't able to begin until the first sentence popped into my head one afternoon, much as it had happened with my mother's book.

My workroom was on the unheated second floor, and I began writing during one of the coldest winters in Oregon's history. This turned out to be strangely beneficial, though I wasn't able to appreciate it at the time. I made it my aim to write one thousand words a day, which I was nearly always able to do by noon. As I worked my quota increased, until on the final day I wrote five thousand words. I completed the first draft in six weeks, and the finished book in eight. I wore thermal underwear and, on the coldest days, earmuffs. Even with a space heater, I doubt the room temperature ever reached 40 degrees.

Through this experience I was given a valuable lesson in identification. With my mother's book I found two tendencies in myself that I knew I had in common with other writers: procrastination and identification. The procrastination resulted in daily rituals of preparation that forestalled the inevitable, and this predilection, when combined with identification, resulted in research-excuses. One came to a point in the story where something needed explaining or defining, that in turn would require information that needed to be obtained. Instead of leaving the research until later and going on with the narrative, this became the perfect excuse to get in the car and drive to the library, or elsewhere, during which time one slowly swelled with self-importance over the beauty of one's mission— which I soon realized was being fueled by the energy obtained during the writing. *This was identification.*

I saw now how identification spoils everything, for the reason that it offers nothing that is needed for the actual work. I also saw that identification is always there, lurking in the shadows, if in fact it is not leading us by the nose. Once at Armonk, one of the old timers stated that he was "identified with everything." I found myself scoffing at the statement. How could someone in the work for twenty years or more still be identified? But now I saw it very differently. Jane Heap had said, "You are going to be identified, so choose your identification." I was too much a perfectionist for that, but I wasn't ruling out the possibility that this *might* be good advice, even for me.

It soon became clear that we weren't going to be receiving manuscripts from anyone connected with the Foundation. This being the case, I accepted the situation and tried to work with what I had, as well as to find out what that might be. I finally concluded that there were two things possible for us in addition to publishing Mrs. Staveley's themes, my own work poems and anything Nonny might produce that was connected to the work: one, to develop whatever talent for writing and illustrating there might be on the farm; and two, to bring the very best work we were capable of to the people on the farm.

I began by trying to encourage others to write for the press. There were those who wanted to write, as well as those who felt they had something in particular they wanted to say. But even those with a discernable talent, as well as a certain—perhaps necessary—ambition, were afraid to expose themselves.

One of the men agreed to write something about the work. This involved long, private discussions, and a great deal of hand-holding, but in the end it came to nothing.

Finally, one of the women wrote a five hundred word essay titled, *The Circle of Our Lives*, about the accretion of work and the slow ascent up the mountain. This became our first memento. It was printed as a tiny pamphlet and given to everyone in attendance at the next Gurdjieff Birthday Dinner.

After the dinner I went around the tables and collected a full fifth of the pamphlets, all that had been left behind, many of which were gravy- and water-stained. But it was a start, and the "author's" pleasure in "being published," as she put it, gave me hope for the future. We had also printed special labels for our wine, as well as menus for each table.

Before I met the work, I had been content to single out those who knew: the ones I thought were sensitive, intelligent, and knowledgeable, and thereby excluding from my attention all those who were not. The idea, new for me, of helping people to see and appreciate beauty and excellent workmanship, was something quite unexpected. For this, Mrs. Staveley had become my example and guide. She spent her time not in picking and choosing among people, but in finding ways to help everyone to understand and learn.

She seemed to be saying that it wasn't enough to know *for oneself*, the important thing was to find ways for others to see and to learn. This was a totally new idea, and when I had first perceived this quality in her, it had given me a necessary shock. She always said that there were two kinds of people on the Path. The first, having become enlightened, ascends the wall and goes over; the other, called *Bodhisattvas* in the Buddhist tradition, after having scaled the wall, return to help others on the Way. I was sure she thought of herself as belonging to the second category. I began to see her in this light.

"I am a cow that gives good milk," she said to me one day,

explaining the constant flow of people that came to see her privately. I also knew that she had long made it her work never to say no to anyone who asked for help. Above all, I saw—as everyone else did—that her approach to people had to do with seeing their potential. Not just what was there, but what they *could* be, what they *would* be, if only they could help themselves to become what they were *meant* to be. This is what attracted us to her. For each of us, she was the other one, the *only* other one, besides ourselves, that cared for and believed in our possibilities.

This was far beyond where I was or even hoped to get, but I could begin with the press, by making beautiful and useful things, for the quiet, private benefit of my fellow travellers who might, I knew, never understand my aim and intention.

The arrival of guests on the farm was far more beneficial than any of us might have imagined. Our harshness with one another, as well as our tolerance for one another—for both were true—were not always conducive to work, to seeing ourselves as we were. For this we needed not familiarity, but shocks. The new people provided this. Gurdjieff had warned that without a constant influx of new people, a group will begin to eat itself.

Strangers had a way of revealing us to ourselves. It was one thing to be offended or annoyed by someone familiar: one could rationalize the reasons based on personal animosities or antipathies, or some other excuse. But being annoyed, puzzled, offended, impressed, disgusted, and so on, with a stranger, and one who was also trying to work on him or herself, had a way of bringing one up short.

One of our earliest visitors was a young woman whose questions seemed to have a single purpose: to bring attention to herself. It was her constant verbal preening, her familiarity with others, her witty banter, that most annoyed me and of course I could see none of these traits in myself.

On her third day there—a Sunday—as we were about to go upstairs for lunch, I approached her to ask a question, and as I did, I put my hand on her forearm. I had frequently touched people when

I talked to them, and I had always attributed this to my being warm, friendly and open. Perhaps it was because there was something in her that repulsed me—a certain phoniness that I could see through—but in that instant, as if by electric shock, I saw exactly what my gesture was saying: *I'm all right, please like me*.

That was what my gesture meant, and what it had *always* meant, *every time* I touched someone in that way.

From that day forward, I was unable to put my hand on anyone again without hearing those words echo in my ear. The gesture itself, though it had long been habitual, was checked in advance by whatever it was that would see and remember, and that was repulsed by the lie.

This not only deepened my understanding of what buffers were, but also what it meant to have a buffer removed. Once removed, it could never return. Seeing could heal as nothing else could, but it had to be instantaneous, without a single thought separating the inner witness from the act that was being witnessed.

Although moments of self-observation as keen as this were rare, I had begun to see that one had to begin by having experiences and challenges of every kind, as well as an openness to whatever might come along.

It was at about this time that I had another very important experience in the work. In giving the exercise for the coming week at the close of our regular group meeting, Mrs. Staveley quoted Gurdjieff, who had once said that each of us must do the thing that was hardest for us, and only we could know what that was.

By the time I reached home I knew what I had to do and, having realized the enormousness of what that was, I managed to put it out of my mind for the rest of the week.

On the day of our next meeting, shortly after lunch, I changed into my oldest clothes and drove to Portland. I could feel Nonny watching me, and intentionally refraining from asking me what I was doing. She knew it had to do with our exercise, but she had no idea what I was up to. She hadn't done the exercise, either, and she told me later that she wished I would invite her along, no matter what it was, rather than leave her to figure out something on her own.

I drove to the section of town called Burnside, Portland's Bowery, and began panhandling. Given my pride and arrogance, and my feelings of superiority, this was clearly the hardest thing for me, especially in that I also suffered from fears of starvation, deprivation and persecution, as a result of my ancestry.

There was a tavern we used to drive by, whenever we were on Burnside, that for some reason always kept its door open. The bar was always lined with drunks, bums, derelicts and the general populace of which that section of town was comprised. I began my exercise by walking into the tavern. After placing a dollar on the bar, I raised my voice and began demanding service. Although I was behaving out of character, I found that I was able to fit quite easily into these circumstances. Before leaving, I struck up a conversation with the man standing next to me.

I wasn't as comfortable in the streets—never having begged before—and yet, before an hour had elapsed, I felt myself being taken over by a mood, and I became aware that I *was* the person I was pretending to be. In that instant I realized that there is really no difference in people: what anyone has been, anyone can become. We may be alienated from one another, but there is no human experience that is alien to us. The prince was in me as well as the beggar, and life's circumstances—chance, accident, calamity—could put me in front of anything at any time.

No man's experience was a thing apart. I was no better or worse than anyone that lived—and no different. Gurdjieff had spoken often of our possibilities, and perhaps all that a man could do was to exercise the possibilities that were open to him. That was all. But that was no small thing. I didn't think I would ever again be able to look upon another human being as a stranger to myself.

I didn't speak about my experience until the group meeting, where I learned what Nonny had done while I was away. She had attempted to open a bank account on play money purchased at the local five and dime.

The film of Gurdjieff's *Meetings with Remarkable Men* had been made and would soon be premiering at the Surf Theater in San Francisco for all the people in the work who resided on the West Coast. Madame de Salzmann would be there, as would Peter Brook, who would introduce the film, and Kathryn Hulme, who had written a note for the program.

The farm had a special investment in the film. Jay Oppen, along with his assistant, Ken Blazer, had been witness to the filming of the movie while it was on location. They had been in Afghanistan buying rugs, and so Mrs. Staveley had provided them with an invitation to meet Michael Currer-Briggs, the executive producer who, like Peter Brook, had been in Jane Heap's groups. His name was familiar to me because I had learned that he had designed the poster for *All and Everything*, a copy of which I had seen many times on display in the metaphysical section of the Gotham Book Mart in Manhattan.

Over tea, Briggs had complained to Oppen and Blazer that there would not be shooting that day, because the necessary funds had not arrived from London. The Afghans would not work a single day without pay, and each day's shooting cost around $4,000. Without a second thought Oppen offered to lend them the money he had brought for his rug purchases and, after Briggs had made a couple of phone calls, they jumped in a taxi and rode to the set.

We had rented five mini-buses, complete with an intercom system, and we set off as a group for San Francisco. I gave the buses the names Farm Barn 1, 2, 3, 4 and 5, and the assistant drivers of each Farm Barn set up their communication system to prevent any of the buses getting lost.

The trip was exciting and eventful, and proved to be the catalyst for two marriages. But the movie itself was a disappointment. Halting and stilted as well as pretentious, I felt that it had made a travesty of the book, with the only believable people on the screen—apart from Warren Mitchell, who played Gurdjieff's father—being the natives, who were not acting but simply being themselves, men and women with real being, unlike the hired actors who, for all their polish, were ineffective and empty.

Except for the movements, it was clearly an unfortunate misappropriation of a great, objective work of art. And yet, in spite of myself, there were moments during the film when I was moved—for somehow, in spite of everything, something of Gurdjieff's great spirit and teaching had come through.

By the time we had walked back to our bus, I was of two minds about the value of the film. I also wondered why it had been made. Was it done to prevent anyone else from doing it? And also, was it intended for life, or for people in the work? Our own people, who were clearly moved by the film, seemed to believe that it was made for the work. They didn't think that people in life would be able to understand it. With this, Mrs. Staveley concurred.

Later, I had the onerous task of introducing the film at the screening for reviewers and media people in Portland. It wasn't well-received, neither there nor anywhere else in the country. But the people in the work had become identified with the film, and it wasn't long before we purchased our own print and began showing it on the farm for special occasions.

I had always felt that Gurdjieff's lectures, collected posthumously in *Views From the Real World,* had been sanitized through Madame de Salzmann's editing. I learned later that she had collected everyone's papers from these talks, advising all work centers and individuals—once the book was published—to destroy any such papers they might still have in their possession. Gurdjieff had not allowed note taking during his talks, but he had trained his people to listen, and the lectures in this book had been compiled from notes taken by his pupils after his talks had been delivered. What I heard, in reading the book, was not Gurdjieff, but a standard version of the man being promulgated for the world by the "Gurdjieff establishment."

I felt now that she had done much the same thing with the film. Gurdjieff's work was slowly being white-washed, and not for the media, but for the followers of his teaching, in an effort to make his work safe and manageable.

I saw now why he had subtitled *All and Everything* "Beelzebub's Tales to His Grandson." He had written this book for his grandchildren, which was our generation, and not for the generation he had personally passed the work on to. That generation is represented by Ahoon, who had been everywhere with Beelzebub, the fallen angel who is sent into exile and must work his way back to the source, or God. By the end of the book, Ahoon realizes that he has missed out, having neither seen nor understood the experiences he had been taken through while at Beelzebub's side.

One of the most telling episodes in *All and Everything* is the description of Tibet, where Beelzebub states that the mountains have become so large that they are beginning to pose a threat to the rest of the planet. The problem is all too obvious: if one portion of the planet—oneself, one's group—develops ahead of the rest, it makes an imbalance and poses a threat, which will eventually result in destructive earthquakes and tremors if the situation is not corrected. Also, while in Tibet, Beelzebub observes that one particular group that were adherents of Buddha, having misunderstood his teaching, had begun to immure themselves in tiny cells for the purpose of perfecting themselves. Of these, and other 'fanatic monks,' Gurdjieff had absolutely no use, and yet this is just what was beginning to happen in his teaching, albeit in a very different guise.

Had Gurdjieff known this would happen? It is certainly what he appeared to be saying in his book. And yet, I could not believe that it would ever happen on the farm.

For all my criticism, I slowly came around to the party line. When I saw the film for the third time, on a trip to New York, it seemed very different to me: still stiff and amateurish, as well as unbelievable as either the book Gurdjieff had written, or as the man himself, as portrayed by Dragan Maksimovic. I did see something I had missed the first and second time: the film was punctuated throughout with work messages, each perfectly formulated and timed, and in these I saw something applicable to my situation. I was struck, in particular, by Prince Lubovetsky's closing statement, in which he states that a man must remain with a teaching long enough to make something that must then be taken out into life and tested, for it is life, at that point, that will show a man what he needs to do next.

What all of this actually meant I did not know, but it had struck a chord. Hadn't Gurdjieff said, "I am colleague of life." Certainly my own teacher could not say that, and yet the Fourth Way was meant to be the way of the sly man, the man who can use the work for life, and life for the work. Christ was saying leave the world to its futile preoccupations, whereas Gurdjieff had said, in so many words, better yet, turn it to your own ends. But who in the work had been able to do that?

Certainly I hadn't. My forays into life had proven to me that I hadn't developed the kind of muscle that would permit me to work on my own. Not so far! I was in fact very much in need of the hothouse environment that had been created on the farm. This is what the farm environment meant to me, but I could see that for many, if not for the majority, it was a place of escape. Their rejection of life and acceptance of the work was a single act.

In the beginning, I had worried that I had come upon the work too late. I found myself admiring all the young people because they had time—enough time, I felt—to make a Being, whereas I questioned if I did. But as the years went by I saw, more and more clearly, that unless one has tried life and has become totally identified with life, until one has seen finally for oneself that life was not going anywhere, that it could not answer for itself, because it was not in itself either the answer or the point, only then could one roll up one's sleeves and go to work. It had nothing to do with rejection or acceptance, but rather, with *metanoia*. One had to *change one's mind about one's life*.

Mrs. Staveley was determined to participate in promoting the film in any way she could. Each of us was encouraged to write our impressions of the film, and she sent the best of these to Lord Pentland. For the screening in Portland she took a selected handful of people. The women prepared coffee and cake for those in attendance. The job of the men, as best I could tell, was to steer those who had questions over to Mrs. Staveley, but we were so nervous that we neither did this, nor were we able to speak intelligently to their questions. I had never felt so inept in a social situation. Had we been so successful at stripping ourselves of our false personalities, and at working for attention, as to forget ourselves? If we were seeing ourselves, then that knowledge, in the moment, wasn't doing us any good. If being here/now was the point of our teaching, then it had delivered us, unwittingly, to far/gone, without our even knowing what had happened to us. Or was it simply being observed by our teacher in life that had turned us into bungling idiots?

The tongue lashing Mrs. Staveley gave me the next day was redundant: she couldn't have been as hard on me as I had already been on myself.

Michael Briggs had returned with us to the farm after the San Francisco premiere. One evening, while we were sitting around the dinner table at our apartment, he mentioned that a number of people had been solicited at Addison-Crescent, the London work center, to write reviews of the film. Madame de Salzmann wanted to get a correct-work-review that could be used for future publicity and as a promo for the film. Apparently, none of the reviews that were submitted were acceptable. "Why don't you try your hand at it?" Michael enquired. "You're a writer, after all."

Nonny had already done a woodblock print of Gurdjieff, as portrayed by Maksimovic, crossing the bridge in the film. Mrs. Staveley had sent this on to Lord Pentland, hoping he would find a use for it.

After Michael left, I went to my studio downstairs and wrote the review. The next morning, I walked over to the Main House and handed him the typescript. He read it while I poured myself a cup of coffee.

"You've done what no one else has been able to do," Michael said, "this is perfect. There are a few minor things that need correcting, and then I want to send copies to Lord Pentland and Madame de Salzmann."

Both my review and Nonny's woodblock quickly came back, which didn't surprise me, although for a week or two I had the notion that I might be able to put my skill to use for the work on a broader basis than the one I was working on at the farm. I was young enough in the work to be flattered by such a prospect, and egoistic enough to be carried away by the thought that this might open a channel— not only for me, but also for the farm—to the major work centers. I hadn't yet completely given up the hope that we might acquire some important outer mission for our press.

If the rejection didn't surprise me, what did surprise me was Michael's open acceptance of what I had done, and his ability to put the need of the moment ahead of considerations of rank and position in the work. It was this that really mattered to me.

Michael soon returned to London. We never saw him again. By the time we heard that he had cancer he was already terminally ill. Before he died he gave Jay Oppen Jane Heap's notes, asking Jay, who had been on a buying trip to London, to deliver them to the farm. Michael had been the executor of Jane Heap's estate.

On his deathbed, moments before he died, he motioned to one of the people in his old group, and using his hands—for he could no longer speak—he pointed first to his friend, and then to himself, and then sweeping his hand in a circle to include the All, he returned the gesture back again to them, to say, *We are all One!*

We met in Mrs. Staveley's living room after a Sunday work day and had our own memorial service, by simply sharing our memories of the man. I told my story of the review, and without knowing I would do so, I began sobbing. I had lost my first brother in the work.

Mrs. Staveley and I began editing Jane's notes, and after our work was completed I began setting in type what would be a 106 page book. Before it was completed and handbound, we would learn to pare leather, to marble paper and to make handsewn headbands. Among the papers, we found Michael's Introduction for the planned English edition. These were the first pages I set in type.

It would take two years to handset and print the book. It was our magnum opus, and soon after it was finished the press began to refuse our work. The truth and meaning of this would only be revealed to me in time.

# · CHAPTER TWENTY THREE ·

The work stated that man's greatest problem derives from his having a dual nature. To understand our higher nature, we must first struggle with our lower, animal nature. One of our aids in this endless quest— for it involves both a search and a journey—is the realization of our own animal nature. Our animal nature is represented by one particular animal on our planet, and we had to discover for ourselves which animal it is that our lower nature is derived from.

As always, Mrs. Staveley attempted to approach the problem of finding our animal in a practical way. As an exercise, we were to write out what we thought each person's animal was within our own group. Mrs. Staveley suggested that we visit the zoo, and begin our work with the study of animals and, even though the zoo wasn't the best place to view animal behavior, it would, nevertheless, present us with a view of a wide variety of animals.

We were given certain clues, the most helpful one being the study of our response to danger. "Some bolt and run," Mrs. Staveley explained, "while others sit and wait. And still others run immediately to the danger and face it." I wondered if the way we wakened from sleep wasn't also a clue. If Nonny was startled from her sleep, especially while napping, she would jump up as if to fend off an attack. She also ran to the source of any disturbance or danger, while I would sit and wait for it to go away, holding off until the last possible moment before doing anything.

No great revelations occurred at the zoo, although it was interesting to look at the animals with humans in mind, because we saw many parallels we hadn't seen before. But it didn't help with our task of assigning animals to the various people in our group, which we did superficially, on the basis of body types, and not psychology. Nor did we have a clue as to our own animal.

The problem, as always, was lack of self-knowledge, which in this case was coupled with lack of knowledge of each animal's habits and instincts. What we saw was not necessarily what was there, though *what was there* was certainly a clue, had we been able to see with greater clarity and objectivity.

I guessed my own animal to be a bear, while Nonny thought I was a bison. I knew only that I was a big animal, not burrowing, not flying, and certainly not swimming. Mrs. Staveley had shown me a couple of stories she had written for children, as a work assignment when she was in groups, and we guessed that the fish—I believed she called him Freddie—was a personification of herself. Was that her animal, I wondered—a fish?

Few people knew their animal. It was understood that we would have to work for this understanding ourselves. And of course it was possible that Mrs. Staveley didn't know everybody's animal either. This further fueled our constant speculations as to the degree of her omniscience.

And then one day, while we were having drinks in her kitchen, she said, without provocation, "Your animal is a water buffalo." The instant she said it, I remembered that years before my sister had actually called me a water buffalo. I hadn't been in the work, and I couldn't find any significance in her remark, beyond the fact that I had a lumbering gait.

"I was close," Nonny shouted, as excited for me as I was for myself. "I said bison. Are you going to tell me my animal, Mrs. Staveley? Am I a beaver.?"

"Oh, no, that was put on you. One's animal is there, ahead of one's conditioning."

"Now I can begin my study," I said.

"Get out some books. And go back to the zoo," Mrs. Staveley advised.

"He *looks* like a water buffalo, doesn't he, Mrs. Staveley?"

Mrs. Staveley laughed. "I think I see a resemblance."

Later, when I read that a wounded water buffalo lays in ambush for the return of the hunter, and then kills him with a cold, malevolent fury, I understood something about my inner violence, and also just how hard—it felt impossible then—it would ever be to come to a place where I was not *just* my animal, but a being that could act independent of his lower nature.

I began to see a little of what I was up against, what we were all up against. I would say to Mrs. Staveley, time and time again, "It is very hard to be a human being," and after sighing, I would add, "sometimes I think, impossible."

"We are given no more nor less than what we need. What man has done, man can do." This was one of her favorite formulations. She said it often enough for it to become a kind of mantra for us, and one I needed to pick up whenever I was discouraged. It was true, this work *could* be done because it *had* been done. And it had been made easier for us for that very reason. I had heard that later groups had picked up the movements much faster than those who had begun movements from scratch, and it wasn't just that we had the music and better instructors. Likewise, theme groups worked better together now than in the past. In the beginning, they quarreled and fought, whereas the later groups learned how to blend the various strengths of each member without picking on each other's weaknesses.

Mrs. Staveley had decided it was time for us to have our first all night work session. It was arranged for a Saturday, with a regular Sunday work day to follow. Those who did not come on Saturday would still be able to work on Sunday, and those of us who chose to work all night were encouraged to work all of Sunday, as well. The Sunday morning sitting would be reserved for those who had worked on Saturday.

There would be no work sheet, but instead a listing of the work areas and projects. Each person could choose their own place of work instead of waiting to be assigned. This meant that each of the projects, including P & P, would probably have new people.

We were a little surprised to find Sol Rubin waiting for us in publishing when we returned from the courtyard where the theme was given. When Nonny was learning how to bind, from a book by Aldren Watson, she had called on Sol for supplementary information.

By this time, however, Nonny and her bookbinding crew had gained a great deal of experience, and probably knew at least as much as Sol did about binding. However, he seemed more interested in straightening out the other people than in doing his own work.

He spent the afternoon and evening examining everyone's work but his own. His constant criticizing and fault-finding finally got to Nonny at about 1:00 A.M. She ran up to him and began screaming, "Mind your own book binding, and stop finding fault with what everyone else is doing. These people have worked very hard to build their skills, and I won't have you tearing their confidence down. If you can't stop criticizing, then get out!"

He was so startled he couldn't speak. He had turned red while Nonny was shouting at him, but by the time she finished her tirade, he was pale white and dumb-struck. Without a word, he turned and walked out of the building.

From that day on he referred to P & P as Printing & Punishing.

But something wonderful came out of the experience. After some time Nonny and Sol became friendly with one another, which was a direct—or perhaps indirect—result of the fight they had had. Time and again, I witnessed this in my own relationships, and in those of others. In life, a falling out separated people forever, but in the work, because we had to go on seeing each other, and were soon working on a project that brought us together for our common work, we were able to transcend our grievances and see the other's possibilities which are, in the end, far more interesting than their difficulties or problems. Even divorced couples came to be friendly with one another, and helpful. This was another example of the work in action, when we were able to put aside petty grievances, opinions, attitudes of like and dislike, for something toward which each of us was working, that we could not attain if we were to work alone.

Whether to help us get through the night, or as a bonus for the super-effort we had been making, we were given a movements class at three in the morning.

I had been fighting sleep for several hours. Our usual rising time was 5:30 A.M., which enabled me to get to work by 7:30. We seldom stayed up past 10 P.M. This routine was almost never broken, in part because there was nowhere to go, but also—and most importantly— because I wanted to be fresh for my work every morning.

Because of the state all of us were in the movements class was a totally new experience. Although my body was tired, I felt light inside, and I was able to do the movements without the usual considering.

At the same time, it was hard in a very different way. I felt completely on my own. Nothing was familiar. All at once, I was in the grip of fear, and I knew, as I had never known before, that *everything is not going to be all right.* I had been an optimist all my life. All my life I had believed that everything *would* be all right—in the end—and now I saw, unmistakably, that nothing would turn out by itself. I was alone with my work and my life and, although this was something I had always known with a part of myself, I knew it now with the whole of my being.

When the movements class ended, I was still shaking inside. I stopped outside the barn and warmed myself at the newly-dug barbecue pit beyond the kitchen, as I watched the kitchen crew killing and cleaning ducks for the Sunday luncheon.

Despite the interview I had given the local paper, rumors were beginning to circulate that we were devil worshippers. This had apparently come about because the various baby sitters had noticed on the shelves of each of our homes, the volume, *All and Everything: Beelzebub's Tales to His Grandson.* Who Beelzebub was, they knew— or thought they knew and even if their curiosity had been suffi- ciently piqued for them to sample the book they would have understood nothing. In fact, the book's very inscrutability would have only convinced them of their worst fears.

Although we were set back from the main road, from which our land was only partially visible, there was another secondary road that ran the entire border of our property and gave a sweeping, if rather distant, view of our land. Our movements classes were visible from this road, as we had never bothered to make curtains. Also from this road our ceremonies could be witnessed. For one or more of the Gurdjieff birthday dinners, we had used candlelight only, walking from the Main House to the barn in procession. If someone wanted to spy on us they would hardly need binoculars, and from a life point of view, killing fowl at 3:00 A.M. must have looked very strange indeed.

The rumors in the following week were rampant, and our neighbors suddenly stopped speaking to us. On Friday, Owen's son, who was friendly with the son of one of our neighbors, warned that an armed posse was being formed and that they would be coming out to the farm the following night.

Even if the rumor were true, we were helpless to do anything about it. We didn't see how we could go to the police; we couldn't reason with our neighbors—this would only have added fuel to the fire—and, needless to say, we were not going to arm ourselves. Doing nothing seemed to be the best defense, as our resistance would only have strengthened their resolve. Gurdjieff had warned that a strong positive evokes a strong negative, just as he had said that people who work on themselves pose a threat, by that very fact, to those that don't. These and similar thoughts were all we were able to entertain as the night drew down on us.

We would simply have to wait and see. Meantime, we would need to go to bed, the same as always. "I think we should leave the lights on and sleep in our clothes," Nonny said.

"Nonsense, put on your nightgown and turn off the lights."

I had an unusually sound sleep that night, but Nonny lay awake at my side. After going over all the possibilities, she decided that the worst thing that could happen to her was that she might die. Once she faced this she knew it was not something she feared. She awoke in the morning knowing she had faced and routed one of her worst enemies.

We heard later that the police had gotten wind of the situation and had put a stop to it at the very last moment.

## · CHAPTER TWENTY FOUR ·

Jeanette Skoulis was our professional musician. She had been an opera singer in her younger days, but she was now semi-retired as a singer. She and Bobby had recently divorced and, with her children grown, she decided to leave Portland and move to one of the villages near the farm.

Soon after we arrived on the farm, she formed a choir that practiced weekly and performed at numerous functions. Thanks largely to her work, as well as the efforts of the choir, the music they produced—because of their inner work—was an inspiration to all of us. Their singing became an indispensable ingredient in each of our celebrations and ceremonies. She had even managed to score the Gurdjieff music for voices, which was reserved for special events, usually for our Easter celebration and Gurdjieff's birthday.

She decided to form a second choir to perform at a crafts sale given by the farm. It consisted of Nonny and me and a handful of others, with perhaps only one good voice among us. The original choir was composed of the best voices available, which meant that no one took what we were doing very seriously. But it was rewarding for us to work together, and when the craft sale was over, we stayed together and slowly grew in size.

Jeanette was, in her own way, as uncompromising and relentless in the pursuit of her goal as I was in the pursuit of mine. She wanted the finest performances humanly possible from what she considered a rather motley and unpromising crew.

Although my voice was an embarrassment to myself and the

choir, I decided to stay on after the craft sale because it seemed to be a good opportunity for inner work.

I had always found Jeanette to be very difficult, and she was, by her own admission, a prima donna. I was not about to indulge another artist, especially since I still felt at the time that I had not been given my due as a poet. Our stand-off relationship seemed to satisfy us both. Although this had begun to change somewhat when she came into publishing, it would change even more dramatically after I joined the choir—for both good and bad. Our difficulties with one another were, in retrospect, both simple and obvious: she was virtually incapable of external considering, and I was touchy to a point.

For all our difficulties, there was something in our situation that was common to the farm, that I came to think of as our signature as a place of work, and that helped keep us sane and in good humor. It had to do with the fact that the person in charge of one project was quite often at the bottom of the class in some other, if not *several* other areas of work on the farm. This meant that we were never able to become comfortable in a single role or position. In publishing Jeanette had to take directions from Nonny, and her hands did not have the intelligence that her voice did. And in the choir the reverse was true, Nonny could not do with her voice what her hands could do as an artist. Jeanette also took her lumps in movements class, and elsewhere. And so it was for all of us. We were the head one moment, and either the foot or the behind the next. As a result, no one was ever comfortable or secure, and it became that much harder for us to fall asleep.

More than anything, it helped us to see that we were not our role, and that there could be no security or safety in the work. Our so called position—if we dared to think of it as that—was no more than a function, and temporary as well. We could never cease to ask ourselves who we were, because we knew—we had our noses rubbed in the fact—that we were not any of the labels that life may have pinned on us, or that we might try to pin on ourselves in the work.

We were seeking our birthright, as well as our right to be.

Singing in the choir had the effect of bringing into focus all of the hidden problems that had resulted from my childhood conditioning. If I had had even a small ability for singing this realization might not have come about so quickly, easily—*or* so painfully.

I had a terrible voice and no musical understanding beyond the very ordinary appreciation of what I liked. As a result—because I felt inept and knew I was a liability to the choir as *a choir*—I was made to suffer, and this suffering made me question myself.

If the choir was a constant reminder to me that this was another opportunity for work, I was even more of a reminder to the other members of the choir, because I held up the practice sessions with my mistakes, and my voice was unable to take its place with the other voices, which in turn was harmful to Jeanette's intentions and ambitions as a teacher.

In grade school I had been flunked repeatedly, labeled stupid, and discriminated against as a member of a minority group. All of this had the effect of making me hate both school and formal learning. Even in sports, which I enjoyed, I was an ineffective team player because I was much more interested in making something for myself than in making something *with* others, and it was my intention to be outstanding—a star!—even if that meant sacrificing the team effort. I had to prove that I was superior in order to establish that I was equal.

Not really believing in myself, hating all forms of group activity and work, convinced I couldn't learn, I had taken the only option left to me in the classroom: I copied and imitated.

It was very different when it came to those things I chose to do myself, but in life there was very little that interested me. It had not entered my consciousness that this attitude was conditioned by my not entering sufficiently into most things enough to appreciate them.

All of this—what I knew and what I didn't know, what I didn't know I knew, and what I knew I didn't know—were suddenly thrown into the pot, and in this case the pot was called The Choir.

Jeanette had her own set of problems, which both helped and compounded my own. Having failed to be a successful opera singer, and urgently needing a livelihood upon her divorce, she turned to teaching in a high school in Portland. As it happened, she was an extraordinarily gifted teacher. She was very slow to see this, but Mrs. Staveley was not. Although she knew her field, and even how to convey her love for music, she did not know how to get along with others. She held grudges, and she was an unrelenting, uncompromising taskmaster. Working with people on the farm, who were undisciplined, unsophisticated and, in many cases, wet behind the ears, would have turned what we were trying to do, and especially what Jeanette was trying to do, into a travesty of false hope, if it wasn't for one thing: the capacity of some of us—even all of us at times—to work on ourselves. At this Jeanette took the lead, as she needed to do in this situation.

She did her research, she prepared her material in advance, she knew exactly what she was working with, as well as what she was working for, and even how to extract excellence from faulty material. She also came early to every practice, and sat and collected herself; and it was from this collected place in herself that she taught. Her efforts were not wasted on us. In her ability to lead a choir, to squeeze the best performance possible out of largely inferior material, she must have been—or so it seemed to me—without peer in her profession.

Because of all this the experiment worked. And what was the experiment? It was that what we were doing could not be separated from how we were doing it, and from *why* we were doing it. Jeanette had been given the opportunity to pass on something she knew, something she had earned, that needed to go beyond the confines of her own sphere of knowledge, and we, in turn, needed to learn something new, to make that effort and contribution, because in addition to our work, the choir provided a very important element in the general mix. It was needed, and we knew it was needed.

But I did not stay in the choir to make a contribution—at least not a noticeable one—and I was not there because I liked to sing. I had continued with the choir because it helped me to see my pattern, and it had shown me a way to work with my problem.

Because of my uncontrollable need to imitate, it was seemingly impossible for me to hold a note on my own once the women's voices came in. This occurred even when I *thought* I was holding the male part. I saw in this my childhood experience at school, and I realized now that this pattern had never left me, that I was an ongoing product of my childhood conditioning. I was unable *not* to imitate. And I was slower than anyone to learn anything that was being taught. Beginning, in this case, with reading music. Also, to make matters worse, I had transfigured Jeanette into a composite of all my grade school teachers.

Now I knew what I had to do. I had to remain in this situation and suffer myself. As the weeks and months went by and nothing seemed to change, I was forced to relive my life, and to see my crippled condition. I had to believe this was healing, even though I had neither proof nor assurance that it would be.

The work, as I had long known, was not about one's strengths, but about one's weaknesses. For once, my weaknesses were so obvious and important to me that my strengths had become irrelevant.

Jeanette was far tougher on me than any of my grade school teachers had been, in part because the choir meant much more to her than the classroom had ever meant to any of my teachers. And she was not just a teacher but a professional musician. But there was also this: Jeanette wanted not only a forum for inner work, but an effective choir that could perhaps do things the first choir could not do.

I didn't tell her, or anyone else, why I was there. I had to work alone, and for myself. This was the message I had received in the movements class the time we had worked through the night.

In general, there was an attitude of forbearance on the farm, which gave each of us the space we needed to work on ourselves. But there were also flare-ups, arguments, shoutings, insults, putdowns and even an occasional fistfight but, in the main, each of us was given ample room to work out our problems. But there were times when Jeanette put me so tight up against myself that I was squeezed beyond my limit. To actually be hollered at and insulted were two things I had never tolerated, even as a child. I had always had a very definite sense of my own self-worth, a sense I had never permitted anyone to violate. Although her treatment of me wasn't any worse or different than anyone else, I felt at one point that she had stepped beyond her bounds, and I told Nonny that I would be leaving the choir.

Nonny had seen something in my departure that I had not seen myself, which was that I was giving up because it had simply become too hard, and not because I was angry with Jeanette. She believed that it would destroy my work, even the whole of my work, if I were to quit the choir now. In my state I could see nothing but my pain and my resolve to put an end to an unbearable situation.

Finally, a meeting with Mrs. Staveley was arranged that Nonny also attended. After hearing both of us out, Mrs. Staveley said, "Well, what interests me is what is going to happen next."

That sentence, by itself, was enough to make me see the entire situation in a new light, and I knew that the only *true* direction for me was to come back into the choir.

I had long known just how delicate a thread our work hangs on, but it would be a long time before I would know fully just how important my decision was. I would come to understand one day just how important self-responsibility is and how without it everything else that one might attain "in the work" was mere window dressing.

One of the things I was beginning to learn about myself was that my individual ability was very different from my collective, or team ability. Jeanette would frequently begin our sessions by having us sit in a circle, and give us a note or phrase to sing, that went around the class. No matter how hard it was for me to sing these notes and phrases, I never flinched and, in fact, I always gave it my full effort. I was always better at this than when I sang in choir with the others. So many others, who *could* sing, when put on the spot in this way, froze and made pathetic squeaking sounds.

Jeanette was both pleased and puzzled. "Why can't you do that when you sing with everyone else," she would constantly demand.

"I try!" I would exclaim. "It's not from not trying."

"Then what is it?"

"I get pulled off."

"And then you quit."

"No, I don't quit. I just get lost and confused, and I can't find my way back."

"And when you sing alone?"

"Then I have my experience. And that's something I won't allow myself to be cheated of. But I would sing better with the others if I could."

"Don't say you can't. You can, you can, you can."

## · CHAPTER TWENTY FIVE ·

Work Week was an important period of work for nearly everyone who was able to attend for the entire time. For some it meant progress on their special project, for others a chance to learn something in one of the classes, the opportunity to teach a class, give a theme, or to work at a task that had always been avoided, or that one simply had never had an opportunity to work at before. But its greatest importance for each of us was that it was a period of intensive work, and therefore a time of heightened experiences, when we could hope for new insights, new understandings, development and growth. The fact that none of this could be articulated, or needed to be articulated, added to the impending drama: we knew it was a special time and opportunity, with the ultimate result, as always, unpredictable.

The first Work Week for everyone was the most special of all. Because it was entered into without any preconceived notions, or any definite expectations, the actual magic of the week could work on one without the usual anticipated result. The magic we all experienced, especially during the first Work Week, was that of people working together toward a common aim, shoulder to shoulder, which often had the effect of reducing us to our essences, where real feelings waited to be released and experienced. No Work Week ever came to a finale without at least one person reporting at a Sunday discussion that they had fallen in love with everyone on the farm. At such moments everyone in the room was able to find at least some measure of this in their own hearts, and the energy that flowed through the room carried with it a common affinity and bond that we knew we had earned, but that was impersonal and did not come from us, that belonged to a source as ancient as the teaching.

That these experiences turned into fading memories as we reentered our ordinary lives was, for us, further proof that this higher truth was a reality we would have to work to make permanent in our lives.

Our living proof for this was Mrs. Staveley. She was always open and warm and giving, and seemed always to put our difficulties and problems, and even our work, ahead of her own. Of course our work *was* her work, and I hardly even wondered if she had any work apart from this. I couldn't imagine that she needed the work as we did, because she manifested a happiness, an inner peace, that seemed beyond my wildest dreams of personal attainment for myself.

From the very first Work Week, Mrs. Staveley asked me to give a writing class. Everyone who had a life skill was asked to do this, and in my case I accepted the assignment on a life level, and presented a class not so different from the way I would have presented it in life. I didn't believe that writing could be taught, and these classes proved my theory correct. I could see no point in the classes, and after the third year I decided not to have another writing class again.

But by the fifth year Mrs. Staveley persuaded me to try once more. This time it was different. It was different because I was different, and because the needs of those who signed up were different. I began to present material not from some idea or theory about writing, but from my own writing experiences. Virtually all of my writing had been autobiographical, and my poetry, in particular, had been a search for self-knowledge. I knew there were patterns in our lives and that these patterns could be explored and discovered through writing. I had tried everything, been down every cul-de-sac, and so, with rare exceptions, I could always find something in everyone's work and experience to relate to, both as a writer and as one who had learned of himself from his writing. I coupled this with a strong intuitive bent that I had never before intentionally exercised.

By the end of Work Week a fever had taken over the class. We saw together a new possibility for work: a new format and form that could accelerate our work. Gurdjieff had told Ouspensky that everyone in his group needed to write an autobiography. He also told them they would not be able to do this. Ouspensky's experiments confirmed my own discoveries, many of which I had made before the work. He saw that something bucked against his attempt to relate his early life, that he wanted to draw on interesting impressions of his childhood memories, and that when he got close to sensitive areas something inside him protested vehemently. These and other stages had to be passed through until we saw that the connections we were trying to make had to do with patterns that were already fixed in us, that controlled our lives, and that were invisible to ordinary sight. But this discipline, or practice, if rightly understood and correctly guided, could be a short-cut to repairing the past and preparing the future.

The class asked if we could continue on a weekly basis after Work Week was over. We were eight in number, including myself.

I had always believed—and hoped—that my poetry would act as a guidepost to those in search of their lives, but I had not seen that this is a search everyone must make for him or herself—and from scratch, on one's own, and that, if anything, what was needed was a guide, not a post; a poet, and not just poetry.

But I wasn't able to luxuriate in this belief for long because I had to wonder, as the weeks went by, if I hadn't gotten in over my head. Did I really know all that I seemed to know, and would it be possible for me to continue to see into people, to know what they needed, and to formulate writing tasks that would help them in their continued search through the labyrinth of their childhoods? I knew, and about this I had no doubt, that our search would have to begin there, and it would only be from there that we would be released into a larger world of growing possibilities and increased being.

One of the women, because of her experiences and her work on herself, became my favorite in the class. Prior to the writing class, we hadn't spoken more than two or three times, and of those occurrences the only one that stood out in my mind was her telling me of her nervous condition when she first met Mrs. Staveley, and that the work had already had the effect of changing her more than she thought it ever could.

The difficulties and problems she had endured as a result of her background surfaced early in the class. For one thing, she seemed to be suffering from amnesia, and I didn't see how we could get anywhere unless she was restored to her memory.

"I didn't have a childhood," she would insist. "I don't remember anything before the age of twelve."

I had to think how to take her back. "You went to school," I said, "somehow you got up, somehow you got dressed, somehow you ate your breakfast, and somehow you got to school. Right?"

"I suppose."

"Fill in just one day by making a composite picture from all of the days. I mean, don't try to remember *a* day, but just *any* day made up of all the days you went to school. The daily ritual that just one remembered detail will reveal, and that will set back into motion again all the lost days of your life."

Her excitement the following week was uncontainable. She almost couldn't wait to read her piece. But if the experience of writing it was beyond her understanding, the experience of reading it only furthered her astonishment at how much she had had, and known, and lost, but that she had suddenly—and very permanently—regained.

The form that I had slowly developed for the class was this: they were to write in the first person, present tense, an episode or experience, which could be nothing more than a smell, the remembrance of someone scratching with chalk on a board, the first taste of ice cream and so on. Or something remembered that could not be forgotten, and that, although not understood, was frozen permanently into a picture that was both unforgettable and unknowable. This then had to be described, as if one were trying as much to paint it as to write it; that is, by carefully describing every remembered detail, for as one thing was remembered it would attract to itself other memories, and these too would need describing. It was also important that they didn't evaluate, interpret or judge what they wrote, and also that they not reread what they had written, but simply put it away until it was time to bring it to the next class. The experience of reading the material aloud had often a more profound effect on them then the writing, for often they did not understand or have any feeling for the writing they had done. It was in the reading, nearly always, that the emotion—that was often the basis of the experience—was able to be released. What I began to see was that no one seemed to understand their own experiences. One could live a whole life and not know what that life meant.

In less than a year she had gone from amnesia to a full-blown childhood. She now had to understand what it means to come into possession of one's life.

Of the many things I learned from working with people in the writing class, the thing that was the most important, as well as being the thing I could not have discovered from my own writing, was this: we are so constructed that we *must* go off, we *must* get lost, we *must* lose our way, down one or another spiraling avenue of hurt feelings and spoiled dreams. For each of us, some particular thing, that manifests in an attitude, occurs early in our childhood and is deter-mined by predispositions that are almost futile to trace, since they are deeply lodged in our essence, conditioned by heredity and ar-ranged by life's accidental experiencings. What is true, what is inescapable and irrefutable, is that we *must* go off, and further, that we must also believe that *if this thing had not happened to me I would have been different.* This is the meaning of mechanicality. We are, Gurdjieff had said, food for the moon, and this is how we become such food. We go through our entire lives trying to correct, or extirpate, or balance this fault. It determines our Chief Feature, and it is the underlying cause of our chief inner attitude, by which Chief Feature is formed.

Only the work could help us to understand that this was so, and that it needed to be so. To see this, to accept it, to slowly separate from it, was to begin our own involution—the slow upward spiral toward real Being.

· CHAPTER TWENTY SIX ·

I had begun to think I would never discover my Chief Feature. From everything I had read, it seemed to be the crux of the teaching, the ultimate lever on which everything rose and fell. In the beginning, I had thought that if I found my Chief Feature my major problem would be solved, although how I had imagined my problems would be solved by this revelation I could no longer remember. Mrs. Staveley agreed with me that my Chief Feature was probably grounded in self love, but of course that was too general to have any meaning. One had to know what it was *exactly* because it was said to manifest always, in everything, and therefore determine each and every outcome of one's life.

From all the reading I had done I felt I knew all there was to know about it, even how to theoretically work on it. Then again, I wasn't sure if one worked on it or with it. Jane Heap had said that Chief Feature was like the magnet in a bowling ball, that always made it go off in a specific way, and that it was only by knowing how to throw the ball—that is, ourselves—could we make it go along *our* intended path.

Mrs. Staveley let me know that it could take years to find one's Chief Feature. She also let me know that there was no hurry. Apparently, Jane had told her what her Chief Feature was long before she was ready to understand it. As she explained it, "I didn't refuse it, but I had no idea what to do with it. I thought I would just take it and put it away, and maybe the time would come when I could understand what it meant to me. I would take it out and look at it then." This was heartening on two counts; one, it gave me something to go on as regards Chief Feature, and two, it was good to know that she had once struggled as I was struggling now. This was as close as she had ever come to sharing her work with me.

And then, on one of our special trips to Portland, where the three of us sometimes went for lunch, she told me what my Chief Feature was: *Complaining.*

"Complaining?" I muttered. "Complaining!" Isn't that amazing, I thought to myself, the one thing I have *never* done. I gave her a puzzled look, but made no comment.

Nonny smiled. "Of course, that's it!"

For a long time I could not see the truth of it. Nor did I wish to see the truth of it. I asked myself how something that was so clear to everyone else could be so opaque for me. And so hidden. Obviously, we couldn't know what we did, if we didn't know how or why we did what we did. It was said in the work that we were an open book to everyone but ourselves. If I couldn't see my own Chief Feature, then what could I see? I had to conclude that my life was perpetuating itself in the dark.

Finally, it dawned on me. What others called complaining, I was calling something else. But, ironically, I had no name for it. What I was probably doing, or thought I was doing, was *correcting the situation.*

I began to observe my complaining as complaining. And this growing ability to see myself as others saw me—which I had only had glimpses of before—began to open a new world for me. In the beginning I had felt so justified in my complaining that I seriously questioned if there was any other possible response. I could see now why I had been blind to my Chief Feature: my response was the only reality I could bring to what I considered an untenable situation. In my view, all of life was crazy, only my response was sane and intelligent.

Gurdjieff had urged us to reason. He said we were to begin from where we were, to use what reason we possessed, and that by doing this our reason would increase. This is what I now had to begin to do.

The first key in my reasoning: I couldn't see what my actual response was because it wasn't intentional or thought out. The second key: I couldn't alter it in any way. Summation: my response was in fact a reaction, a *mechanical* reaction. Although I was powerless to stop it, I *could* attempt *not* to express it.

An exercise that we were given around this time was a big help. Whenever we were disturbed by something, or someone, we were to hold our disturbance by remembering neither to express it, nor suppress it—but simply to contain it.

I learned from this exercise that my reaction to everything is partial, that even if I am correct in what I see, I am only correct about my view of it, which is always limited because I look at everything from myself, from my own self-centered point of view. By practicing this exercise I began to widen the picture and, aided by the disturbance and the friction I caused in myself by neither expressing nor repressing my disturbance, I kept it alive in myself as a question, which sooner or later revealed a truth which, if it was not the final truth, was a definite step in the direction of reality.

Eventually I began to see that my Chief Feature spoiled my life. My repetitive response or reaction to life's offerings began to sound in me like a single note played *ad infinitum* on an overused instrument, an instrument that had been constructed, ideally, for much finer music.

As my understanding of my affliction began to deepen, I was able to refine the definition of my Chief Feature, for I had come to understand better and better where it came from, and even how it had occurred.

Complaining was the manifestation, but what I was really doing inside was *assigning blame*. This is how I had responded to the criticism and prejudice that were imposed on me in school. Instead of accepting the discrimination I had suffered then, I turned the arrow against my tormentors: I was not at fault, they were. And it was just here that I took my twist. From then on, everything that seemed off was someone else's fault, not mine. I realized now why I never apologized, even when I was able to concede that *maybe* I was *partially* to blame, and also why I was always scowling.

I was slowly building a muscle for self-observation, and when we were given again the exercise of observing our inner attitudes, which had always been so difficult for me to see, I decided this time that instead of observing my behavior, I would attempt to ponder for long periods of time, asking again and again to be shown.

And then one day, again mysteriously, it was given to me to see—and in the most amazing way. It felt as if I was plucking up my inner attitude—my chief inner attitude, which felt as significant for my work as the knowledge of my Chief Feature—from out of a deep, dark hole in myself. This attitude, I saw now, was something very real, as real as some inner, secret entity that is cloaked in silence and is able to operate without word, utterance or articulation, but that in fact defines itself, but never in words, so as not to be detected. But there *were* words for this, an exact phrase that fitted perfectly the action, the very life of this inner attitude. And the words were: *I've been cheated, they owe me.*

Just that—but *exactly* that. Now I saw how my life was controlled. This, more than self-love and vanity, as Gurdjieff had said, marched ahead of me and arranged my life. When this button was touched, as it often was, I went into a mode—that the work called an "I,"—in which I could do things such as stealing, lying, falsifying, and in which I was totally justified. And I saw that I was able to commit these acts of violence—as I saw them now, on reflection—because I had felt myself wronged.

This one gift had the effect of changing my life to the extent that I could now see when I began to fall into this mode of self-pity which was always coupled with self-justification. Repeating the phrase, *I've been cheated, they owe me,* to myself had the effect of exorcising this demon which, although it had been tamed, still resided in the black chamber of my unbecoming, apparently conquered, but not yet subsumed.

All of my struggles with my poetry began to make sense to me now, as did the training I had committed myself to as a writer, for I had made it a practice to listen, to watch everything, to observe my inner reaction to things and, above all, to remember all that I could, especially anything that disturbed me, that seemed a little off or unusual or incomprehensible, for I had learned that it is from these hidden regions in myself that some new truth could be revealed in time.

Now I would be able to write what I was certain was the concluding volume of my trilogy of autobiographical poems. I called this volume, *Place of Birth*, taking as my subject, for the most part, all the faint and tenuous, strange but irreducible occurrences that had played over my sensibilities, and had left in their wake a pathway of markers, that I now needed to go back over and name.

I saw in all these hidden fragments of memory: each tiny jewel, each aspect, as my essence, that lay there, hidden and waiting to grow. A passing cloud, a sea shell held to the ear, lost pennies on the sidewalk, forgotten pantry smells, a mustache on a lined Armenian face, all of them revealing lost time, the ancestral past, the broken promise of earthly existence.

The more I learned about myself, the more useful I became to my writing class. The word had gone out, and before long I had a second class, and then a third. I was told that the people in my classes were sharing this material in their groups, as well as discussing its benefits with Mrs. Staveley.

I consciously and intentionally made the writing class an arm of the work, buttressing my own insights and knowledge and experience with Gurdjieff's teaching, because clearly my own life and work would have come to nothing if my struggle had not been informed by his ideas, which had the effect of transforming all the experience of my life into an intelligent order, with any inherent limitations being mine and never his.

Mrs. Staveley credited my life experiences and my practice as a writer, by saying that I was effective as a guide in my classes because I had become as a clean knife, sharpened by life.

## · CHAPTER TWENTY SEVEN ·

A live spark from the chimney of the newly constructed sauna nearly caused us to lose our barn. Although the smoke stack extended high above the roof, no one had thought to treat the wooden roof shingles, and after a rare, rainless month, the summer sun had baked the roof to tinder dryness.

Miraculously, by our own efforts as well as the help of the local fire department, we saved the first floor of the barn. The second floor was reduced to studs and a charred floor that was saved only because we had just laid a new oak floor, that was now burned through, but leaving the sub-floor untouched. The third story had simply disappeared.

We joined hands in its reconstruction, a messy, dirty job that went on for several months. In the meantime, the school had to be set up for sittings, while the outer bay of the barn, previously used for preservation, needed to be converted into a dining hall. We met the challenge with, if anything, more enthusiasm than was required. This experience taught me that outer work is always easier than inner work, and although, ideally, they should conjoin, with each taking its proper place, in practice the outer work too often becomes a let-off for the inner work. Our enthusiasm was fueled in great part by the emotional energy that was released by the heightened anxiety and tension that followed in the wake of the fire. I observed that at such times the teamwork that takes place can result in total sleep, however much it may appear from the outside that the opposite is occurring.

Some of the older people saw that the work they had put into the construction of the barn had not been taken away by the fire. The barn had nearly disappeared, but the inner work remained. It had taken the near loss of the barn for them to see this—a valid and valuable example of the meaning of inner work.

One day, coming out of a sitting in the school, I stopped in front of the children's lockers to put on my shoes. As I bent over, I noticed that one of the handwritten children's names, attached to the locker I was standing in front of, had been smeared. A voice inside me very quietly said, "If that were mine, I'd make them do it over." This was the still, small voice of essence. It had appeared, unobtrusively, because of my state of inner quiet. There was no considering. Nor was there any hesitancy or doubt. This was my sensibility, grounded in essence, that had spoken. I had known that my poetry came from my essence, just as I always knew when I had written a poem from my personality. But I was in a different state when I wrote poetry, just as I had been in a different state following this sitting.

As I walked across the orchard, I asked myself what I would have to do to make essence appear during my ordinary states. I reasoned that for this to happen, personality would have to become much more passive than it was now. The sittings were there to help us build our kesdjan (astral) bodies. Personality, made passive, could produce a similar result.

Once the barn was reconstructed it was seen that a new drainage system was needed. It was decided that the school also needed dry wells, as did the Main House. Since this project alone would take three days of continuous work, it was planned for the Labor Day weekend, one of our traditional work periods.

Each hole was to be dug to a depth and circumference of seven feet. I was part of a team that included Len Bolton and Fred Ginsberg. The dry well we would be digging was at the corner of the barn, just beyond the entry-way. By mid-morning Fred Ginsberg went off to find a wheel barrow and never returned.

Len Bolton was a man of the earth. He could make anything grow, and had learned how to make a living by extracting organic material from wooded areas, that no one else wanted, or even knew were there.

By day, he was able to transform dead or misused space into beautiful garden lots. On one occasion he flew to Scotland to study stone cathedrals and, after returning, he single-handedly erected his first stone edifice. It was intended as a tool shed, but turned out so magnificently that he decided it would be more effective as a miniature temple.

The first day of digging was hardest. I was out of shape and Bolton was hung-over. Mrs. Staveley had told me that I should try to last for two days. She must have thought that I couldn't make three days, and that therefore two days would be my maximum possible effort. I myself hadn't made a plan; I had simply wanted at the start to be in on the work because it was a farm project and I didn't want to exempt myself.

By the end of the first day I made a decision. Either one of two things were going to happen: I would be there at the finish, at the bottom of a 7' x 7' hole, looking up; or I would perish in this effort.

Aside from the fact that I was fifty years old, the exact age of Bolton's father, my greatest obstacle was my hands. I had always prided myself on the fact that my hands were as soft as a woman's. I had done as little physical work as possible all my life, and now this "triumph," as I had viewed it before the work, was being put to its ultimate challenge.

I went off by myself and had a talk with my hands. "You know, don't you," I pleaded, "that if I get a blister I won't be able to do this work. And you know how much it means to me to complete this task. Help me to do this now and I will see that you get what you want when it is over."

We had accomplished very little on our first day, but by the middle of the morning of the second day we had coordinated our effort, and we were now digging, pitching dirt, and hauling it away with an established rhythm. We also began to make a relationship, for although I had admired Bolton from a distance, I had never had any reason to spend much time with him. We discussed at length our very different relation to physical work and, every hour or two, he would stop, feel the palms of my hands, note that I still didn't have a blister and shake his head in disbelief.

It was extremely important to me that I keep up with him, shovel for shovel, and this I did, drawing strength, not from my body, it seemed, but from my wish.

The women in publishing stopped by, one by one, on their way to lunch or coffee break, and stared down in disbelief at the work we were accomplishing. "How can you go on like that, David?" Bea asked, with Alice beside her, shaking her head in disbelief. "You'd better come out of there, David!"

Nonny was visibly worried but refrained from speaking. I knew she was pulling for me. Bolton said, "You can't pay attention to them, women find working men attractive. They display their pride by showing worry."

I was well aware that Mrs. Staveley was avoiding us, and I knew that this was her way of giving support.

We finished exactly fifteen minutes before the official close of the work weekend. As we washed off our shovels, before sharpening and returning them to the tool shed, Bolton looked down at my soft, unblemished hands for the last time, and said, "I have just witnessed a miracle."

## · CHAPTER TWENTY EIGHT ·

Faye and Owen Hammond, our neighbors in the hop barn, had bought a house and would soon be moving away. No one was more shocked than we were. Although living on the farm was uncomfortable from a life point of view, it was considered a privilege because of the opportunities it afforded for inner work.

It felt as if something had been torn away from us. Although it was said that no one is indispensable in the work, and further that no one is missed once they are gone, it simply wasn't true in this instance, as it had not been true when Bobby Skoulis had left groups. Bobby had been in the work for years, and I did not take his leaving the farm as a sign that he had stopped his work.

Although they were only leaving the farm, and not the work, it was emotionally disturbing for us because something irreducible had taken place, although we didn't know what that might be. Perhaps we realized, if only dimly, that they would someday leave the work. Owen had been a key figure in the early years, but more important than that, he and Faye, like us, were "elderly" members within the group, and now, once again, it looked like our numbers were about to shrink. I sensed that their leaving the farm was a form of withdrawal, and that we would be seeing less and less of them in the days ahead.

The Murphys—Patrick and Wendy, and their two boys—were Mrs. Staveley's obvious choice to replace the Hammonds. Our relationship with them was bound to change, for better or worse we couldn't tell.

It was at this time that I had two inner experiences that were both startling and inexplicable. I had done something against my better judgment in one instance, and in another I had refused to make an extra effort in solving a difficulty having to do with Jane Heap's *Notes*, that was now in production. I had made a mistake in typesetting that was going to cause a flaw in the book. I couldn't go to Mrs. Staveley with the problem because I knew inside what I needed to do, but I didn't want to listen to my own inner voice.

In both instances, I had blamed Mrs. Staveley inside, and at one moment I had declared to Nonny that I was going to leave the work.

But within a day, once the smoke had cleared, I realized what had happened. Mrs. Staveley had been the representative of my conscience, and for as long as this was the case, I could go to her and get "straightened out" whenever things became too difficult for me. But something had clicked, something that had been building for years that I had not even been aware of. And that certain something was the development of my own conscience, which had now come alive in me.

I had *wanted* to blame Mrs. Staveley because I *couldn't* blame her. This was my way of getting out of this new responsibility that I had earned, but was unaware of. From now on it was up to me to be responsible for my own life. I *had* to say yes to my own conscience, and perhaps my reflexive no was simply the refusal of something new and unexpected. It was also the shock I needed to let me know that I was no longer between stools. I might have only one buttock on, and the other hanging precariously over the edge, but I had made a shift.

My work had reached a new intensity, in great part because of my involvement with my writing classes. When we were visited by an older member of Madame de Salzmann's French group, I was quick to cancel my appearance at the Portland Poetry Festival, so as not to miss a talk he would be giving.

It was soon after this that William Saroyan died, and I was asked to speak at his memorial service in Los Angeles. I had refused but, the following day, while talking to Mrs. Staveley, and after I had mentioned the invitation and my response, she said, "Oh no, you must go. This is also your work. You've demonstrated time and again that you can choose work over life, and so now you need to do this, not just to keep a balance, but because it is something you need to see through. He was an important part of your life once. This is your chance to look at that again and maybe bring something to a finish, or resolution. I say this not knowing what will happen. I mean, I can't know for you what all this means, but I do think it is important that you speak at his memorial service."

"I was thinking it was just another life affair."

She smiled. "Funerals are interesting; they're important. In the olden days, when the funeral procession moved through the villages and countryside, the workers would stop in the fields and remove their hats to honor the soul that had just passed."

"That's really touching," I said.

"Something was passing that would not pass that way again," Mrs. Staveley said.

When I got home I called the committee to say I would like to attend the service after all. The next morning I wrote my memorial speech. I had Mrs. Staveley to thank for the concluding paragraph:

In the olden days, before we were afraid of death, when funerals were enacted in the open, on the road of life, the citizens would stop when a funeral procession went by and tip their hats to the departed. One aspect of the human essence of all life had come to an end, and its like would not be seen again. Something that was, was no more, and needed to be honored and mourned for this reason.

Saroyan, here is my hat.

As Saroyan's son, Aram, had suspected, Saroyan may have thought of me as the son he wished he had had. I do not know if this was true, but I do know that for me he was the father I never had. When I had asked my own father, after high school, if he had any ideas about what I might do, he had said, "Work in factory, like me."

I don't remember if I was surprised by this or not, but I can imagine that I was at least a little disappointed. I thought to myself, All right, if that is your understanding, we won't speak about such matters again.

I also needed a father who could challenge me, whom I would have to overthrow. That Saroyan was far too much for me—given that I had the father I had—was probably just as it should have been. He made me stretch, and he made me grow. And then one day I stood on my own two feet and walked away from the influence he represented. I still loved him deeply, and thought of him often, but I'm not sure there was any need for us to meet and talk again. In any case, we hadn't, but this did not mean that our business with each other was finished. This is what the memorial service had shown me. By going there and participating—in addition to paying my respects—I went through the entire relationship one last time, consciously, and I suffered. This I needed to do, for all that had passed, and had not passed, between us. I also needed to honor his influence and his support when it had meant so much to me. And I needed to have all this transpire inside of me one last time because, as it did, I saw that we are none of us a thing apart, but connected to something so vast it is outside of our comprehension, and therefore requires ceremonies, suffering and loss, before our eyes can be even partially opened.

· CHAPTER TWENTY NINE ·

Another year had come and gone, our seventh on the farm, and we were back in New York for what would be our final trip; though I never would have guessed this at the time.

Armonk had become so crowded that some of us were assigned to work at the Foundation on Sunday. The small maintenance crew and the people in the kitchen were given work to do that was more or less real, but for the rest of us it was make-up work, as usual. It was an opportunity to work on non-identification, if nothing else, because, as the reasoning went, it doesn't matter what you do but "how you are in front of it."

It was easy to be non-identified when repairing useless junk that would never be used again, as I once did at Armonk, or making a Shaker cradle for a tentative craft sale that never came about, or grill work on the forge for some other craft sale. It was no wonder, I thought, that the people there looked emotionally dead. Between meaningless work and a pose that was meant to telegraph to others that one was remembering oneself, it seemed to me to be a dead-end voyage to nowhere.

On my fateful, final Sunday, Lord Pentland presented me with the task of writing a review of all the published reviews of the film, *Meetings with Remarkable Men*. Needless to say, he had them all on file. He brought them out and spread them across the table in front of me. I couldn't be sure if he was serious about wanting such a review, or whether he felt it would serve some purpose or function, or if this was some kind of subtle—or not so subtle—put-down of me.

I took it as an opportunity for work. For this to be possible I had, despite my inner reaction, to treat it perfectly seriously. I would say yes, intentionally, and thereby become active about my work. This was my freedom. The assignment had not just been given, I had *chosen* it!

I saw from this experience that the idea of "obedience" was both misunderstood and misused in the work, perhaps not only in the Foundation, where it was obviously so, but everywhere else as well. Obedience was a very high thing, and *did* belong to the realm we were, or thought we were, participating in, for it was only through obedience—by submitting one's self-will to a higher will—that our own Real Will could be attained. Perhaps I should say developed, for it would take years, and the process, by necessity, would have to go on in the dark for the pupil, because otherwise one would either resist, or mindlessly submit or, worse yet, involve the devil in the process, which would be enough to sabotage the entire operation.

It was obvious to me now that this transformative process could not be accomplished alone, but only with a teacher, with or without his assistance, and in a school in which one's self-esteem was constantly being chipped away. It was just as clear that the teacher was, if anything, in greater danger then the pupil, for if he or she were to forget that this obedience was being made to something higher—to the student's higher part, that is—and not to the teacher's authority, then it would be the instructor, not the instructed, who would soon find themselves in the devil's camp.

As I reflected on my experience and the understanding it had brought me, I remembered the day the subject of will first came up during a group meeting in my first year at the farm. Apropos of something someone else had said, I said to Mrs. Staveley that I was strong-willed. She had hesitated for a moment, and then smiled. "I would call it willfulness, wouldn't you?"

Our yearly trips to New York were a great joy and opportunity for us because of the concentrated time spent with Mrs. Staveley. It felt at these times as if we were being given a private teaching. We were able to talk to her at length about our work, and we were given special exercises that were far harder and more demanding than anything we were given on the farm.

Although it was good to return to the farm after our final trip to New York, I began to feel, as Nonny did, that something had changed, whether in us or in the place, we couldn't tell. It was apparent that Mrs. Staveley was also going through something, because she sometimes seemed a little distant and preoccupied. One Sunday, toward the close of the work day, she walked into publishing and sat down at one of the tables, something she had never done before. Only Nonny and I were still in the room, cleaning up before the reading that would conclude the day. Mrs. Staveley said, "There is something in the air. Everyone is feeling it. How does it seem to you?"

I thought a moment before speaking. "It feels like the calm before the storm." It was a gut feeling, and I didn't try to fathom its meaning. Mrs. Staveley, by her silence, seemed to assent.

Just before we had returned home from New York, Mrs. Staveley had said something to the effect that she wished Jane were there because she needed to talk to her. It was obvious that she was pleased about something, but also troubled. From the little she said, and from what we were able to put together, it appeared that she had been offered something—some work, or task, or assignment—perhaps even a "position"—and there was something in the inherent temptation that disturbed her. She needed, apparently, to have her teacher's approval and advice. But Jane was long dead, and she had no one else she could confide in.

She now began speaking of her need to travel. A shift was needed, she said, and we could take care of ourselves, because there were people in other places that needed someone to guide them.

Before we could even consider what this might mean to us personally, she announced at the end of a work day that "the experiment on the farm is possibly over." We were sitting in the arbor, following the reading that concluded the work evening. She rose from her chair and walked slowly to the Main House.

In the following days a new energy began stirring on the farm.

Nearly everyone had gone into a frenzy of worry and self-doubt, as well as deep, serious questioning. Was it really over, or was there something being demanded of us that we just couldn't see?

For the first time in the seven years that we had been there, the farm had been put into question.

We had, each of us, to ask what her statement meant to us. Nonny and I asked ourselves if it was over and, if so, where would we go, and whether alone, or with others, to start another group, or carry our work into life. It seemed so confusing, and yet, although there was no immediate or obvious answer, we soon saw that we had been challenged, that we *needed* to be challenged. We had not come to the farm in order to stay permanently, we had come out of a need and for a reason, not to find a way of life. But, like everyone else, we had become comfortable and had grown used to the place. With a part of ourselves—that we knew was our better part—we felt that perhaps the time had come for all us to go out and test ourselves, as Prince Lubovetsky had said in the movie.

But almost as quickly as the offer or challenge had been made, it was forgotten. The questions it had raised in Nonny and me were very real questions, important to our work, but we were apparently alone in our concerns, for after a few days the subject had been dropped and was never picked up again.

Mrs. Staveley began to plan her trip East for the following winter. She would spend more time away and stop at cities where groups needed a strong leader. Wendy and Patrick would spend the New York part of the journey with her, then we would meet her and travel with her from there.

We received a call from Patrick the day before they were to leave New York, to inform us that Mrs. Staveley was very ill and that we should cancel our tickets and meet their plane with a wheelchair. He said he would explain everything when they arrived.

We watched as Patrick and Wendy walked with her through the long tunnel leading to the waiting area. They were holding her sagging body up as best they could, their faces showing signs of strain and deep anxiety. We rushed forward with the wheelchair. Nonny wrapped a shawl around her upper body, which was jackknifed forward and being supported now by Nonny and Wendy, who were holding onto her shoulders. I could not see into her eyes, hooded by her wrinkled brows, or make out the words she was muttering to herself.

She improved slightly once we got her into the car and began driving back to the farm. She began to say something about the negative vibrations she felt when the plane flew over Colorado. "I didn't think I would survive that," she muttered. Patrick's expression was trying to tell me that she had nearly died.

He explained now that Mrs. Staveley had been invited, with Group I, to see the film, *The Dark Circle*, which was a devastating film about the misuse of atomic energy and the fear of an impending holocaust. Patrick whispered that she had been visibly distressed not only by the film but by the reactions of the Foundation people to the film. Patrick leaned back and looked out the window.

As I drove, Nonny turned and looked at Mrs. Staveley, wanting— I knew—to find some way to comfort her and help her in her illness. I could see Nonny out of the corner of my eye, and those in the back seat through the rear view mirror. The noise of the windshield wipers was pounding in my ear. We were all in our own thoughts. I wondered if she would recover. She had been sick so many times before. In fact, each crisis on the farm seemed to send her to her bed for a week or two, but even from her bed she was able to guide and direct our work. Could she do that now, if she recovered, or would we have to get along without her?

I pulled into the driveway. "We're here," Nonny said. "I've made some fresh soup and bread, and your bed is ready, Mrs. Staveley." There was no answer as I made the long, slow drive up to the Main House. For once, the presence of the farm had no effect on her. I watched her in my rear view mirror. She looked neither right nor left. Nonny slowly turned forward in her seat to be ready when the car came to a stop.

Her health remained in a precarious state for several months.

During this time she remained cloistered in her room, where she saw only Nonny and Wendy, who were caring for her, and Patrick, to whom she gave instructions. She did not want to see me, she told Nonny, until she was well.

The extent of her illness was known only to the four of us. At one point we converged to discuss what we would need to do in case she didn't recover, and to talk about future plans for the farm should she die.

I still hadn't visited her when Patrick reported one day that she had passed her crisis. She had been invalided for two months. She had told him that her spirit was now ahead of her body. This was apparently to be seen as something positive, as if the better part of her had now to endure somehow the lesser part of her. Patrick said that she was going to be all right, but that she would no longer be seeing people as before. He let Nonny and me know that we needed to cut down on our visits to her.

Everything was going to change. Her occasional forays into the "great world," as she had once teasingly called it, would now stop altogether. Her spirit could no longer process the "raw material" it had once required, albeit in very tiny doses.

The farm began to stabilize, more or less, but she seemed more and more remote. She had left the guidance of the youngest people to her older pupils. She had always promised that I would participate in this work, but used the excuse of my writing classes, saying that I was better needed there.

That fall, for the first time, we didn't have enough new people to start a beginning group. "Maybe the tide has gone out," she said one day, as we sat in the library having drinks. Always in the past we had sat in the kitchen, which was the most private room in the house but, since her illness, she had taken to sitting in the library. I felt that she needed to be nearer the activities and energy of the farm, which she was able to view from the library windows. She seemed to have less interest in us and often looked surprised to see us, and would make statements about how busy we must be with our own work.

"She's always hoping Patrick will come along," Nonny said one day, as we walked back through the orchard to the hop barn. "Have you noticed that? Whenever she sees him she waves him in. I don't think she's comfortable with us anymore."

"Uh-huh," I agreed. But my mind was going over her comment about the tides, and I couldn't help but think of the backwater, the still tidal pools, where the water was trapped after the waves had gone back out to sea. And what of the water *there*, I thought, how long can it support the life that is trapped in those pools?

· CHAPTER THIRTY ·

One of the first things Mrs. Staveley did, after her convalescence ended, was to begin talking in private about our need to pay off the mortgage, so we would never have to worry about losing our place of work. Several of us were finally called to a meeting to discuss the problem. All of those at the meeting were considered eligible to contribute. We gave what we felt we could afford, as did some of the others, but we never heard if we had come close to paying the mortgage or not. The subject was closed and, apparently, forgotten.

We were now beginning our eighth year on the farm. Her statement that the experiment was possibly over had been working in both Nonny and me and, although I never thought of it again as the farm experiment ending, I was beginning to believe that perhaps the two of us had gone as far as we could under these conditions and circumstances. She had said, over and over again, that a group is only good if it serves your needs, and a group—one's own group—*was* the work. The group, of course, included the guide or teacher. The meetings had definitely begun to run down for us, and I was beginning to question whether there was anything more I could learn from Mrs. Staveley. We had absorbed all we could from what she had to teach, just as we had exhausted all the possibilities inherent in this particular setting. I could no longer learn anything new of substance from repeating the tasks I had been engaged in for all these years.

One could not be a student forever. At some point the ideas took hold, were incorporated, and became a part of one's living reality, but only if they were practiced, tested and forgotten—as ideas—and simply lived. Life had to replace the Group Leader as the teacher. Until that moment came one deferred a great part of one's initiative and self-responsibility but, having arrived at the threshold of that possibility, I realized that I would have to leap into the abyss or become a perpetual student.

Increasingly now, the talk began to center on the form of the work, and how we had to be grateful for the form, because without it there could be no work. A great part of the form was the farm itself, and the weekly sittings, group meetings, the movements, at which we had not only improved, but had provided instructors and able musicians from within our own ranks, all of which resulted in more and more movements classes. And of course the themes, that were shared by more of us, and possibly even the ceremonies: one for each solstice, Gurdjieff's birthday and even Easter Sunday. Our time was well filled.

All of these made up the form, and we were reminded again and again of the importance of the form, and of the impossibility of work without the form. What was never said was that the form cannot guarantee work, that it too could turn against itself.

That winter I put on the Gurdjieff birthday celebration. The coordination of the birthday dinner always came under the guidance or leadership of a single person, someone who either volunteered, under Mrs. Staveley's urging, or who had pushed themselves forward in advance.

The dinner that had always stood out in my mind was the one Ken Blazer had put on, the first year I was there. I had signed up to be a waiter, and also to work on clean-up afterwards. Ken worked to capture the atmosphere of the Middle East and Central Asia. The room was decorated with Oriental rugs on the floors and walls, with low tables and cushions, with the menu consisting entirely of Middle Eastern dishes. The overall effect was stunning and, although I had worked on it off and on during the week, it still delivered a powerful impact upon completion.

But the biggest, the most important experience of the evening, was yet to come. I had never served as a waiter before, nor had any of the other men with the exception of Stewart Rees, who was a waiter in life, and was therefore able to guide and instruct us. Stewart gave us a simple task: try to see what is needed without being asked, he had said, and put the needs of the people you are serving ahead of your own.

The effect was transformative, for both the servers and the served. I was aware that everyone was sensitive to the way we were working and, instead of being made self-conscious by this, I felt that we were engaged in a dance, in which everyone in the room was participating.

Giving and receiving could not be separated, only the roles could, and if life was a stage, then it was possible that one could choose not merely to strut through one's brief performance, but to play one's part consciously, as a participant, who was in turn aware of the other participants in the drama.

And now, several years later, I was ready to head a Gurdjieff dinner. I had no idea what was involved, nor did I know that I would have to develop quickly the ability to delegate work, coordinate a great body of people and keep their work moving in the direction of my vision. What I hadn't counted on was my ability to visualize forms and to manipulate the ingredients that belong to any given form into a coherent, artistic whole. I chose for our theme The Sarmoung Brotherhood, where Gurdjieff had gone for his initiation. I wanted everything to be quiet and austere and beautiful in its simplicity.

Nonny became my troubleshooter, ranging among the decorators and cooks, as well as in publishing, where we would be printing our traditional memento, as well as menus for the tables and wine labels for Jeff Scooter's farm-produced wines that had been enjoying a slow progress toward table-wine status.

We decided on an all-white dining room, with white walls and tablecloths, white sheets draped from the ceiling, the room lit entirely by tallow candles on wall mounts, with each individual carrying his own candle to the table. The choir would sing by candlelight, and we would walk in procession from the Main house, across the swinging bridge that Len Bolton had built after extending the pond he had created earlier, that bordered the northern side of the Main house.

Immediately following the toast to Gurdjieff, the choir would slip out and go to the barn. Our candles would be arranged on a table, that we would pick up as we filed out in twos, led by Mrs. Staveley and myself. The choir would be singing Gurdjieff's, "The Fall of the Priestess," that would not be audible until we reached the bridge.

In the anteroom that had been used for storage, Nonny fashioned a gallery. She had long been studying Gurdjieff's *Meetings with Remarkable Men* with the idea that Gurdjieff's journey could be traced on the Enneagram. Based on her theory, she had begun a painting that would be completed by the time of the dinner. Meanwhile, Julius McMahon had begun a series of drawings based on the Enneagram. Mathematical and design possibilities had long been his hobby, and they were now reaching fruition in his perceptions of the various visual possibilities in the Enneagram.

In keeping with our theme, Nonny and Pete Goska decided to create a replica of the movements apparatus Gurdjieff had spoken of seeing at The Sarmoung Brotherhood, and in the process of their work they discovered that the "Vesanelnian trees" were forms in proportions of the various sizes of man. The student of movements then could take the movements position by following the bends in the apparatus exactly. They first made a replica on paper, and then from wood.

I wanted to create a dinner without a single highlight, but with everything flowing into a unified fabric that would hold the evening in its protective care.

My work on the dinner, the long process of team work that brought it to fruition, and the atmosphere we had created, had the effect of placing me before my life and instilling in me a sense of completion. One octave of my work had been completed on the slow, mysterious, unending journey of life.

The purpose of a monastery is to teach its adherents, and not to bind them to the form. We had been given this incomparable teaching because one man alone had come out of that monastery at Sarmoung and, in coming to the West, had provided us with a western formula based on an ancient teaching that now needed to be transmitted to a new and changing world.

I knew now that my leaving the farm was inevitable. I began hinting to Mrs. Staveley that I would be leaving before long, but I wasn't sure if she was able to hear me. She seemed to agree that I would be leaving one day, but she didn't feel that I needed to be in a hurry. It was clear that she did not understand what I was going through, that it was a painful and necessary step, and that I was ready. Although she agreed in theory that it was necessary—at least for some people—to leave their school, it wasn't something she seemed able to think about. Jane had told her to leave when it was time for her to go. That was her experience. Gurdjieff had said that even if we have the being of an angel, we cannot understand another's experience if we have not had that experience ourself.

Although we didn't feel anxious about leaving, both Nonny and I, separately and together, did feel a sense of frustrated purpose, as if there was something we needed to do but didn't know yet how to do. At least I had my writing classes, to which I felt a deep attachment. But Nonny, in addition to not having a major responsibility that kept her occupied, was also somewhat homeless on the nights of my classes—she had a choice of sitting in our small, unheated bedroom and reading, or going down to P & P, lighting a fire, and working by herself on binding.

Earlier, when I had felt that there was a loss of energy in some of my writing classes and went to Mrs. Staveley for advice, she always said the same thing, "Kill it!" At first I took her at her word, until I realized that she had never done this herself with her own groups.

And then one day she let slip her true feelings. Apropos of sharing leadership, and in reference to my writing classes, she said, "It's not easy for me, you know." All I could do was contrast this statement, which on reflection was not as shocking as I took it to be at the time, with her earlier attitude, as well as her support then, when the writing classes had first begun. I knew at that time that no other teacher in the work that I knew of, with the possible exception of Bennett, would have allowed someone under them to create a new form for the work, nor to run this project on their own, without interference or input from above, as had been the case with my writing classes, thanks to Mrs. Staveley. I had been deeply grateful to her for this, and I was still. Her jealousy now I only took to be human. In any case, teaching was her life, it wasn't mine. She had never come to any of my classes, nor would I have allowed her to, and I rarely shared my experiences with her. I knew from her own inability to respond to my childhood material that this was not her area of interest or expertise. Everyone must pass on the work from their life experiences, and from whatever it is they have perfected in life. Mrs. Staveley was a pre-school teacher, and she ran her work as a school teacher would, hence her references to us in beginning groups as "toddlers," and "infants" and so on. Once we moved past dependence on her she felt either threatened by our growing independence, or she grew disinterested. She had also apparently been a good cook, and food was also very important on the farm. It all made sense.

Our trips to Portland with Mrs. Staveley were now confined to trips to the doctors and the bank. We no longer went out to lunch in one or another of our favorite restaurants, as we had done in the past. We couldn't help but contrast these obligatory journeys with the joyful trips we used to take. But ordinary life no longer interested her if, in fact, it didn't offend her. I think she felt that she had moved beyond it or, perhaps it would be more accurate to say, she had finally created what she had wanted for herself on the farm.

Some of the visitors who came and could feel the energy there thought we had created a very special environment, but there were those who said that although it looked like a good life, they questioned whether it was the work. But they hadn't seen the farm in the beginning years, when we were alone, unvisited and unknown, with the work concentrated: pure and uncompromising, and with Mrs. Staveley our constant, living example.

We had no problem as a school. Our problems began when—for reasons I didn't understand—no one graduated to the next step.

On one of the last trips we took together to Portland Mrs. Staveley removed the rest of her money from the bank, in order, she said, to put it down on the farm mortgage. Although we had given half of what little money we had left during the "mortgage crisis," we had, on my mother's death, come into a tiny inheritance. Just enough, I told Nonny, for our eventual departure. Since Mrs. Staveley was putting the last of her money into the farm, Nonny felt honor-bound to put another chunk of our money down also. But I refused to give in. Mrs. Staveley, of course, had said nothing to us about our contribution—and all past contributions had been kept secret—but she had made her intentions clear by having us drive her to the bank. In fact, we never did learn who had paid into the mortgage and who had not, nor what the remaining mortgage was. Everything that was given, was given "no strings attached," because, as she often said, "In the work there can be no deals." About this she was certainly right.

· CHAPTER THIRTY ONE ·

Once again life was about to bring us what we needed for our work. What happened next would be seen by both Nonny and me as one of the most important gifts we had ever received in the work, and it would prove to be a turning point in our lives.

We had been invited to speak about our life work at a state library convention in Pendleton, Oregon. An interesting format was set up for our talk: Nonny and I were placed together on one platform and, from another adjacent platform, someone asked us questions, to which we answered, speaking directly to the audience. This allowed us to play off one another, and it was the kind of relaxed, personal and informal atmosphere that we always attempted to create when we appeared before large audiences. At one moment, Nonny said something about working from her essence rather than her personality.

Immediately following the talk we were taken to a table where we were to sign our books, that were being purchased at the end of the hall, before being brought to us for signing. The usual procedure consisted of being handed one of our books, that we then opened to the page we chose to inscribe, and then, looking up, we would ask the purchaser their name.

"Your name?" I asked the young woman now, who was leaning forward, slightly apprehensive, but smiling.

Before I had finished signing her book, she asked, in a very quiet voice, if I knew the work of Maurice Nicoll.

I was startled. "Of course!" I replied.

"We read his *Commentaries* on the Gurdjieff work." She hesitated. "When I heard Nonny's comment about essence and personality, I wondered..."

"Do you have a group?"

"Yes, we're on our second time through the *Commentaries*."

"Where is this?"

"In Bend, Oregon."

I was trying to write and talk at the same time, to accommodate the anxious crowd, that was now beginning to push forward. "Do you have Sunday work?" I asked her.

"Ah—no."

I told her where our group was located. "You're welcome anytime."

"I'll tell my teacher, she'll write to you, if that's all right," she said, and all at once her excitement broke out into laughter.

Nonny had heard most of the conversation, and tried now to speak, but it was difficult for her to make herself heard. I asked for the young woman's card, quickly wrote our address on a scrap of paper—and then she was gone.

We didn't see her again, but our brief encounter fueled the rest of our stay in Pendleton. As the weeks rolled by we wondered who these people were, and where they had come from, the nature of their work, and how it had been that we had never heard of them before—nor they of us.

And then, two months later, we received a letter from their teacher, Cari Kimler, apologizing for her long delay in responding. It turned out that the original teacher of this group was Nan Mc-Curdy, a psychologist, who had never been in the "official" work but, having read Maurice Nicoll, had established a work of her own, that had been going on for over ten years. She had died some time ago, turning the reins over to Cari Kimler, one of her prominent students.

After talking to Mrs. Staveley, I wrote to Cari Kimler, inviting her, and a handful of her people, to our Sunday work.

Being an offshoot group, Mrs. Staveley tended to look at them a bit askance. They were given short shrift on the farm, although they did fit into her program of nurturing beginners—as she thought of them. I began to see, as a result of her attitude towards these people, who were interesting, bright, sophisticated city dwellers—that Mrs. Staveley's purist approach to the work was really a form of parochialism.

Perhaps I was identified with the Bend people because we had found them, and although I agreed that they had things a bit askew, I could see that they had qualities that we were missing, such as the ability to externally consider with one another, as well as an interest *and* an ability to take their work into life. Also, they were fresh and wholesome—and attractive, and they were never abrasive, and a non-abrasive Gurdjieffian was something I thought I would never see. In short, they seemed reasonably well-adjusted and happy. But it was more than that: they were a breath of fresh air, at a time when our lungs felt polluted from stale impressions.

Mrs. Staveley allowed eight of them at a time to come for the weekends, that would include Saturday movements. We put them up in the newly finished apartment that adjoined the Main House, which had been converted from the original garage.

Mrs. Staveley had spoken to me about sending Bea Greer to Bend, which disappointed me in a way I was scarcely able to disguise. She had always told me that I would be going out to teach, and here was my opportunity. Bea had more than enough responsibility as it was. But the next Sunday, Cari—who worked with us in publishing—asked if I would come to Bend and give one of my writing classes. She had heard about the writing classes, not from me, but from several other people on the farm. I agreed at once, and wrote out an assignment for her to read to all those who would be attending.

I told Mrs. Staveley about the invitation and my acceptance. She gave her approval, and changed the subject. The following Saturday, Nonny and I drove to Bend.

Cari divided her twenty-five people into two groups. I asked Nonny and Cari to sit in on both groups and to speak whenever they felt they had something to say.

By the end of the second class I knew that I had come into my own as a teacher. The differences between the classes in Bend and those at the farm was simple and dramatic: not knowing me, the Bend people held nothing back. And not having an assigned place in their lives, I could be exactly who I was, and *all* that I was. Here I was not "supporting" someone else's work—as Mrs. Staveley liked to say about my classes—but I was doing my own work.

I was now ready to emerge with a real function, thanks to the long years of study and work I had received at the farm. One must know for oneself when one is ready. Equal to this insight was the realization of just how far I had come in making these classes a force for inner work for those who chose to work with me in this way.

I returned to the farm a changed person. I was no longer a dependent, a cog in the machinery of someone else's design. Nor could I have fit myself back into that machinery, even if I had wanted to. But the change was more profound than that, for it involved not just my perception of myself, but my perception of the Gurdjieff work, as well as all other spiritual disciplines.

In my excitement, on the evening following our return, while having drinks with Patrick and Wendy, I said, in mentioning the Bend people, that when we got to the pearly gates, Peter would not check our passes to see if we were Gurdjieffians, that in fact God was not interested in any of that, but only if we had become what we were meant to be, and *all* that we were able to be.

Although I could feel Nonny agreeing at my side, neither Patrick nor Wendy responded. Was this heresy, as the looks they were giving me seemed to indicate? I should have known to stop talking when no one answered, but I rambled on. "It seems to me that all too often, instead of taking the work into our life as a help, we merely exchange our outward life for the garment of the work, and then we say that we have an inner life, when in fact it is only our outward life that has been exchanged—that we now *call* our inner life."

Wendy got up and went to the sink and began doing her dishes. Patrick said, "Without the form, nothing is possible. You know that. What people do with it is not the work's responsibility."

"But the farm isn't the work, it is only the condition within which work can occur."

"And without which work *cannot* occur."

"But forms change, and the work can be practiced anywhere. It's true that in the beginning most people need extraordinary conditions in order to work, and we can't work without guidance for a long, long time, *and* special conditions. But eventually, one has to test one's work in life."

Wendy turned from her soapy water. "I'm not there—are you?"

"All I can say is that I was the equal of that situation. *That's* what I learned there."

"It was different from the classes here," Nonny said. "I wish you could have sat in on them, Wendy, as I did."

"But that's not life," Patrick jumped in, "that's the work again. You're taking responsibilities, what more can you ask for? We need to provide for those who are coming along. Like a chain..."

"Jacob's Ladder," Wendy interjected.

So. The form had become the farm. And the farm had become the work. As I sat there staring at our friends, I was reminded of Jane Heap's statement that with some work people she knew she could communicate up to a point, until suddenly there was this great gulf between them that no words could bridge.

## · CHAPTER THIRTY TWO ·

The person I had wanted most to talk to about my experience was Mrs. Staveley. The summer before, she had said that Nonny and I were being passed over for certain duties and responsibilities. "You two," she had said, "and Jeanette Skoulis I won't be putting in front of groups. You three have other responsibilities." I stared at her, without answering. After a short pause, she continued. "You'll be going out someday. I have to train the ones that will be staying."

My first reaction was one of hurt. She had told me, from my first year, that I would one day be in her chair, that is, in the same role that she was in. I didn't believe it then, or since, but of the many changes that had occurred in me over the years, one thing alone was certain: I was no longer a pupil. Her statement came as a mild shock, but it should not have been a surprise. It was my fate to be a loner, to do my own thing in my own way and by myself. To be without a place in the established order or structure of the work was no different than being unplaced in the world of poetry. But I had put time in here, had even come to accept and finally to love these people, and now I would have to walk away from all this.

But hardly a day had gone by when—once it all sank in—I realized that the inevitable next step had presented itself. We had, whether we knew it or not, prepared ourselves for such an eventuality when she had first proclaimed that the farm experience might be over. In the days and then months that had followed, the life at the farm slowly began to shift and change. Once she realized she would not be going out to other groups, as she had expected, and had returned to the farm in a sick condition, she began, upon her recovery, to solidify her holdings on the farm. She began to delegate authority, with Patrick the acting administrator, issuing orders and policy, and—for the first time—there began to be rules and codes of conduct, that extended not only to the adults, but to the children as well.

There were mumblings, and some dissent but, in the end, everything settled down. It was from this time that the farm began to be referred to by others as Mrs. Staveley's Farm.

I was also aware that she no longer corresponded with Madame de Salzmann, and that there had been a rupture with the Foundation. Don Hoyt was no longer giving us movements.

Two things had occurred during this time that made all the other happenings insignificant for me. I had outgrown my need for a teacher, and our social visits with Mrs. Staveley had become awkward. I certainly thought I was still her friend, but it became obvious, though I was slow to realize it, that our friendship could not exist outside the confines of the teacher-student roles that had been in place since we met.

The week following her surprise announcement, Nonny and I began to think about relocating our lives. Seattle seemed close enough for an easy move, and far enough away that we would be independent. We both liked Seattle.

When we told Mrs. Staveley of our tentative plans, she shouted, "What! Are you planning to run off again? This isn't the time for that." Three years before we had grown homesick for New Concord, and had hinted at leaving. She convinced us then that it was not the right time—that we were not yet ready—and perhaps it was true, then. But it was not true now. We were not homesick for a particular place any longer. What we needed now was not a place, but rather to be on our own, to be tested and to find a way to practice our understanding in life, without the buffers of the work.

"When will it be the time, then?"

"When there's a sign." I watched her as she fished inside her head for a better explanation. For the first time I realized that she had never had any intention of letting us go. But why, I thought; she's holding us down, she's holding us back, what is the meaning of our being here beyond this point?

Now, a year later, with the Bend experience behind me, I had the confirmation I needed. When we went to see her immediately upon our return, I said, "I know now that I am ready to leave. I'm ready to go out on my own. I can work with people, I have something to pass on, and I know how to present my understanding in a way that is beneficial to others. I want to give back to the work, and what I am doing here isn't enough."

"You need more experience. Don't be impatient." Her face seemed composed, but she was opening and closing the top button of her sweater, a mannerism that had always annoyed me. I knew not to argue. She was always right, she always knew best, she always won. No one had ever stood up to her before, and there was no point in my trying now. I needed to have her agree with me, because I didn't want to oppose her.

I felt—mistakenly, as it turned out—that I would need the assistance of others, as well as papers and open communication with those in the work, including the people on the farm, if Nonny and I were to start groups on our own. I somehow knew that she would blockade this in any way she could—and about this I was not mistaken.

In the past it had always been assumed that those who left groups had left the work. There had even been themes delivered on the subject by Mrs. Staveley, in which those people who had left the farm, but not the area, were characterized as parasites and not people to associate with.

In addition to everything else, I cared for her and I wanted her blessings. I also wanted to say my own good-byes to the people on the farm, with whom I felt a kinship that was in some ways closer than blood.

"I don't want to tell her next time," Nonny said, when we were alone.

"But I don't want to be cut off. What would happen to us if we left without her blessings? All I want is her blessings. I don't want to cut myself off from the work."

"I don't want to go this way, either, but there's nothing left for us here anymore, and we can't make her listen to us. You at least have the writing classes, but I have *nothing* anymore."

I knew what Nonny was going through. Three nights a week she had to go down to the first floor, build a fire, and do edition binding by herself. She was an artist who brought something to perfection, and then left it—to publishers, to make a book with, to others to make a craft of. She had taught herself binding, silk screening, marbling, leather paring, each for a purpose, but not to do herself. Very little would have been possible without her in publishing, but her function was not that of edition binder. She had never even made an extra print of one of her own etchings: as soon as she brought something to perfection she dropped it and went on to something else.

"I can't even entertain anymore," Nonny said. "The Bend people are bringing their own food. Why did Mrs. Staveley stop us from feeding the Bend people? I feel like that was the last responsibility I had left, and she took it from me."

"That's the way she wants it."

"But this has never happened before. We were always hospitable. Why aren't we being hospitable with them?"

"Because she thinks they're not quite right."

"They are not only feeding themselves, they're starting to bring food for us. I almost can't bear the embarrassment of being fed by them in our own place."

"Maybe, just maybe, she's telling the truth. Maybe there *is* going to be a sign, and we need to wait for it to be revealed."

Whether or not she was right, we *were* given a sign. Joseph Rael, a medicine man whom we had met at a work seminar in Cave Junction, Oregon the summer before, was coming to pay the farm a visit.

Patrick had gone to the airport to pick him up. We were invited to breakfast at the Murphy's with Joseph Rael. Wendy and Patrick asked about another recent illness of Mrs. Staveley's that she was still recovering from. She had blamed this illness on the fact that her spirit had moved ahead of her body. Joseph said, very simply, that Mrs. Staveley was out of balance.

"What can we do for her?" Wendy asked.

"Have a group of women rub her body down with warm castor oil," Joseph said.

Almost in one voice, the women exclaimed, "Oh, she would never allow that."

"Then have one woman do it."

"Who?" Wendy asked.

Joseph stopped for a moment and then looked at Nonny. "You do it," he said.

The following day, Nonny prepared lunch for Joseph and Mrs. Staveley. She had left the roast lamb in the oven at home, and asked me to carry it to Mrs. Staveley's in twenty minutes. Nonny walked to the Main House to work on the vegetables. At one point, Mrs. Staveley had walked into the kitchen and said, "What are the two of us going to talk about during lunch?" Nonny was puzzled at first, but attributed her unease to her illness and depression. "We could invite a third person," Nonny said.

"Who?" Mrs. Staveley questioned.

"Patrick. I'm sure he would love to come for lunch." At that moment Patrick was walking through the orchard. Nonny called out to him at the same moment that I walked in the door with the roast lamb. Patrick followed me into the kitchen, and walked past me into the library, while I carried the roast into the dining room.

Several minutes later, Mrs. Staveley walked into the kitchen and said to Nonny, "Why don't you and David stay and have drinks. Joseph should be here any minute."

I thought the lunch began awkwardly, in part because Nonny and I were sitting at the end of the table and trying to involve ourselves in the conversation but without intruding on their lunch. Mrs. Staveley was ill at ease but was doing her best not to let it show. Fortunately, Joseph was so completely himself, and so able to be all things to all people, that it wouldn't have mattered to him what anyone did, or did not do. I knew that he had already been to the school and had given all of the children their Indian names—names that had been so accurate, and so telling, that many of the parents would have to revise the way they had always related to their children. For several minutes I toyed with the idea of asking him my Indian name.

I had never had my hand read, gone to a card reader or clairvoyant, had never thrown pennies at the *I Ching*, or consulted the Tarot. I stayed away from these things, not because I didn't believe in them, but because I did believe. I wanted to find out about my life by *living* my life, and I did not want to know more than was good for me. But something kept niggling at me. Was it because I really didn't have a teacher anymore? Or did I simply suspect that this ability at giving names was as valid and as legitimate as was the finding of one's animal, or the learning of one's Chief Feature? I screwed up my courage, and asked. "Joseph, can you tell me my name?"

"Hu tai," Joseph said, without hesitating.

"Hu tai?"

"It's a game played with a stone and hollowed out rock, in which the stone fits perfectly. This makes it very difficult. You throw the stone ... and throw the stone ... and throw the stone ... and then you make it. It goes in, and stays in ..."

"Yes," I answered, puzzled.

"Then you do it again, another game. That's all. Sometimes the stone goes in the hole. Sometime it misses. But you just play the game, and when it is over you move on to the next game."

It was a revelation. Suddenly, I saw my whole life. This is exactly how I had gone through my life. When I had "finished the game," I simply moved on and without looking back. Once accomplished, a thing was over. It was time for the next game, just as Joseph had said. In the work it was called, Doing the next thing.

I felt joyous. I was *Hu Tai*, the man who enjoyed the game, who had the possibility not to be identified, to enjoy the process, not the product. I realized that all the things I wished for from the work I had in potential, if only I could let go and simply be myself. I had always been free inside, but it had taken something like an act of magic to make me see this for myself.

So this was the freedom I had come in search of. It had been there, right under my nose all that time, I just hadn't seen it. Perhaps I had to be *prepared* to see it. That was what the work had done for me.

All at once I started chattering, not because I had a question, or any doubts, but because I was deliriously happy. How could he have known—how could he have known *so much*? He had looked inside me and pulled me inside out, and shown me myself as I really was, not as I imagined I was, or as I thought I should be. If there was more to enlightenment than this, I couldn't imagine what it was.

After lunch we went into the living room with our drinks. I had been the only one to ask a question, but now Mrs. Staveley said, and I could feel that her question was one she had been carrying around for a long time, "What happens when this life ends?"

"We do it again," Joseph answered, and laughed. "What else is there?"

"I was afraid of that," she said. I could feel her withdrawing from us. It wasn't long before we excused ourselves and returned to the hop barn.

All at once an image came into my mind, an image that had always troubled me. I pictured Mrs. Staveley standing over a baby carriage in the arbor, staring at a child's face, without speaking. She just stared into the buggy for a long minute, and then raised herself up and walked away. Now I knew what that look had meant; she was considering her own death and rebirth. But I was as puzzled now as I had been then, because the work had always taught a form of reincarnation, although Gurdjieff had tried very hard to downplay it, on the theory that the only time is *Now*, and that it didn't matter how many chances we might have if we didn't use the opportunity that was available to us at this very moment. So what did all this mean to her, I wondered.

The day after Joseph's visit she seemed even more sullen. I stared at her troubled face, trying to understand her moodiness. I wondered why we had come again to see her. It had been such a very long time since we had had anything of importance that we could share with her.

Were we really so completely at odds? If so, was it only that our natures were different, and that underneath we were just two human beings struggling for the same things, but in completely different ways? She had wanted to have her farm brought to a final point. She had never tired of working for its perfection, believing it could become a model for the work, a place were people could come and be regenerated. But I was destined to keep moving through life without looking back, unless there was something in the past that impeded the present. How different we were, or had become—how totally different—and yet, for a time, we were indispensable to one another. She herself had always said that Nonny and I knew how to "do the next thing," and how could we have ever known she would some day try to prevent us from doing just that?

Orage had said, "Hang on tightly, let go lightly." With us, it seemed, she had done the opposite, by hanging on much too lightly, and letting go, if she *could* let go, much too tightly.

The scales had fallen from my eyes. In the days that followed, I saw her plain, in the way I was able to see everyone else on the farm, and in the same way that they were able to see me. Although it was to my great sorrow that I saw her this way, it did not alter our long relationship. We had been through too much together. She was no longer my teacher, but she was, I felt, still my friend. And even more importantly, she had been my teacher, my guide and my link to Gurdjieff and his Work. That could never change. Without her I could not have come to the place were I was now, ready to take the next step, wherever it might lead.

I was determined to stand, psychologically, on my own two feet, and I could see that she was just as determined that I stay put and go on being one of her dependents.

## · CHAPTER THIRTY THREE ·

Mrs. Staveley had made a decision not to go to any more group meetings. She had announced some time back that it was time for peers to work with peers. She had also said a number of times that the work shouldn't be a crutch, that our dependence had to be broken, that we had to throw away our crutches once we learned to stand on our own. But if she was preaching "crutchless," she was certainly teaching "crutches."

When the inner work was effective on the farm, it was not only because of her, but also because of our need. We had sensed that higher influences were making themselves felt in us, but for reasons we could scarcely comprehend. It had been magic, but there wasn't any magic anymore. And it wasn't just me. It wasn't only that I had outgrown her and the conditions of work here, it was—as she had said so often—the tide going back out. What she didn't say, and what I am sure she couldn't face, was that we seemed to be one of the abandoned tidal pools, left to perish in the backwater.

We would perish unless we were able to hoist ourselves out of the wash and get back on land, to do what we could with what we had been given. This *was* Gurdjieff's intention, I was certain of that, or he wouldn't have thrown out some of his best people: Thomas de Hartmann, Ouspensky, Orage and Salzmann, and all the others about whom we knew so little. He would never allow dependence, by him or on him. And he had been determined to see his work go out into life, where it was needed. I could not say anything of this to her, or to anyone else. I simply had to get out myself. I didn't want to leave as others had, I didn't want others to think that I was "leaving the work," which was the conditioned response when someone left, as I well knew, having been conditioned myself.

There was also this: having lost all of my animus toward the people on the farm and, having accepted them completely, the thought of slinking away, with their not understanding why, was just too painful for us both. We had even come to accept Oregon, something I thought would never happen.

I had been waiting for a sign, and I had been given not one sign, but three: my name, from Joseph; my acceptance of the people on the farm, for whom I now felt love; and, finally, my acceptance of Oregon.

Our first group meeting without Mrs. Staveley was a bit awkward, but good. It was decided that each of us, as an exercise, give everyone else in the group some assignment that each person needed for his or her work. We had done this in beginning groups, when it had been very effective, for it showed us that we were fairly transparent to others, and also just how hard it was for us to see ourselves. It made us see how badly we needed each other.

In time, as we built muscle, some of us had asked others, usually the person we perceived as our arch-enemy, how they saw us, or why they were put off by us. I had begun to see the various stages within the work that we had passed through, and how the work was layered, and even how it needed to be transmitted.

But now, to go back like this? Both Nonny and I refused to work on making a list, but we went to the meeting, where Nonny, in typical fashion—for she never contained her objections or feelings, but managed always to spit them out—said, "This is ridiculous, after ten years in the work, and more, each of us knows what our work is. I certainly know what *my* work is, and I don't need to be told by someone else *what* it is."

With that opening, I couldn't help but speak myself, "A lot of what I'm hearing is just vindictiveness, people getting back at one another, putting one another in their place. It's childish."

Not too much was said at the meeting, but in the end we

wondered for ourselves if there was any point in our going to another meeting.

When we had complained to Mrs. Staveley that the group no longer served a purpose for us, she said, "Don't speak. Go to the meetings, but don't speak."

Of course, I thought, this was your experience, and now you are putting it on us. After twenty years in groups, and after Jane Heap had dropped hints that she should leave, Jane finally said in a group meeting, "Whatever happens, don't speak." Mrs. Staveley knew that those words were for her, that no one else in the room had heard them. Being an obedient student, she never spoke again. As the weeks turned into a month, and then two, the other members of the group began complaining, louder and louder, about Mrs. Staveley's silence, until Jane finally said, "That's right, if you don't speak, you must leave." What could Mrs. Staveley do? She had been told not to speak, and now, that if she didn't speak she would have to leave. This was Jane's way to get her to stand on her own, which, after twenty years in groups, she needed to do.

Now, not knowing what to do herself, she was giving advice that was neither appropriate nor transferable.

But her reaction to Nonny's outburst was unequivocal. She charged into our next meeting and, looking straight at Nonny, she said, "When we get to the place where we think we can work by ourselves, we're in our egos. To go up the mountain, we must go *round* the mountain and, although we feel that we've come back often to the same place, we are different, or we should be different, but the place is *not* the same, is *never* the same, *if* we are ascending."

Once again, we were in her living room, and once again I was trying to tell her why we needed to leave. "The milk is running down my chin, it won't go in anymore. I don't need my mother any longer."

"Just because you've crawled down from my lap, it doesn't mean you have to leave the room."

I didn't think to say that children do change schools, and they do eventually leave home. Instead, I said, "I need to forage for my own food. If I can only understand one thing in a month, in a year, by myself, that would be better than having the same formulations rammed down my throat."

"You're not feeding me anymore," Nonny said. "I need to begin to feed myself."

"You *are* feeding yourself. That's what this farm is all about, a place were people are being fed in the *right* way, in all three centers."

"But it's not working for me anymore," I said. "I need to stand on my own two feet, and find out for myself what I know and what I don't know, and what I need to know and do next. I don't have any answers, but I do have questions that I don't want you to answer for me. What I do know is that this place doesn't work for me anymore."

"Maybe you're right."

And I could see that she *had* understood, however painful it may have been for her to admit this to herself—or to us.

But that tiny part in herself from which she could understand, and even somewhat empathize with us, would soon be crowded out by the larger parts—the many "I's" that would never understand a viewpoint that weakened its own stronghold.

The next time we saw her I had to go through it all over again—and again and again—until, in the end, she agreed. But inside of an hour, I knew that she would have forgotten once more everything that we had told her.

"I can't seem to make her understand," I said to Nonny one evening, "and yet she does understand something. She keeps talking about peers working with peers, about how the work shouldn't be a crutch, and even, lately, that she is standing in everyone's light."

"She can't bear to have her children grow up. I've never been a mother, but I *have* been a daughter..."

"You were?" I interrupted, and laughed.

Nonny smiled. "Yes, I was. My own mother couldn't let me go, and now my spiritual teacher can't let go either. I'm beginning to see a pattern here that I don't like."

"This should really be a cause for celebration ... a banquet!"

"I think you mean it."

"Of course I mean it. I love these people. We've done time together. We may never see any of them again. And now, I suppose, we're going to be forced to slink away in the night. How could anything that was so right for us once, be so wrong now?"

"It *hasn't* gone wrong. This is right. Maybe this is how it is meant to be, but the pain of it is almost unbearable."

We had always had our Christmas dinner with Mrs. Staveley. Despite her downplaying of the Holiday as a commercial assault on the senses, as well as an outrage to the spirit of Christ, nearly everyone went to their families, in town or out of town, for the holidays, except perhaps those like us who were simply too far away, though we had gone to Fresno once or twice when my mother was alive.

At Christmas time the farm was always deserted. We had spent nearly every Christmas with Mrs. Staveley, and we invited her once again to have Christmas dinner with us in our home. Nonny had spent two days cooking. We were happy to celebrate a holy day with her, and we also hoped that we could speak openly about our next step. But, as Nonny would say later, "My heart sank, almost from the minute she walked in."

The moment she had reached the top step and caught her breath, she said, "This is a great Christmas for me, my family has finally agreed not to exchange presents." And as she said this, she handed us a small box of chocolates.

She walked into the living room, to the stiff-backed chair I had set up for her in the middle of the room. As she walked to her chair she passed by Jenny, our sick cat, who was lying, fully awake but immobile, on the couch. We had found Jenny in a pet store two months before, and for the past month she had been unable to walk. We knew by now that her condition was incurable. The two cats before her, Missak and Sossi, had both died of feline leukemia—Missak from the stress caused at my Mother's death because of our frequent trips to Fresno. Missak had been with us for nearly all of our married life, but Sossi had lived with us for just four years. We knew that Sossi had died because of our inner turmoil over leaving the farm. But we didn't know at the time that Jenny was dying for the same reason.

Joseph Rael had said that animals, like humans, did not perish with their physical death, but continued, just as we did. We were sure that Jenny was an evolved being, but we didn't know then that she was somehow, mysteriously, providing our passage from the farm. Although we were torn apart by her suffering, there was something in her being that consoled us and companioned us at a time when we had been thrown back completely on ourselves.

Mrs. Staveley had phoned nearly every day to ask about Jenny but now, when she was actually seeing her for the first time, she walked by her without so much as a comment, or even a glance in her direction. I didn't know what to make of it. I petted Jenny and sat down beside her.

Mrs. Staveley was talking again about how she felt she was standing in everyone's way, and that we had to learn to work together and for ourselves. When she said, without looking directly at either of us, that she felt that she was standing in our light, I said, "Yes, that's how it feels," and Nonny said, "It feels more like someone is sitting on my chest."

"I'm getting out of the way of people. Of course, everyone's different. Patrick argues with me. But you're not Patrick. Naturally, everyone has their own way."

"Then you see how it is for us, especially if you are changing yourself," I said.

"Children grow up," she answered. I realized with a start that she was speaking of herself.

"The next time," I said, "I'm not going to talk to you about leaving, I'm just going to go."

She nodded her assurance, feeling on top of everything again, with that look that meant, I know and see everything, it's all under control.

I don't know if anyone tasted their food. We were so far apart that, for the first time in years, we had to search for something to talk about. She didn't stay after the meal, but asked to be taken home after she finished her coffee, which she allowed herself on special occasions.

I was so depressed that I lay down on the couch and fell to sleep.

On New Year's Eve, unable to bear Jenny's suffering any longer, we took her to the vet and had her put to sleep. We held her and talked to her while the needle was being inserted. She looked at us in full acceptance, and we were certain she understood what all of us were going through much better than we did.

We drove directly to the Main House to tell Mrs. Staveley we were leaving. We no sooner got in the door then Nonny began to sob over Jenny. "Let's have a drink," Mrs. Staveley said, and walked into the library.

After Nonny and I had calmed down, and we had turned the subject away from Jenny, I said, "We feel the time has come for us to go." At that moment, Mrs. Staveley spotted Patrick walking up the gravel path toward the stairway. She got to her feet and said, "Let's drink to it, but first let's see what Patrick wants."

I didn't trust the smile on her face. She of course knew that we wouldn't say anything in front of Patrick, and so, once again, we felt that we had been thwarted.

## · CHAPTER THIRTY FOUR ·

We felt that Jenny had released us to leave, but neither her merciful death nor our final meeting with Mrs. Staveley had lightened our hearts or our minds.

We had begun to mourn our departure, and for good reason: we had finally accepted our fellow-travellers, and now we had to leave them, and it seemed unlikely that we would ever see any of them again. But more than anything we were mourning the way we had to leave, with the knowledge that our relationship with our former teacher had been terminated, and we knew it could never be renewed.

But the worst was yet to come.

It was Sunday, another day of work on the farm. I no longer had my heart in the work we were doing in publishing. The press hadn't run well for more than a year, and I had despaired of ever printing anything respectable on it again. Mrs. Staveley asked us to print her little fable on Christmas for this year's birthday celebration on the 13th. I had half-heartedly been setting the type and Nonny was struggling equally hard with a woodcut for the broadside format we had chosen.

I felt so far away from everything at the luncheon discussion that I couldn't believe that this place, these discussions, and Mrs. Staveley's words of wisdom and teaching, had once fed me. I looked around the room and wondered at the rapt attention of so many of the faces.

After the reading we dragged ourselves across the orchard, washed up, changed our clothes and went upstairs. "I'm going to call Patrick," I told Nonny. "I think we need someone to talk to about our leaving."

"Wendy too?"

"If he wants to bring her, but I doubt that he will."

Patrick came over at once. I made us drinks and we sat down. "I suppose you know we're leaving," I said.

He nodded his head yes, and then no, and then, when his face became still, it registered a puzzled look of surprise. "I always knew you would leave someday. I told Wendy, it must be a year ago, the Kherdians won't be here forever. But I'm shocked. I really am."

"We're ready to go, we've been ready for a very long time."

"But why? Tell me."

"You mean she hasn't told you," I said.

"Not a word, I swear it."

"There's just nothing for us here, anymore."

"She told David she wasn't going to put either of us in front of groups because we'd be leaving someday, and she had to train the ones that were staying. And yet she's told David for years that he would teach these ideas one day, but she won't train him, and now that he is ready she doesn't want us to leave."

"Is that why?" Patrick asked.

"No, that has nothing to do with it. There's just no work here— for us—anymore. How long can we go on with the same exercises?"

"The group meetings are kindergarten," Nonny said. "It seems like there is *only* beginning work, on and on and on, until there's no purpose to any of it anymore."

"But what if she put you in front of groups, would that make it different?"

"I think it might have prolonged it a little, but that's all."

"I feel like we're being eliminated, and yet she won't let us go," Nonny said.

"Have you spoken to her?"

"For a whole year!" Nonny shouted.

"We don't want anything, Patrick, that's not the point. It's just that there's nothing for us here anymore, and she will neither recognize that nor do anything about it. We're beginning to feel like prisoners. You know, when we tell her why we have to leave—in order to keep our work alive—she agrees, because she knows it's the truth. And then, five minutes later she turns around and calls us impulsive Armenians, or tells me I'm a quitter. The *work* in her understands, but *she* won't, or can't, or refuses to understand."

"How long can one go on being a student?" Nonny asked.

"I don't know the answer to that. I still have a lot to learn, I know that. But it sounds to me like you're making the right move. I feel for you guys. Gee, I'm going to miss you."

Suddenly all three of us were crying. We pulled at our drinks and looked at each other and then down at the rug. There was so much to say, but no one wanted to say it.

Finally, Patrick got up and walked to the stairs. "I know you're making the right move, but I need to tell you that I might not be feeling this way tomorrow, after I talk to her."

The following morning I phoned Mrs. Staveley. She answered as she always did; cheery, open, inviting, until I said, "We've made our decision and want to tell you about it." Her voice fell, and turned instantly cold. "Come over then," she said.

She led us into the living room. "We've decided to leave," I said, with finality. Until that moment I had been shaking, but my combined resolve and determination were suddenly anchored by that single sentence of speech.

"If you've made your decision, that's it then."

I had wanted to say something more, but I was so troubled by her darting eyes, and the tick over her left eye, that I was suddenly speechless.

She began speaking now, but so incoherently I couldn't follow the words, nor did I wish to. She had been our teacher and our best friend in the work, and now it was all being washed away in a flood of anger and resentment.

This is the terror of the situation, I thought, no one's work can mean anything to anyone else. I felt overwhelmed, not only by what I was seeing, but because I knew now, if I hadn't known it before, that it was up to me, entirely up to me. I could never look to anyone again, or count on anyone again. Gurdjieff had said, "Trust no one," and I knew it was true. I had always counted on her being conscious: on there being someone who knew me, who understood me, and for years that had been enough, a necessary illusion that had been replaced by my own understanding of myself. The teacher was the mirror who—by not judging—held us up to ourselves. And because we had not been judged we could dare to look at ourselves *as we were*, if only for single moments. It was these moments that we built on, and that, with her help, became amplified, until one day we had learned to be fearless and daring—and responsible—for our work.

We left as quickly as we could. We were still in a state of shock when we reached home.

"Between her fear of abandonment, and her need to always be right and to always win, it was just too much for her," Nonny said. "I feel horrible."

"I think we all become mad when our buttons are pushed, especially if we are unable to work on ourselves at that moment."

"I don't want to think about it anymore. Let's not talk about her again, okay."

The next day Mrs. Staveley called us back to talk to her again.

She was in control now, and ready, I could see, to calculate her next move. We spoke again, as we had so often, about our reasons for leaving, and once again she nodded her assent. In order to mollify her I mentioned that she had left Jane's groups when she was ready to go out on her own, and that if she hadn't she never would have had her own groups. I said that, like her, we were now ready to go out on our own, though we didn't have any plans for the future.

"How soon will you leave?"

"Just as soon as we can. We've already contacted the movers. We thought we would stay through the Gurdjieff birthday dinner, so as not to disrupt things."

"That's good. It's always good to leave quickly once a decision has been made. And it is best to keep it to yourselves."

"We would be leaving even sooner, if it weren't for the dinner,"

I said.

"If anyone asks," she said, "just in case word gets out, I want you to say that you are leaving for life reasons."

"But Mrs. Staveley," I pleaded, "we are *not* leaving for life reasons, we are leaving because of the work."

"Because of *our* work," Nonny corrected.

"Yes, I know, but it's important we have a smooth transition. When you say life, you can think big 'L', but say little 'l'."

I could feel Nonny crying at my side. Mrs. Staveley turned and looked at her. Her eyes were locked in their sockets, her face expressionless. Nonny said, "What hurts me most is Wendy's not knowing. More than anyone, I wanted to speak to her and tell her why we were going."

"There will be plenty of Wendys," Mrs. Staveley said, and looked out the library window.

"One final thing," she said, "you'll need to write to everyone on the Two Rivers Press mailing list and tell them you are closing down the press because you have been called away for some life emergency, and that we will be filling orders for all the books we have, but that there will be no more publishing. One or both of you will need to sign the letter."

I knew better than to argue, and I knew now that there would be no more understanding between us.

The next eight days would be the longest period of our lives, each day a separate, hellish eternity. We took to locking our door for the first time, so that no one would stop in on us and see us packing. We closed off the bedroom, my workroom and Nonny's tiny studio, because as things were boxed and packed they were stored in these rooms. we had to keep the downstairs hallway and the entire upstairs free of any signs of disruption.

Patrick never spoke to us again as a friend, and Wendy slowly became distant. I was determined to print the broadside for the dinner. I had decided that I would not compromise my standard, however important it was for me to do this final printing job. One of the things I had learned from Mrs. Staveley, years before, was that other people's behavior should not influence our own. One should know what one believes, and stands for, and wishes—and resentment, revenge, or any other negative emotion should not prevent one from being one's self.

Time and again the printing press had faltered, but always there was a reason, and it seemed in each case that it had to do with negative emotions. The minute I threw someone out of publishing who didn't want to be there, or who was there for the wrong reasons—wasting my time and holding things up—the balking press would get back on track again. But for the last year it had been going gradually downhill. We had tried everything, and I even called in a specialist, who came not once, but twice, all to no avail. I should have known now that the problem was me, *I* didn't want to be there anymore, and the press picked up on my vibrations, and had gone on strike. I had always hated machines, but somehow, I loved this one. I asked it now to perform for me one last time. I wanted to leave the place clean, and printing this job was an important part of my overall plan.

Miraculously, it happened. Not great printing, not fine printing, but acceptable printing, and this was all I had asked for.

Our countdown didn't help. The days grew blacker and blacker. Jeff Scooter, our lawyer, along with Bea and Patrick, came to take care of publishing's legalities, and to remove our names from any legal documents. Scooter was cold and distant. Only Bea hadn't changed in her feeling for us.

Nonny came down with walking pneumonia, and I began to wonder if we were going to get out of there alive. We went to Clifford Page, the only doctor in the group, who had sewn us both up at different times, and asked that he give Nonny anything and everything, because we had to get through a crisis, which meant staying on our feet through the dinner that was now a few days away.

Somehow, Nonny was able to keep going. The Bend people had come two days ahead of the dinner, and when we told them we were leaving, without any extra questions, they pitched in and helped us to pack.

A part of the birthday celebration included movements demonstrations by each of the five classes. It was the one time in the year that we were able to observe each other's work at movements. It was as excruciating to do movements under these circumstances as it was wonderful to watch all the other classes, and to see everyone else's work. Nonny and I were both in the front row of class five, and one of the movements we had prepared for the dinner was *Arch Dificile*, which was appropriately named. In addition to everything else, we had to practice this movement on our own every day. I didn't see how we were going to remain collected for the movements, but we were determined to put a good face on it because we didn't want to spoil the movements for the rest of the class.

By the time of the dinner we were numb. We got through the movements and, for the rest of the evening, we clung to Bea, who stayed by our side.

We began early the next day with our packing, with Patrick and Wendy joining us, for they had no doubt been assigned the task, as we had been before, when someone left the farm. It was the afternoon of the 15th before we were completely packed and on the truck, with our apartment cleaned and ready for the next occupant. At the very end, when we were sweeping and scrubbing the floors, one of the women burst in and, hugging us and weeping, said, "Oh, you brave people." By the time the words were out of her mouth, we were all crying and clinging to each other. She repeated the phrase once more, before turning and running out of the apartment.

As we were leaving Patrick said, "Let us know where you end up. I may need a place to go to someday." I turned at the door and looked at him and then at Wendy one last time, knowing we might never meet again.

On our way out we turned into Mrs. Staveley's driveway to pay our respects and to say good-bye. She offered us a drink that we had to refuse. It had taken all day to load the van. It was now 4:30 P.M., and we had to make a stop in town before heading East. We were hoping we could drive out of Oregon before stopping for the night. She led us into the living room.

"I feel good about leaving," I said. "I came here for something that I was able to receive, and now it is time to leave. I want to thank you for everything you provided that made that possible."

"Yes," Nonny said, "We can't thank you enough."

I didn't think she heard us. "Do you know where you are going?"

"No. We're not sure," I said.

"Did you get the letters off that you were going to send?"

"Yes," I lied. They were in the car and I would mail them on the way out. I hadn't signed my name to the letter, and had said simply that Two Rivers Press had accomplished what it had set out to do, and now it was time to end that project, but that the press would continue to fill orders.

"Have you told anyone here why you are leaving?"

"No," I said, which was partially true. That afternoon I had told Len Bolton that we were leaving the farm but that it was a happy day for us. He had said, "It may be a happy day for you, but not for me." I had said, "Well, if it's any consolation, we're not leaving the work." He said, "Yes, that's what they all say. Time will tell."

"I'm sure you'll have interesting lives," Mrs. Staveley said. I looked at her, surprised. "You leave a legacy of good work behind..." she was saying, but her voice trailed off.

Nonny began to cry and I got up from my chair. We all stood there for a moment, awkwardly, and then Nonny ran and threw her arms around her. I hugged her next, and when she released her arms, ahead of mine, she threw them down at her side in a slashing movement, as if to dispel any attachment she might still have to me.

At the door I turned one last time, for myself, and said, Goodbye, by which I meant to convey that it was a leave-taking that was good, because I *had* received the work and I was ready now to go back into life.

Her earlier gesture had belied her feelings, which now showed on her face. Perhaps in that moment I had opened myself enough to see what I hadn't seen before. All along I had prayed that it was not too late, that she would sit down and talk to us like equals, like the friends we had once been. But it was not to be, and I accepted that now.

Many times in the past I had said to her just how hard I felt it was to be a human being. The more I worked and suffered, the more I saw the suffering of others until, at one point, it became clear to me that human life *is* suffering, and that none of us can know enough or *are* enough to construct a life that is certain of meaning, and that we can be assured will be free of failure. Sooner or later we all come up against the same thing: ourselves. And no one could know for us, or speak for us, or understand for us. We must suffer our own lives. This was the final gift she had given me. In one of the very last group meetings when, on the verge of tears from frustration and anxiety, I had said that however much I tried to work on the limitations imposed on me by my heredity, however much I tried not to be what I seemed unable not to be, the stronger the grip of that heredity became. She had said, very quietly, very simply, "Take up your burden."

Although it hadn't sunk in at once, when I finally understood what that meant I knew that I could never be free if I didn't accept myself *as I was*.

The point was not to rid ourselves of our faults, but to know ourselves. The big things never go away, but we could learn to work with them.

There was a reason Gurdjieff pushed his followers out of his work, away from himself, forcing them to go back into life, with the double-edge of suffering that came from knowing something they had not known before, and knowing because of it that life did not answer, and then finding in life a way to live that was purposeful, dignified, intelligent—and finally, useful.

Now I stood on the steps, outside the door that divided us, and said good-bye again, for the third time. I didn't know what would come next, but I wasn't concerned. I only knew that I was taking the next step.

One Sunday in November, nearly four years after we had left the farm, Nonny and I took a Sunday stroll through the downtown mall in the city we had recently moved to. We had stopped in our walk to read the newly painted name on the window of the store we were standing in front of: *Rubaiyat*. Because it was a Sunday, we were surprised to see that its door was standing open. We walked inside, and while I took a seat in the back of the store—it was a woman's dress shop— Nonny browsed among the racks.

Later, as we stood at the counter, waiting to have our credit card processed, I found myself looking down at an open copy of Omar Khayyam's familiar work. Almost absently, I began reading the two facing quatrains:

> Alike for those who for To-day prepare,
> And those that after a To-morrow stare,
> A Muezzin from the Tower of Darkness cries,
> "Fools! your Reward is neither Here nor There."

> Why, all the Saints and Sages who discuss'd
> Of the Two Worlds so learnedly, are thrust
> Like foolish Prophets forth; their Words to Scorn
> Are scatter'd and their Mouths are stopt with Dust.

As with all seeming accidents and small acts of fate, those two poems reached me at just the right moment in my life. For some weeks, if not months, I had been wondering why I was finding all thought and mention of the "spiritual life" repugnant.

My repeated thoughts on this subject had carried me back in my thinking to my brush with religion as a child, when I had refused all participation in the church even though the church, in the American diaspora at least, was as much our cultural, as our spiritual, home.

These early feelings, and the refusal that accompanied them, had remained intact until I met the Gurdjieff work, when they began to be transformed—correctly, I had felt—into a reverence of and a need for something higher, that belonged to a spiritual dimension that had not been corrupted, because as yet it had not been codified.

Words like Higher and Spiritual had, from that time on, a very different meaning for me, and so why did the mere mention of these and similar words cause revulsion in me now, and why had I stopped reading spiritually-oriented and consciousness-raising books, with the sole exception of Gurdjieff's *All and Everything*?

Standing at the counter and reading those two poems, the reality and truth of those vaguely familiar poems were reaching me for the very first time, as an experience completely new and fresh. Certainly, I knew—had learned—that man has two natures: higher and lower, and that he must keep them in balance, as well as in safety from one another. This was the meaning of Gurdjieff's parable about the wolf and the lamb. But what I saw now, with such clarity and certainty, was that we were neither. We were *from* both, but *of* neither. Our reality—our True Reality and Home—belonged to neither of these conditioned worlds. I had never thought of the spiritual world as conditioned because I had never seen before that our yearning for it alone automatically conditions it. At the same time, I recognized that if the spiritual has to be a reality for us  and neither ambition nor dream—it would have to be attained at the conjunction of the two worlds, with ourselves the meeting point. And this could only be arrived at by a series of steps.

Gurdjieff had said that we needed to be spoiled by life; that it was only when we were thoroughly disillusioned with life that we could begin to work for Real Being. Only then could we experience our own nothingness. One could not occur before the other. Having seen the world—that is, ordinary life—and having seen ourselves, we could then begin to actualize something real within the framework of the ordinary world, but ultimately not for this world only. For this to occur there would need to be a leap of faith, a journey into the abyss of which all the great teachings speak. One had to give up what one had made, to let go completely, to risk everything before something new could enter. This is exactly what had not been done by those whom Gurdjieff had instructed and who had been charged with passing on the teaching to us. Perhaps they could not make that step. Perhaps it was ordained that the form of the work would slowly grow moldy, on its way to becoming another religious sect. It was this that had been the cause of my revulsion, and the reason I had been thrown back to my memory of the staleness of the church, and its religious bankruptcy, that I felt as a boy when I had attended the services of the Armenian church.

I needed now to review in my mind all that I had been through—that *we* had been through—since leaving our school in Oregon. I had learned a great deal since that time, both about myself and the work, but I had not yet attempted to align my thinking around a single point, and to place those experiences and my insights into a useable order.

In the painful, closing days, when we were leaving the farm, one of the last, and certainly the most important thing I had said to my teacher was that I needed to begin to understand things for myself, and *by* myself, without her counsel, or the work's exegesis and heavy breathing.

Within a year of our departure from the farm—after we had gotten on our feet and had earned enough money—we bought a farmhouse in upstate New York on forty-five acres, where we were able to expand the small group we had already formed. But we saw, after a very short time, that we were imitating the form we had inherited with the teaching: a farm, acreage, projects, Sunday work and so on, and it soon became evident that none of us were farmers, nor were any of us interested in instituting make-believe projects in order to simulate conditions for work. Further—and this helped Nonny and me to see our own needs and feelings and beliefs—that the people who were coming to us were not interested in having the work separated from life and carried on in artificial conditions. Their questions were as real as their lives, and as urgent. The work meant nothing to them if it couldn't help them to begin at once to grapple with their own lives.

It was obvious now that the tide of the sixties had gone out to sea, and that the sea had changed colors, bringing with it a new cargo into port.

We put everything again into question. It soon became clear that we were not where we were meant to be, and we could no longer carry on the work in the same way, that even the press and the chapbooks and broadsides we were printing were no longer appropriate. We decided to sell everything and move. But for some unknown reason we didn't sell the press.

After a long and frustrating search for a buyer our property finally sold. Before we were able to move we were literally *struck* by an omen. Driving through our village one early afternoon in July, a large deer came charging out of a stream bed, just as we were about to cross a narrow bridge, and crashed through our windshield, knocking me unconscious. Our car hurled from side to side across the bridge and came to a stop at the end of the guard rail, bordering a steep ravine.

Not long after we had moved a friend of ours on a visit brought us a copy of Tom Brown, Jr.'s book, *The Vision*. I was not surprised to read in Brown's book that certain animals—deer, fox, owls—are to be taken as omens when they behave in a way that is out of character for them. This confirmed what I had already believed: that the accident had marked and underscored our decision, by declaring our act—that is, our decision to move from that area and to settle in a city for the first time in our married life—to be both inevitable and true.

We were now comfortably settled in our new home, in a place that was right for us, and it seemed we had found our place at last. But our press, and all our pressroom equipment remained in the cellar, slowly rusting, and again we were faced with an inner frustration resulting from a need to participate in something—we knew not what. Although I was writing again, and Nonny continued to illustrate, and even though it was clear that our work was not being done just for ourselves, there was a need to be active in some way that we could not yet see.

As we pondered our situation it gradually became clear that we needed to make practical use of our training, as well as our skills, along with the beliefs that were personal to us.

We waited for a sign, and at last one came. An article appeared in the local paper concerning a new community center that was getting under way in our neighborhood. The drug problem was escalating in our city and the new center was preparing to offer alternatives to those in need.

We phoned the center at once and offered our press, along with our binding and marbling equipment, as well as our services, to work with children at printing, writing, art; in short, whatever was needed.

It appeared now that the Gurdjieff teaching had come full circle for us. We had returned to a new beginning. We were part of life, and the drug problem was, therefore, also our problem. When there is a strong negative force there needs to be an equally strong positive force. I was reminded by something I had read many times before in *All and Everything*, that I had always assumed I understood; that man needed to serve God's higher purposes. This had been ordained for us, but of course it could not be done for us. This was something we had to do ourselves. I had always taken this to mean an action that would occur in other worlds, other times, something so distant that I could only dream about its ultimate reality and truth. I saw now that Gurdjieff was talking about right here, right now, each of us as we are, *once we have been prepared*.

This, then, was the meaning of Gurdjieff's message and teaching. He had expelled those around him, after a certain training, so they would not whither within his protective sphere, but take their places in life, in positions and in work that was true for them, to become the influences they could not help but be.

# . G L O S S A R Y ·

BEING *Everything a person is; the overall quality of one's internal and external responses to life, and the degree to which consciousness has become manifest within one.*

BUFFERS *Mechanical, internal "appliances" that keep one's picture of oneself intact.*

CENTERS *Functions of the human machine, separated into intellectual, emotional and instinctive-moving divisions, each of which has an intelligence of its own.*

CHIEF FEATURE *The main axis of personality (qv), on which all our decisions hinge, and around which almost all our behavior circulates.*

CONSCIENCE *If activated one's objective conscience can direct the needed action or appropriate response in every situation of life.*

CONSCIOUS SHOCKS *The first conscious shock applies the effort to remember oneself (qv) to individual moments of life, thereby producing higher materials than are ordinarily created in normal human functioning. The second conscious shock continues this process by transforming negative or unpleasant emotions.*

CRYSTALLIZED *Fixed in form.*

DIVIDING ATTENTION *Simultaneous awareness of self and other; mindfulness.*

EMOTIONAL CENTER *Functions responsible for all feelings other than physical feelings.*

ENNEAGRAM  *A nine-sided figure inscribed in a circle which, according to Gurdjieff, embodies the two most important laws of the universe; The Law of Seven and The Law of Three.*

ESSENCE  *Those traits that we are born with, as opposed to personality (qv) which is entirely learned. That part of man that contains his highest spiritual potential and experiences.*

EXTERNAL CONSIDERING  *The ability to psychologically put oneself in the place of another and to act with regard for the needs of others by putting aside one's own desires. Also see Internal Considering.*

FEELING CENTER  *see Emotional Center.*

FOOD, FIRST  *Food for the body in the form of ordinary foodstuffs.*

FOOD, SECOND  *Air.*

FOOD, THIRD  *Impressions.*

FORCE, FIRST  *Positive, or affirming, force, as the plus in electric current.*

FORCE, SECOND  *Negative, or denying, force, as the minus in electric current.*

FORCE, THIRD  *Neutralizing, or reconciling, force, e.g., electricity, which occurs when the two forces are equal.*

IDENTIFICATION  *The tendency to lose or forget oneself in an object, activity, sensation or product that one has created and cannot respond to objectively.*

INTERNAL CONSIDERING  *One's inner thoughts concerning other people's thoughts or attitudes toward one, always imagined and often untrue.*

LAW OF RECIPROCAL MAINTENANCE  *Action by which everything in existence is designed to be both a necessary support for some other entity, and is supported by other entities, in an immutable web of mutual* interaction. "Feeding and being fed." The Law of Three, as described above in three Forces.

LAW OF SEVEN  The variations in any movement through time or space determined by the variations in vibrations as can be seen in the musical scale, with the intervals created by half-tone steps in that scale.

MAGNETIC CENTER  The part within a person that contains the actual desire for spiritual development.

MECHANICALNESS  Tendency of human beings to act in a repeatable and predictable manner, and for the same stimuli to almost always produce the same responses.

MIND CENTER  see Centers.

MOVING-INSTINCTIVE CENTER  That group of functions that includes both learned movement of all kinds (moving center), and all instinctive functions.

PERSONALITY  The learned part of human behavior drawn from knowledge gained throughout life; behaviors imitated or learned which are thought to benefit one's life. See also Essence.

REAL I  A higher state of being which brings with it freedom, love and existence beyond the confines and lifespan of the physical body.

SELF-REMEMBERING  One of the basic practices of the Gurdjieff work, in which divided attention (qv) is accompanied by an emotional response to each moment.

SLEEP  The condition, according to Gurdjieff, in which man exists. He delineated four possible states of consciousness; physical sleep, as ordinarily understood; waking sleep, in which we think we are awake and perform all ordinary human activities; self-consciousness, when a higher faculty is activated and is capable of seeing oneself objectively, and; objective consciousness, in which all laws of the world are apparent to one, and all one's higher functions have been actualized.

SUPER-EFFORT  Going beyond the ordinary demands of life, and beyond *the usual practice of the Gurdjieff work, for the sole motivation of perfecting oneself.*

THREE LINES OF WORK   *In group work, three types of efforts are deemed necessary; work for one's own evolution; work with others in the group, and; work for the Work as a whole.*

VESANELNIAN TREES   *Described by Gurdjieff as being in the Sarmoung monastery. They were made in proportion to the human body and could be moved to various positions so a student of the movements could initiate a correct position for the sacred dances.*

WILL, SELF   *Our ordinary desires or wants, over which we believe we have control.*

WILL, REAL   *Freedom of action unencumbered by cultural predispositions, opinions of others, or any outside influence, as manifested by a person in whom consciousness, reason and conscience have become activated.*

# GLOBE PRESS BOOKS

Globe Press Books publishes works of philosophical, psychological and spiritual importance. You can stay informed about our forthcoming publications by simply mailing us the Order Form on the last page of this book. Some of our other titles are detailed on the following pages. These books are available at fine bookstores or they can be ordered directly from the publisher using the Order Form.

The Body of Light
*History and Practical Techniques for*
*Awakening Your Subtle Body*
by John Mann and Lar Short.
A concise guide to the use of chakras for self-development. Combines easy-to-read scholarship with step-by-step practices for a better understanding of *all* spiritual traditions. Reviews Hindu, Buddhist, Taoist and other traditions, and includes beginning, intermediate and advanced exercises. With 60 illustrations by Juan Li. Softcover, 192 pages, $12.95.
*This is in many ways a hands-on manual which bridges theory with experiment in the area of spiritual practice. Recommended for all who are devoted to the fulfillment of meditation.*—Shri Brahmananda Sarasvati

New Horizons; Explorations in Science
by P.D. Ouspensky, with an Introduction by Colin Wilson.
Thoughtful "new science" readers will enjoy this remarkable book's treatment of physics; the fourth dimension; mystical states of consciousness; and dreams and hypnotism. By the author of *In Search of the Miraculous*. 222 pages. Softcover, $14.95.
*A great achievement, a work of genius*—Saturday Review

Body Types
by Joel Friedlander. *The Enneagram of Essence Types*.
Learn how to recognize the physical and psychological tendencies of each type. Explore the automatic thoughts, attitudes and motives of your type, and discover the dynamics behind your relationships and the people you know. 168 pages. Hardcover, $19.95. Softcover, $9.95.
*Written in such an easily read style you will wish it were longer. Recommended*—The Unicorn

## Maurice Nicoll, A Portrait
by Beryl Pogson.
An account of Maurice Nicoll's life as a student of Gurdjieff and Ouspensky, and his teaching of the Fourth Way. 288 pages, 19 photographs. Softcover, $12.95.
*The most detailed published account of Nicoll's life as a student and teacher of the Gurdjieff work.* —J. Walter Driscoll

## Gurdjieff's Fourth Way: An Introduction
by Joel Friedlander.
Verbatim transcripts of seven lectures given at the New York Open Center designed to introduce the major ideas of the Gurdjieff system. Topics include states of consciousness, negative emotions, self-remembering and self-observation, cosmology, and more. *Note:* These lectures are available only by mail, and are not sold in any store. 183 pages, illustrated. $65.00.

## The Training of the Zen Buddhist Monk
by D.T. Suzuki.
This is perhaps the best introduction to Zen and the life of the Zen monk. By means of a direct and succinct description of the training that a Zen Buddhist monk undergoes, Dr. Suzuki has given us the most precise picture possible of Zen in life. Forty-three illustrations depict the disciplinary measures pertaining to the life of Zen. 176 pages, 43 illustrations. Softcover, $9.95.
*The best introduction to Zen Buddhism available. (After) writing this book, Suzuki published more than 20 books in English on Buddhism, yet this still stands as one of the very best.* —Choice

## On A Spaceship With Beelzebub
*By A Grandson of Gurdjieff*
by David Kherdian.
288 pages. Hardcover, $24.95. Softcover, $12.95.

# Order Form / Mailing List Request

**How to order:**

Payment must accompany order. Please remember to calculate shipping charges according to the Shipping chart. For shipment to addresses in New York State, please add appropriate sales tax. Mail the completed order form (or a copy) with your payment to Globe Press Books at the address below. *Foreign Orders:* Surface shipping takes 2-15 weeks. Checks must be American Express or international checks drawn on a U.S. Bank. *Mailing List:* Simply fill in the name and address portion of the order form and return it to the address below.

| Qty. | Title | Price | Total |
|------|-------|-------|-------|
|      |       |       |       |
|      |       |       |       |
|      |       |       |       |
|      |       |       |       |

|  | | |
|--|--|--|
| Subtotal | |
| Tax | |
| Shipping | |
| **Total** | |

### SHIPPING CHARGES

|  | Surface | Air |
|--|---------|-----|
| U.S.A. | $1.75 first item, .50 each addtl. | $3.50 first item, 1.00 each addtl. |
| Canada & Mexico | $3.00 first item, 1.00 each addtl. | $4.50 first item, 2.00 each addtl. |
| Europe | $3.00 first item, 1.00 each addtl. | $8.50 first item, 3.00 each addtl. |
| Southern Hemisphere | $3.00 first item, 1.00 each addtl. | $10.00 first item, 5.75 each addtl. |

> *Our Guarantee*
> Return any book in saleable condition within 30 days for a prompt and friendly refund.

Name _____

Address _____

_____

City / State / Zip _____

Country / Postcode _____

Mail to: Globe Press Books, P.O. Box 2045-B, Madison Square Station, New York, NY 10159.     *Thank you for your order.*

SB